R.S. GRANT.
JUNE 1987.

# HOW TO
# UNDERSTAND AND USE
# COMPANY ACCOUNTS

# HOW TO UNDERSTAND AND USE COMPANY ACCOUNTS

## Roy Warren

*Partner, Robson Rhodes Chartered Accountants*

**HUTCHINSON BUSINESS**
London   Melbourne   Auckland   Johannesburg

Hutchinson Business

An imprint of Century Hutchinson Limited

Brookmount House, 62-65 Chandos Place,
Covent Garden, London WC2N 4NW

Century Hutchinson Publishing Group (Australia) Pty Ltd
16-22 Church Street, Hawthorn, Melbourne, Victoria 3122

Century Hutchinson Group (NZ) Ltd
32-34 View Road, PO Box 40-086, Glenfield, Auckland 10

Century Hutchinson Group (SA) (Pty) Ltd
PO Box 337, Bergvlei 2012, South Africa

First published 1983
Reprinted 1983, 1985, 1987

Set in Times

Printed and bound in Great Britain by
Anchor Brendon Ltd, Tiptree, Essex

**British Library Cataloguing in Publication Data**

Warren, Roy
  How to understand and use company accounts.
  1. Corporations—Great Britain—Accounting
  I. Title
  657′ .95′ 0941     HF5686.C7

ISBN 0 09 145890 0 (Cased)
     0 09 145891 9 (Limp)

# Contents

# Introduction: purpose of the book

This book is written for you. Its purpose is to provide the businessman with an understanding of his accounts, an insight into what they can tell him and how they can help him to plan for a more profitable business.

To do this we shall be looking at Dovetails Limited, a well established, medium-sized company which is in the business of making furniture.

Although a manufacturer and although medium sized, Dovetails is used as no more than a convenient vehicle for illustrating the themes of the book. The objective is to provide an explanation of accounts and the uses to which they can be put: the description in these pages applies equally to the largest of companies and the smallest of traders, and it will be as relevant to service companies as it is to those engaged in the manufacture of a tangible product.

Dovetails' 1982 accounts are set out on the pages that immediately follow. At first sight they may make daunting reading; many businessmen may well have experienced the same sense of bewilderment – and possibly frustration – when presented with their own accounts. Before we go any further, therefore, we would do well to answer the charge 'Why bother?'. Books are rarely seen on subjects such as bridge building for the non-engineer, or pension valuations for the non-actuary – so why accounts for the non-accountant businessman? Why does a businessman *need* to understand his accounts? There are at least three compelling reasons.

● The first is that he simply cannot do without them. More than anything else, of course, a successful business depends on the flair of the businessman – and that flair in turn requires a knowledge of the product, an eye for a market, and a range of managerial skills. But no matter how good the product, or how well it is packaged, or how committed the workforce, or caring the management, a businessman only *stays* in business if he makes a profit – and the only way he knows whether he is making a profit is by drawing up a set of accounts.

● Second, accounts can do much more than that. With careful examination, they are potentially very informative documents; and by careful analysis, they can show a businessman not only whether he has made a profit but why that profit was not as good as it might have been, and how he might make it better in the future. A good businessman will not only want to make a profit, he will want to control his business, monitor its performance, and lead it to greater profitability. The surest way in which a businessman can control the performance of his business is by watching his **accounts, and** by listening to what they are telling him.

● Third, an understanding of accounts will lead to better business decisions. If he wants to decide whether to borrow more money from the bank, or whether to invest in new machinery, or whether to tender for a new contract, the first thing a businessman needs is a full appreciation of the business's current financial state of affairs – what its present resources are and how its existing funds are presently deployed. That can only come from an assessment of his accounts. He can be sure that his bank, or suppliers, or competitors, will themselves be looking at his accounts and making their own assessment, and the businessman is at a clear disadvantage if they understand more about the present state of his business than he does himself.

Of course, by being able to understand his own accounts the businessman will also be able to understand the accounts of other people: he can make his own assessment of whether his competitors are really as strong as they make out to be, or whether a new customer is as creditworthy as he claims, or whether a potential supplier is likely to be in business long enough to ensure a continuous source of essential materials. A proper understanding of accounts will therefore not only help a businessman to plan and control his own business but will also give him an insight into the operations of other businesses.

A final reason – and perhaps the most compelling of all – is that the understanding he needs is really not that difficult to acquire – as the following pages will hopefully show.

# Outline: how to use the book

The book assumes no accounting knowledge but the layout, in six separate parts, is constructed in a way which will hopefully take those who wish to read the whole of it to a well advanced level of understanding.

As far as possible, the intention has been to avoid technical jargon and to explain the meaning and interpretation of accounts in straightforward language. That is not to say that matters of accounting concept or principle have been totally avoided: coverage is given to them in so far as they are necessary for a full understanding of the sort of information that accounts are intended to convey. Indeed, in this respect an awareness of certain of the fundamental principles on which accounts are drawn up is essential, for in many respects they act as limiting factors on the alternative uses to which accounts can be put.

This should not, therefore, be taken as a technical textbook on accounting theory, but it may nevertheless serve as a guide to a practical understanding of what accounts are all about.

Part One prepares the ground. Accounts such as Dovetails' are prepared in the first instance from underlying accounting records. In order to understand accounts we need first to understand the procedures by which business transactions are recorded. Of the two chapters in Part One, the first provides an introduction to the accounting process and explains how, for example, the technique of double entry produces a 'balance' sheet that has two equal sides.

The second chapter in Part One describes the transition from accounting records to the preparation of a set of accounts. Accounts tell a story about a business and, if the story is to be as fair and complete as possible, the raw data provided by the accounting records may need to be amended and adjusted. The way in which these amendments and adjustments are made is governed by a small number of fundamental accounting concepts. Chapter 2 describes them and underlines the degree of judgement and estimation involved in applying them. These concepts set the parameters for the story accounts are designed to tell. Anyone who really wants to understand accounts needs to understand where these parameters are drawn.

With this background, Part Two takes the reader *line by line* through Dovetails' accounts. The general purpose is to explain what the words mean and how each of the figures is arrived at. For ease of reference, the relevant extracts from the body of Dovetails' accounts are reproduced beside the paragraphs that describe and explain them. Separate chapters are devoted to the contents of the balance sheet, the profit and loss account and the funds statement.

By the end of Part Two the reader should have an appreciation of how accounts are made, what they mean, and the manner in which they describe the financial position and performance of a business. All of that is offered as the necessary precursor to the practical core of the book contained in Part Three, which explains how the businessman can use his accounts – and his understanding of them – to the practical benefit of his business. The techniques of ratio analysis are explained and the calculation and interpretation of key ratios are illustrated by applying them to a full analysis of Dovetails' accounts. Considerable emphasis is placed on the assessment of trends as well as the sources of comparison by which the businessman might evaluate his own performance. By this means Part Three explains how the intelligent and informed use of accounting information can help business managers chart the route to greater profitability. A separate chapter is devoted to the equally important question of business liquidity, and on the means of avoiding cash crises. A further chapter deals with the needs of proprietory and other shareholders and describes how they can use the information provided in the accounts to assess the value of their investment, its growth, and the level of risk attaching to it.

Using Dovetails as the vehicle, Parts One to Three are concerned with accounts drawn up on the traditional basis (historic cost) and in the sort of traditional format with which most businessmen will be familiar. Parts Four to Six widen the focus. Part Four tackles the question of inflation and analyses the shortcomings of historic cost accounts when prices are rising. It includes a description of some straightforward methods by which businessmen can adjust their historic cost figures to account for the effect on their business of changing price levels. By way of illustration Dovetails' accounts are restated in current cost terms; the step-by-step workings are set out in an Appendix for those who wish to follow the calculations in detail.

Part Five covers the new accounting law introduced in *The Companies Act 1981,* which will in future affect the accounts of all companies. Dovetails' accounts are represented in their future, required format, and in a manner which highlights the new disclosure requirements and other areas of significant change. The Appendix to Part Five provides, in the form of a checklist, a working document for those directors who wish to ensure that their published accounts do include all the information they should. The checklist comprises a comprehensive statement of statutory and other disclosure requirements as they will stand once the new law has been brought into effect.

Part Six reverts to the question of accounting principles. Its particular relevance will be to businessmen and others who are concerned to read the accounts and assess the performance of other companies. It picks up some of the accounting themes developed in earlier sections and underlines the importance of the reader being aware, when assessing a set of accounts, of how alternative accounting treatments can lead to alternative measures of profit: being able to assess the reliability of the figures shown in a set of accounts depends on being able to assess the propriety of the accounting policies which have been adopted, and that in turn requires an awareness of the choices available and the degree of estimation inherent in each of them. Summaries are provided of those accounting principles which have been codified in Statements of Standard Accounting Practice and coverage is given to those – often highly significant – areas where no standard treatment has yet been developed.

There are two concluding appendices. The first offers a glossary of some of the more important accounting terms used in the book. The second provides notes on some of the possible sources of comparative business statistics against which a businessman can assess the relative performance of his own business. It includes a summary of the sort of information made available by a cross-section of trade associations.

# Dovetails Ltd: accounts for year ended 31 December 1982

**DOVETAILS LIMITED**

**Balance sheet
at 31 December 1982**

| | Note | 1982 £ | 1982 £ | 1981 £ |
|---|---|---|---|---|
| Fixed assets | 7 | | 488,061 | 454,384 |
| Investments | 8 | | 26,000 | 22,000 |
| **Current assets:** | | | | |
| Stock and work-in-progress | 9 | 435,289 | | 404,095 |
| Debtors | | 584,537 | | 416,756 |
| Cash | | 26,333 | | 29,745 |
| | | 1,046,159 | | 850,596 |
| **Current liabilities:** | | | | |
| Creditors | | 461,958 | | 329,877 |
| Taxation | | 46,061 | | 16,831 |
| Bank overdraft | 10 | 111,966 | | 85,599 |
| Dividend | | 21,600 | | 20,400 |
| | | 641,585 | | 452,707 |
| Net current assets | | | 404,574 | 397,889 |
| | | | 918,635 | 874,273 |
| *Represented by:* | | | | |
| Share capital | 11 | | 120,000 | 120,000 |
| Reserves | 12 | | 559,528 | 519,373 |
| | | | 679,528 | 639,373 |
| Long-term loan | 13 | | 140,000 | 140,000 |
| Deferred taxation | 14 | | 99,107 | 94,900 |
| | | | 918,635 | 874,273 |

**DOVETAILS LIMITED**

**Profit and loss account
for the year ended 31 December 1982**

|  | Note | 1982 | 1981 |
|---|---|---|---|
|  |  | £ | £ |
| Turnover |  | 2,424,900 | 1,993,400 |
| Operating profit, before taxation | 2 | 129,833 | 134,218 |
| Taxation | 4 | 49,736 | 71,408 |
| Profit after taxation |  | 80,097 | 62,810 |
| Extraordinary item | 5 | 18,342 | – |
| Profit after tax and extraordinary item |  | 61,755 | 62,810 |
| Dividend | 6 | 21,600 | 20,400 |
| Retained profit transferred to reserves | 12 | 40,155 | 42,410 |

**DOVETAILS LIMITED**

**Statement of source and application of funds
for the year ended 31 December 1982**

|  | | 1982 | 1981 |
|---|---|---|---|
|  | | £ | £ |
| Source of funds: | | | |
| Profit before taxation | | 129,833 | 134,218 |
| Extraordinary item | | (18,342) | – |
| Adjustments for items not involving the movement of funds: | | | |
| Depreciation | 65,404 | | 59,926 |
| Profit on sale of fixed assets | (3,907) | | (1,320) |
| | | 61,497 | 58,606 |
| Funds generated from operations | | 172,988 | 192,824 |
| Other sources: | | | |
| Sale of fixed assets | | 5,500 | 3,250 |
| | | 178,488 | 196,074 |
| Application of funds: | | | |
| Purchase of fixed assets | | 100,674 | 83,499 |
| Taxation paid | | 16,299 | 12,101 |
| Purchase of trade investment | | 4,000 | – |
| Dividend paid | | 20,400 | 18,000 |
| | | 141,373 | 133,600 |
| Increase in working capital | | 37,115 | 82,474 |
| Comprising changes in: | | | |
| Stock | | 31,194 | 28,967 |
| Debtors | | 167,781 | 52,390 |
| Creditors | | (132,081) | (33,523) |
| Net liquid funds | | (29,779) | 34,640 |
| | | 37,115 | 82,474 |

## DOVETAILS LIMITED

### Notes to the accounts
### year ended 31 December 1982

1    *Accounting policies*
The principal accounting policies adopted by the company in the preparation of its accounts are as follows:

(a)    *Depreciation*
Depreciation is not charged in respect of freehold land. On other assets it is charged in equal annual instalments over their anticipated useful lives. The rates of depreciation used are as follows:

| | | |
|---|---|---|
| Freehold buildings | – | 2 per cent per annum |
| Tools and equipment | – | 15 per cent per annum |
| Motor vehicles | – | 25 per cent per annum |

(b)    *Stocks and work-in-progress*
Stocks and work-in-progress are stated at the lower of cost and net realisable value. Cost comprises materials, direct labour and attributable production overheads.

(c)    *Deferred taxation*
Provision is made for taxation deferred because of timing differences between the treatment of certain items for accounting and taxation purposes, but only where there is a reasonable probability of payment.

2    *Profit before taxation*

| | 1982 | 1981 |
|---|---|---|
| | £ | £ |
| Profit before taxation is arrived at after charging: | | |
| Directors' emoluments (Note 3) | 43,500 | 42,000 |
| Depreciation | 65,404 | 59,926 |
| Hire of plant and machinery | 16,416 | 12,210 |
| Auditors' remuneration | 5,000 | 4,500 |
| Bank interest | 13,686 | 11,008 |
| Interest on long-term loan | 12,600 | 12,600 |
| and after crediting: | | |
| Income from trade investments | 2,278 | 1,741 |

**DOVETAILS LIMITED**

**Notes to the accounts**
**year ended 31 December 1982**
**(Continued)**

| 3 | Directors' emoluments | 1982 | 1981 |
|---|---|---|---|
| | | £ | £ |
| | Fees | 500 | 500 |
| | Other remuneration including pension contributions | 39,000 | 32,500 |
| | Compensation for loss of office | – | 5,000 |
| | Pension paid to former director | 4,000 | 4,000 |
| | | 43,500 | 42,000 |
| | Remuneration of chairman | 9,500 | 8,500 |
| | Remuneration of the highest paid director | 13,000 | 10,000 |

| | Scale of directors' remuneration: | Number of directors | |
|---|---|---|---|
| | Up to £5,000 | 1 | 1 |
| | £ 5,001–£10,000 | 3 | 4 |
| | £10,001–£15,000 | 1 | – |

| 4 | Taxation | 1982 | 1981 |
|---|---|---|---|
| | | £ | £ |
| | Corporation tax at 52% | 45,015 | 15,538 |
| | Transfer to deferred taxation | 4,721 | 55,870 |
| | | 49,736 | 71,408 |

| 5 | Extraordinary item | 1982 | 1981 |
|---|---|---|---|
| | | £ | £ |
| | Redundancy and other costs relating to the closure of the Scunthorpe factory (less related taxation of £19,012) | 18,342 | – |

| 6 | Dividend | | |
|---|---|---|---|
| | Proposed Ordinary dividend of 18p (1981 – 17p) per share | 21,600 | 20,400 |

## DOVETAILS LIMITED

**Notes to the accounts
year ended 31 December 1982
(Continued)**

| 7 Fixed assets | Freehold property | Tools & equipment | Motor vehicles | Total |
|---|---|---|---|---|
| | £ | £ | £ | £ |
| Cost: | | | | |
| At 1 Jan 1982 | 227,575 | 391,789 | 35,557 | 654,921 |
| Additions | 50,715 | 43,913 | 6,046 | 100,674 |
| Disposals | – | (18,866) | – | (18,866) |
| At 31 Dec 1982 | 278,290 | 416,836 | 41,603 | 736,729 |
| Depreciation: | | | | |
| At 1 Jan 1982 | 27,309 | 159,161 | 14,067 | 200,537 |
| Charge for the year | 5,058 | 50,483 | 9,863 | 65,404 |
| Disposals | – | (17,273) | – | (17,273) |
| At 31 Dec 1982 | 32,367 | 192,371 | 23,930 | 248,668 |
| *Net book values* | | | | |
| At 31 Dec 1982 | 245,923 | 224,465 | 17,673 | 488,061 |
| At 31 Dec 1981 | 200,266 | 232,628 | 21,490 | 454,384 |

| Capital commitments | 1982 £ | 1981 £ |
|---|---|---|
| Contracted for but not provided for in the accounts | 4,600 | 28,100 |
| Authorised but not yet contracted for | 8,900 | 1,900 |

| 8 Investments | 1982 £ | 1981 £ |
|---|---|---|
| Listed investments, at cost | 14,000 | 14,000 |
| Unquoted trade investments, at directors' valuation | 12,000 | 8,000 |
| | 26,000 | 22,000 |

The market value of listed investments at 31 Dec 1982 was £17,963 (1981: £15,236).

The trade investment comprises 12,000 Ordinary shares in Legato Limited, representing 15% of the issued share capital of that company.

**DOVETAILS LIMITED**

**Notes to the accounts
year ended 31 December 1982
(Continued)**

| 9 | Stock and work-in-progress | 1982 | 1981 |
|---|---|---|---|
| | | £ | £ |
| | Raw materials | 211,579 | 195,026 |
| | Work-in-progress | 202,993 | 187,792 |
| | Finished goods | 20,717 | 21,277 |
| | | 435,289 | 404,095 |

10   *Bank overdraft*
The bank overdraft is secured by a fixed charge on the freehold property of the company.

| 11 | Share capital | 1982 | 1981 |
|---|---|---|---|
| | | £ | £ |
| | Authorised: | | |
| | 150,000 Ordinary shares of £1 each | 150,000 | 150,000 |
| | Issued and fully paid: | | |
| | 120,000 Ordinary shares of £1 each | 120,000 | 120,000 |

| 12 | Reserves | 1982 | 1981 |
|---|---|---|---|
| | | £ | £ |
| | Non-distributable: share premium account | 243,336 | 243,336 |
| | Distributable: Revenue reserves | | |
| | At 1 Jan 1982 | 276,037 | 233,627 |
| | Retained profit for the year | 40,155 | 42,410 |
| | At 31 Dec 1982 | 316,192 | 276,037 |
| | Total reserves | 559,528 | 519,373 |

| 13 | Long-term loan | 1982 | 1981 |
|---|---|---|---|
| | | £ | £ |
| | 9% Unsecured loan stock 1990/95 | 140,000 | 140,000 |

The 9% Unsecured loan stock is repayable at the company's option between 1990 and 1995 with a final redemption date of 31 December 1995.

**DOVETAILS LIMITED**

**Notes to the accounts
year ended 31 December 1982
(Continued)**

| 14 | *Deferred taxation* | *1982* | *1981* |
|----|----|----|----|
| | | £ | £ |
| | Accelerated capital allowances | 108,364 | 103,643 |
| | Advance corporation tax | (9,257) | (8,743) |
| | | 99,107 | 94,900 |
| | If full provision were made, the potential liability would be as follows: | | |
| | Accelerated capital allowances | 147,500 | 138,000 |

# Part One

# CONSTRUCTION OF ACCOUNTS: HOW ARE THEY MADE?

# 1 The accounting process: recording business transactions

Dovetails is an ordinary, medium-sized business. Nevertheless their accounts stretch out over eight pages. They are a formidable and rather uninviting set of documents, and the businessman may well be forgiven if he dismisses them as no more than a riddle, wrapped in a mystery of technical jargon.

In Chapter 2 we shall examine the figures, and begin to unravel some of the jargon. Before we can examine the accounts in detail, however, we need to understand where they come from, and why they take the shape that they do. In particular, we need to understand the difference between the accounts as they are set out and the accounting records from which they are derived and prepared. We also need to understand the small number of fundamental principles that are applied in preparing them, for these set the parameters to the quantity and quality of information that accounts can provide. This chapter provides the necessary background. It explains how accounts are made.

**THE ACCOUNTING RECORDS**

Dovetails provides the vehicle for this book, so for the background we might go back ten years to the week when John Dovetail first set up in business. What happened in that first week?

JOHN DOVETAIL – BUSINESS DIARY
Jan 1    Paid in £5,000 savings
Jan 2    Bought workshop £4,000
Jan 2    Bought tools £300
Jan 3    Borrowed £1,000 from FD
Jan 3    Bought timber £100
Jan 5    Sold table £130

An examination of John Dovetail's business diary shows that on the first day he opened a business bank account and paid in his savings of £5,000. Then he bought a small workshop for £4,000, spent £300 on the tools of his trade, and borrowed £1,000 from his father (FD). Next, because he was a carpenter, he bought £100 worth of timber and set to work to make it into a table. By the end of the week the table was finished and he sold it for £130.

How did John Dovetail's business stand at the end of its first week? Although he hadn't done very much, Dovetail may have found that question difficult to answer. He could probably confirm how much he had in the bank, or what he had spent his money on day by day, but he may have found it difficult to put the whole story together. He would have found it easier if he had kept proper accounting records, but he hadn't yet discovered the accounting process of double entry.

## DOUBLE ENTRY

The technique of double entry is not as mysterious as it may sound. It can be observed in everyday transactions. If a man owns a car, for example, he knows – unless he was very lucky – that he had to pay cash for it. He acquired one thing – a car – in exchange for another – cash. Alternatively, he may have borrowed the money from the bank. In that case he acquired the car in exchange for a commitment to repay the bank. There are two aspects to be observed in any transaction; double entry merely records both of them.

By keeping financial records on this basis, e.g. by recording both the acquisition of a car and the payment of cash or the acquisition of the car and the amount borrowed from the bank, the accounting process enables us to record, for each transaction, the two equal and opposite effects that it has on the financial standing of the business. And it is because the accounting process is based on double entry that a 'balance' sheet can be prepared which has two equal sides.

## ASSETS, LIABILITIES AND CAPITAL: THE BALANCE SHEET

When Dovetail first set up in business, there were only two places he could have obtained the money: used his own or borrowed someone else's. He did both, and then he used the money to buy the things he needed to run the business. These simple events describe the three main components of any balance sheet:

ASSETS = what the business owns
LIABILITIES = what the business owes
CAPITAL = the owner's interest in the business

The two sides of a balance sheet therefore arrange these components in a way which shows 'where the money came from' (on the one hand) and 'where it is now' (on the other) – see Frame 1.

**Frame 1**

**The balance sheet equation**

| *(Where the money came from)* | | *(Where it is now)* |
|---|---|---|
| CAPITAL + LIABILITIES | = | ASSETS |

The balancing of the balance sheet results from the process of double entry. More particularly, it results from the fact that the two sides of any transaction can be recorded in terms of their effect on any one or more of these three main elements: assets, liabilities and capital.

Consider John Dovetail's first week of business. The payment of his savings into a bank account would have been recorded (from the point of view of the business) in terms of both John Dovetail's capital interest in it (£5,000) *and* the acquisition of an asset (cash £5,000). When he bought the workshop, the double entry would have been to record the acquisition of one asset (workshop £4,000) *and* the reduction in another asset (cash £4,000). Similarly when he bought tools for £300: the accounting process would have recorded both the acquisition of those tools *and* the reduction in cash he had to pay for them. The same when he borrowed money, increasing the business' cash holding by £1,000 *and* recording the liability to his father for the same amount. And again when he bought the timber: increase in one asset (timber); decrease in another (cash).

And then he worked on the timber, made it into a table and sold it for £130. The business received £130 cash, but the asset given in exchange was only in the records at £100. What has happened of course is that Dovetail has made a profit, and that is what he is in business for – to see his capital grow. Everytime he exchanges one asset for a bigger asset he makes a profit, and everytime he makes a profit his capital grows. Profits are increases in the owner's capital interest, and that is how the accounting entry for this transaction would be completed: an increase in one asset (cash £130), a decrease in another asset (timber £100), and the difference representing an increase in capital (£30).

With his records on a proper accounting basis, Dovetail can readily draw up a balance sheet to show where his business stands at the end of the first week (see Frame 2). Note that the balance sheet shows where Dovetail had

**Frame 2**

| Dovetail's balance sheet end of first week | | | |
|---|---|---|---|
| *Where the money came from* | | *Where it is now* | |
| | £ | | £ |
| CAPITAL | 5,000 | ASSETS | |
| Profit | 30 | Workshop | 4,000 |
| LIABILITY | 1,000 | Tools | 300 |
| | | Cash | 1,730 |
| | 6,030 | | 6,030 |

got to at the end of his first week, but not how he had got there. It shows that he had made a profit, but not how that profit was made. It says nothing about buying timber and selling furniture, but that's what his business is all about – he hopes to buy a great deal of timber and sell a great deal of furniture.

That is exactly what happened. The business flourished, and very quickly Dovetail found that he couldn't manage on his own. He employed another carpenter and as well as the wages he had to pay he was of course soon paying as well for power and light and rates for his workshop. Profit was no longer a simple comparison between the cost of timber and the price he obtained for a piece of furniture. Indeed he started buying timber in larger quantities, enough for several tables and of different qualities and length, and it became even more difficult to assess the cost of the timber that went into each piece of furniture that he sold. With all these costs to be accounted for, the calculation of profit on any one sale would be an extremely complicated exercise, and the accounting records would quickly be reduced to a state of almost indecipherable complexity.

## REVENUE AND EXPENSES: THE PROFIT AND LOSS ACCOUNT

To avoid that, two further sections are introduced into the accounting records. Every time Dovetail sold a piece of furniture he recorded the increase in asset (cash) and maintained the double entry by noting that the cash came from 'sales'. And every time he incurred a cost connected with those sales, he recorded the reduction in asset (cash) and maintained the double entry by noting that the cash went on 'cost of sales'. These two further elements in the accounting process are usually described as:

REVENUE = Money received from selling the product of the business

EXPENSES = Costs incurred in making and selling that product

If from time to time total revenues are compared with total expenses, the difference will be the profit or loss which has been made not on any one

**Frame 3**

| Dovetail's profit and loss account for first week | |
|---|---:|
| | £ |
| REVENUE | |
| Sale of furniture | 130 |
| *Less:* EXPENSES | |
| Cost of timber | 100 |
| PROFIT | 30 |

**Frame 4**

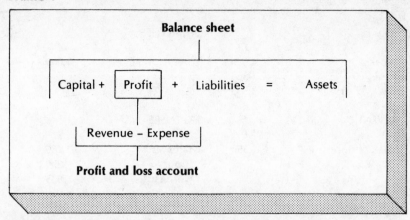

individual sale but on all the sales that have taken place since they were last summarised.

Extending the accounting records in this way provides the basis for preparing a profit and loss account. That for Dovetail's first week would look as in Frame 3. It summarises the results of trading during the week, and shows how the profit disclosed in the balance sheet arose.

There are now five main elements to the accounting records: assets, liabilities, capital, revenue and expense. It is important to remember, however, that profits accrue to capital; that revenue and expense are no more than sub-components of capital; and therefore that the profit and loss account is no more than a sub-analysis of the capital section of the balance sheet. This can be illustrated by extending the balance sheet equation as shown in Frame 4.

Alternatively, the equation can be rearranged in simplified form as follows:

Capital = Assets − Liabilities

The right-hand side of this equation (assets − liabilities) is often described as 'net assets', and this form of expression provides the basis for the accounting description of profit (an increase in capital) as representing an increase in net assets.

These five components provide the framework for keeping full and comprehensive accounting records. Any business transaction, no matter what its apparent complexity, can be described and recorded in terms of its effect on assets, liabilities, capital, revenue or expense; and the double-entry process keeps the equation constantly in balance by recording the dual aspects to any transaction in terms of their effect in increasing or decreasing any one or more of these five main elements.

Accounting records also provide the means by which day-by-day control can be exercised over the affairs of the business, and for this purpose the businessman will want his records in as much detail as possible. Dovetail

**Frame 5**

| ASSETS | | LIABILITIES | | CAPITAL | |
|---|---|---|---|---|---|
| | £ | | £ | | £ |
| Workshop | 4,000 | Loan from FD | 1,000 | J. Dovetail | 5,000 |
| Tools | 300 | | | | |
| Cash | 3,985 | | | | |

| REVENUE | | EXPENSES | |
|---|---|---|---|
| | £ | | £ |
| Sales of furniture | 5,350 | Materials | 1,260 |
| | | Labour | 970 |
| | | Overheads | 835 |

**Frame 6**

**Dovetail's profit and loss account for first year**

| | £ | £ |
|---|---|---|
| REVENUE | | |
| Sale of furniture | | 5,350 |
| | | |
| *Less:* EXPENSES | | |
| Materials | 1,260 | |
| Labour | 970 | |
| Overheads | 835 | |
| | | 3,065 |
| Profit | | 2,285 |

**Dovetail's balance sheet at the end of the first year**

| CAPITAL | | ASSETS | |
|---|---|---|---|
| CAPITAL | 5,000 | ASSETS | |
| Profit | 2,285 | Workshop | 4,000 |
| | | Tools | 300 |
| | 7,285 | Cash | 3,985 |
| | | | |
| LIABILITY | | | |
| Loan | 1,000 | | |
| | 8,285 | | 8,285 |

would want to know not just how much his expenses were in total, but how much he was spending on timber, or electricity, or wages. So he would keep not just one cost of sales account but several expense accounts – according to the nature of the expenses he incurred. Similarly, he will want separate records for each of the business' assets, and separate details, for example, of transactions with each person to whom he might owe money, or who might owe money to him. Accounting records will become detailed in their analysis, but no matter how extensive or sophisticated they might be they will always be organised under these five main categories – and it is because of this ordering of the accounting process that accounts take the shape that they do.

Frame 5 summarises Dovetail's accounting records as they stood at the end of his first year of business. Of course, these figures are not the records themselves but totals extracted from the records, representing in some cases the accumulation of several hundred entries made during the year to record the several hundred transactions that Dovetail entered into. It is these totals, however, which provide the basis from which we can prepare accounts. The profit and loss account set out in Frame 6 compares Dovetail's sales with his expenses to reveal that as a result of all of his trading activities during the year Dovetail had made a profit of £2,285; and the balance sheet which follows shows that at the end of the first year the business had assets totalling £8,285, owed liabilities totalling £1,000, and that Dovetail's capital interest had been increased from its original £5,000 by the profit of £2,285.

# 2 Preparing accounts: describing a business

**MEASURING BUSINESS PERFORMANCE**

The process of summarisation draws out the essential difference between keeping accounting records and preparing a set of accounts. The records are rather like a diary: look up any one page and you will find all the detail you need about each event and transaction that took place. But, like a diary, accounting records have the same limitations: they only provide the detail of each event; they don't draw the events together.

Accounts condense and summarise the information contained in the records into the form of a story. The story has two main chapters: the balance sheet, which assembles information in answer to the question 'Where are we?'; and the profit and loss account, which attempts to answer the question 'How did we get here?'. (Later on, we shall come to a further chapter – the statement of source and application of funds – which explains a little about 'What happened on the way?')

Unfortunately, the process – from accounting records to accounts – is not quite that straightforward. Anyone looking inside John Dovetail's workshop on the last day of the year would find a supply of unused timber – timber which Dovetail has had to pay money for, and which is included in the cost of materials in his profit and loss account. But that timber is not an expense of this year's sales – it will go into furniture that he hopes to sell next year. Similarly with the tables which are not quite finished – are they not as much an asset of the business at the end of the year as the workshop and tools are? And the bill outstanding for the latest supply of materials, or the amount due to carpenters for the last week's wages – are they not liabilities of the business at the year end?

The answer to all these questions is, of course, yes. The point is that the accounting records do not necessarily contain all the information needed to prepare accounts. If the story told in the accounts is to be as fair and complete as possible, the raw information provided by the accounting records may need to be amended and adjusted. The need arises because, whereas the activities of the business continue from day to day, the act of preparing accounts happens only occasionally: in order to prepare them, we have to 'freeze' the flow of the business – rather like taking a still frame from a moving picture. We split the life of a business into periods, usually of one year, and in this act we move from the exact science of noting transactions in the accounting records to the rather more imprecise art of describing the financial position of a business and measuring its profit to date.

This process will often involve a considerable degree of estimation and opinion. (If Dovetail's half-finished tables, for example, are to be regarded as an asset of the business at the end of the year, what cost should be attributed to them?) In order to provide some consistency in the estimates that are made, and to provide a framework within which to exercise their judgement, accountants have adopted a number of generally accepted principles and conventions. Some of these are specific and are concerned with particular types of asset, revenue or expense. Others are more wide-ranging in their effect and it is these we shall look at in the remainder of this chapter. Their importance is that they imply certain assumptions about what accounts are and are not intended to convey. If we want to understand accounts, we need to understand these conventions. And if we want to make use of the information contained in accounts, we need to understand the degree of estimation that goes into preparing them.

## 'REALISATION', OR HOW TO MEASURE REVENUE

There are only a small handful of broad rules that we need to be concerned with. The first is the principle of realisation. Its effect can be observed in the results that were reported for John Dovetail's first week in business.

We said then that he had made a profit because he had *sold* a table, but Dovetail might well claim (and most economists would agree with him) that he started to earn that profit as soon as he started to *make* the table, and that the earning process continued during the making of it. In terms of economic theory that is no doubt true; for accounting purposes, however, it would be impractical to attempt to calculate how much profit was earned on each of the three days it took to make the table – even if we could reasonably assume in advance what the total amount of the eventual profit was likely to be. Such a measure would be too subjective, and open to widely differing estimates and interpretations. For accounting purposes the measure of revenue needs to be objective, and so we adopt the principle of realisation: a profit isn't recognised until it is 'realised' in the form of a sale.

There are certain extreme circumstances in which this rule has to be bent. An engineering company, for example, might take four years to build a bridge, and it would clearly be a distortion to allocate all of its profit to the fourth year and none to the first three. For this reason there are exceptional rules which apply when accounting for long-term contracts; but they are the exception. The general rule remains: profit is not recognised until the earning process has been completed and a sale has been made.

## 'HISTORIC COST', OR HOW TO MEASURE ASSETS: 1

The convention by which accounts are based on historic (or original) costs is the mirror image of the realisation principle. The consequence of not recognising a profit until the point of sale is that, while they are still held, assets will always be shown in accounts at a figure based on their original cost.

Thus Dovetail's half-finished tables – his work-in-progress – will be shown at cost – even though the tables are very nearly complete. The supply of timber he bought a year ago will, if unused, be shown in his balance sheet at the end of the year at the same original cost – even if its price has doubled in the meantime. The saw bench he is still using will be shown in this year's accounts at a figure which is based on the amount it cost him many years ago – even though it might cost him three or four times as much if he wanted to buy it now.

It is therefore important to appreciate that the amount at which assets are shown in the balance sheet does not necessarily represent their current value, nor what it would cost to replace them, nor what we could sell them for. Under conventional accounting, assets are shown at the historic cost of acquiring or producing them.

The twin principles of historic cost and realisation have important consequences for an understanding of accounts. Consider two garage owners, Bill and Ben. Both start the week with 100 gallons of petrol in their tanks, and both have paid £1 a gallon for it. On Tuesday, the price of petrol doubles. Bill thinks it might go up further, and decides to hold on to his stock. Ben sells, and invests the whole of the proceeds in bicycles. On Wednesday the price of bicycles doubles, as does the price of petrol once again. Bill still decides to hold on. Ben sells his bicycles and invests the whole of the proceeds (£400) back into petrol – which now costs him £4 a gallon. On Friday they both draw up their accounts. Bill's show no profit, and assets of £100. Ben's reveal a profit of £300 and assets worth £400. Yet they both started and ended the week in identical positions – with 100 gallons of petrol in their tanks.

The difference is, of course, that Ben entered into two market transactions during the week: he made two sales, and he therefore realised an accounting profit. Nevertheless, his wealth in 'real' terms at the end of the week was identical to Bill's.

The example illustrates how the principles of realisation and historic cost act as limiting factors on the type of information that accounts are intended to convey. An appreciation of them will serve the businessman well when he comes to consider such questions as the value of his business and its profitability.

## 'MATCHING', OR HOW TO MEASURE EXPENSE

Profit is the difference between the total revenue of a business and its total expenses for a given period. The purpose of the 'matching' principle is to ensure that, in arriving at that profit, revenue is compared or matched with *all* of the costs that have been incurred in earning it.

The matching process is sometimes referred to as the 'accruals' basis of accounting. This is merely to differentiate it from a simple cash basis, and it means that expenses should be recognised in the period in which they are incurred, rather than that in which money happens to be paid for them.

It is quite clear, for example, that if it costs £1,000 a year to rent a warehouse, then there is an expense of £1,000 to be recognised each year, regardless of how and when the rent is paid. If it was paid in lump sums of three years, £2,000 should, at the end of the first year, be carried forward as an asset – ready to be matched against the revenues of Years 2 and 3. It would be quite wrong to charge the whole of that payment as an expense of Year 1. Similarly the power used in the last quarter of 1982 is an expense of 1982's trading – even though the electricity bill might not be paid until 1983.

The matching process does not create any difficulty when the expense is identifiable with a particular period of time. But that is not always the case. A large-scale advertising campaign, paid for this year, might be expected to boost sales over the next two or three years. How much of that cost to recognise as an expense of Year 1, and how much to carry forward and match against the revenues of Years 2 and 3 is a matter of judgement, involving a good degree of estimation.

Much the same principle applies to plant and machinery. John Dovetail might hope that his saw bench will last for many years, and its use will therefore contribute to several years' revenue. But it won't last for ever, and one way or the other its cost has to be allocated against the revenues it helps to earn. He might expect it to last eight years, in which case one eighth of its cost will be charged against the revenues of each of those years. This process is what is usually referred to as depreciation, but essentially it is no more than a further element in the matching process – the attempt to compare revenues with *all* the costs incurred in earning them.

## 'GOING CONCERN', OR HOW TO MEASURE ASSETS: 2

The idea of 'going concern' is not so much a principle of accounting as a general assumption which supports other, more specific, accounting procedures. The assumption made is that, in the absence of any evidence to the contrary, the business will continue to operate in the future and in the same trade. This may not of itself appear particularly startling, but the assumption of the going concern lends support, for example, to the historic cost basis of valuing assets. If we can assume that the business will continue to operate in future years, it will be appropriate to carry assets forward at their full cost; and it will therefore be unnecessary – indeed inappropriate – to state these assets at what might be a much lower disposal or break-up value.

Take for example the production of this book, and assume it to be in the course of production at the publishing company's year end. It started off life as sheets of clean and rather costly paper, which were then cut up into smaller pieces for printing. At the year-end it comprised a collection of half-printed pages, worth no more than scrap value – and certainly worth far less than the original clean sheets of paper. But by assuming a going concern, we assume that the company will continue in business next year, will finish printing and binding the book, and will sell it at a price which (in normal circumstances) would recover all the costs that have gone into it. So at the year end the going-concern assumption allows the half-processed paper to be carried forward not at its scrap value but at an amount based on the full costs incurred to date, including all the material and production costs that have so far gone into it.

Alternatively, take the table which John Dovetail had only half-finished on the last day of the year. The original length of timber from which he was making it had considerable value, but now he has sawn it, drilled it and chiselled it, although it hasn't yet taken the shape of a table. It lies around his workshop as a collection of odd bits of wood – suitable for the fire but, in their present shape, not much else. But we don't value it as firewood, we value it at the full costs that have so far been put into it – because we assume that he will finish making it, and sell it, and recover all of those costs next year.

## ALLOCATING COSTS TO ACCOUNTING PERIODS

In other words the unfinished table is regarded as an asset. The costs that have gone into it will not be written off as an expense of past trading but will be reflected in the balance sheet, and carried forward to be written off next year and matched against the revenue to be derived from its sale.

This illustrates a theme which is central to the preparation of accounts: whether costs – regardless of how they are described in the records – are properly regarded, for the purpose of preparing accounts, as assets to be carried forward or expenses to be written off. If we could have waited a week or so before preparing Dovetail's accounts, there would have been no problem – the revenue from the sale of the table would automatically have fallen in the same period as the costs of making it. If we could have waited eight years, all the costs of the sawbench would have been used up and automatically matched against the total revenue generated during those eight years. But accounts have to be prepared at least annually, and the allocation of costs to the appropriate accounting periods is one of the finer arts involved in their preparation – and one which will often involve a good deal of estimation.

## 'PRUDENCE', OR HOW TO ESTIMATE

The last of the conventions we need to consider – prudence – is more an attitude than a principle of accounting. Prudence says that whenever you have to exercise judgement, or make an estimate, or assess an uncertain outcome, take the pessimistic view.

We can see prudence in the principle of realisation: don't take a profit until it is certain, until it is realised in the form of a sale. More particularly, we can see it in the converse, in the rule which says provide for all known losses – whether they are realised or not. So Bill the garage owner was not able to show any profit because he hadn't sold any petrol, even though he knew he could sell it for £4 per gallon. But if the price of petrol had halved instead of doubled twice, prudence would have required that Bill's stock be written down to 25p per gallon. He would have shown a loss for the week, even though he hadn't sold anything.

Prudence has its roots in the purpose that accounts have traditionally served in providing financial information about a business to creditors, shareholders and other interested parties who, of necessity, do not have day-by-day control over the credit they have given or the money they have invested. For these purposes there is some virtue in adopting conventions such as prudence in order to temper the terms of uninhibited optimism in which management might otherwise be inclined to report. But prudence does imply 'at least as good' rather than 'most likely' or 'at best'. It does tend, on balance, towards a relative understatement of both profits and asset values, and it adds a further dimension to our understanding of accounts.

**SUMMARY**

To understand accounts we need to understand their derivation. Accounts are derived from accounting records, and accounting records – the means by which a business keeps a record of the transactions it has engaged in – are maintained on the basis of double entry.

The process of double entry results in a balance sheet that has two equal sides, which describe and compare assets (what the business owns) with liabilities (what the business owes) and capital (the owners' interest in the business). The balance sheet is a statement of financial position: it describes where the business stands at any given time.

The process of double entry also leads to the profit and loss account, which compares the revenues and expenses of a business for a given period. Profit is represented by an increase in net assets, and the making of a profit results in an increase in the owner's capital interest. The profit and loss account summarises how that increase arose; it analyses the movement in the capital part of the balance sheet equation. A balance sheet shows where a business stands; the profit and loss account shows how it came to stand there.

In order to make use of accounts we also need to understand the bases on which they are drawn up. A summary of the accounting records provides the starting point but, because the act of preparing accounts requires the flow of business transactions to be frozen, figures extracted from the records will need amendment and adjustment if the balance sheet is to provide a fair picture of the financial position of the business and if the profit and loss account is to provide a fair measure of its performance to date.

The process of transformation – from accounting records to a set of accounts – is one that involves accountants in a good deal of estimation and opinion. The rules that govern the estimates which are made are dominated by a sense of prudence: the principle of realisation gives a prudent measure of profit; the convention of historic cost normally results in a prudent measure of assets.

These rules serve their purpose in providing a framework in which accounts can be drawn up on a reasonably objective basis; but they also serve as limiting factors on the type of information that accounts are intended to convey. An appreciation of them is essential for an understanding of the uses to which accounts can be put.

# Part Two

# CONTENT OF ACCOUNTS:
# WHAT DO THEY MEAN?

# 3   Introduction

In Part Two the accounts of Dovetails Limited will be examined in detail. Since its modest beginnings, John Dovetail's furniture business has expanded considerably. Others have joined him in forming a company, which has been trading successfully for a number of years.

The company's accounts for 1982 are set out on pages xv to xxii. They comprise two things – words and figures. Our purpose in this chapter will be to look at what the words mean, and how the figures are arrived at.

First, however, it should be emphasised that the accounts reproduced are extracts from the company's published annual accounts. Because they are extracted from the published accounts, they are drawn up in a manner that complies both with the Companies Acts and with Statements of Standard Accounting Practice (SSAPs) issued by the accounting profession.

For the most part, the accounting requirements of the Companies Acts seek to establish the minimum amount of information that should be included in accounts, and the manner in which it should be presented: until very recently (see Part Five), company law has not been concerned with how the figures are arrived at. SSAPs also regulate disclosure, but their main purpose is to establish the principles by which certain of the figures are calculated. Although, for the most part, there will be no need here to refer to the detailed requirements of either the Companies Acts or SSAPs, the reader should be aware of their governing influence on the accounts to be examined.

It should also be noted that in addition to the statements that are reproduced here, Dovetails' full set of published accounts would include two further reports: one by the directors and one by the auditors. The first provides a narrative commentary by the directors on the company's activities during the year (usually in highly cryptic form), but is otherwise concerned to disclose details to the outside world about the directors themselves and their interests in the company. The second report contains confirmation from the auditors that they have carried out an independent examination of the company's accounts, and includes their opinion as to whether the accounts provide a 'true and fair view' of both the company's financial position and its reported profit or loss for the year.

The accounts are in four parts: a balance sheet, a profit and loss account, a statement of source and application of funds, and supporting notes. Earlier sections described how the balance sheet and profit and loss account are derived from the accounting records. Later, we shall examine how the statement of source and application of funds provides a re-analysis of this information in different terms.

The fourth part to the accounts – the notes – serves two purposes. First they are the traditional means of disclosing more detailed information can reasonably be included on the face of the balance sheet or the profit and loss account. The notes can be very useful in the explanation and supporting information they provide; indeed they will often contain information which is critical for a full understanding of the main accounts. Secondly, the notes will disclose the accounting treatments adopted by the company in areas where alternative treatments would have a significant effect on the figures. For our purposes in 'walking through' the accounts of Dovetails Limited, we shall be looking at each item in the accounts in conjunction with any notes which support it.

# 4  The balance sheet

**DATE AND FORMAT**

The balance sheet is a statement of position. It attempts to provide the financial answer to the question 'Where does the business stand?'. The first point to be noticed about a balance sheet, therefore, is that it is drawn up as at a particular moment in time – in Dovetails' case, at the close of business on 31 December 1982.

We have already noted that the business itself does not of course 'stop' on 31 December. Its trading activities are continuous. If the preparation of a balance sheet is to be compared to the taking of a still frame from a moving picture, we should also note that if we take the frame a moment earlier or a moment later, the picture will be different. In the case of the financial picture in a balance sheet, any difference will depend on the extent to which the business has engaged in any transactions of unusual significance during the days and weeks immediately surrounding the date of the balance sheet. In normal circumstances, assuming a steady pattern to the flow and terms of trading, the difference may only be marginal, and we can usually regard the balance sheet not only as a summary of affairs 'as at the balance sheet date', but also as a reasonable representation of the company's affairs on or around that date.

The second general point to note about Dovetails' balance sheet is that it is really two balance sheets, presented under the columns 1982 and 1981. The amounts appearing under the 1981 column are referred to as 'comparative figures' or 'corresponding amounts' and they summarise the position as it stood on the same date last year. Their inclusion is a legal requirement, but they also provide a very useful basis for comparison: it is one thing to know where the business stands on 31 December 1982, but it is much more useful to be able to assess that position in the context of where the business has come from. The comparative figures show where the business was twelve months ago.

Thirdly, it will be noted that Dovetails' balance sheet is presented in a vertical format. This presentation differs only in shape from the simple examples of horizontal balance sheets that were illustrated in Part One. The substance of the two formats is the same: the totals of Dovetails' vertical presentation (£918,635) retain the same, essential balance sheet equation.

**FIXED ASSETS**

The first line of Dovetails' balance sheet shows fixed assets of £488,061 (and £454,384 for the previous year). The one characteristic that distinguishes a 'fixed' asset is that it is held because the business intends to use it rather than sell it.

**Frame 7**

| 6 Fixed Assets | Freehold property | Tools & equipment | Motor vehicles | Total |
|---|---|---|---|---|
| | £ | £ | £ | £ |
| Cost: | | | | |
| At 1 Jan 1982 | 227,575 | 391,789 | 35,557 | 654,921 |
| Additions | 50,715 | 43,913 | 6,046 | 100,674 |
| Disposals | – | (18,866) | – | (18,866) |
| At 31 Dec 1982 | 278,290 | 416,836 | 41,603 | 736,729 |
| Depreciation: | | | | |
| At 1 Jan 1982 | 27,309 | 159,161 | 14,067 | 200,537 |
| Charge for the year | 5,058 | 50,483 | 9,863 | 65,404 |
| Disposals | – | (17,273) | – | (17,273) |
| At 31 Dec 1982 | 32,367 | 192,371 | 23,930 | 248,668 |
| Net book value: | | | | |
| At 31 Dec 1982 | 245,923 | 224,465 | 17,673 | 488,061 |
| At 31 Dec 1981 | 200,266 | 232,628 | 21,490 | 454,384 |

'Fixed' assets are those which a business intends to retain for a number of years, and put to use repeatedly in the production and distribution of its products. They will normally comprise buildings in which to make and store the product, plant and machinery to make it with, and vehicles to deliver it in.

A breakdown of Dovetails' fixed assets is given in Note 7 to the accounts and reproduced in Frame 7. It shows that Dovetails have three main categories of fixed assets and (in the penultimate line) that the balance sheet figure of £488,061 is made up of freehold property (£245,923), tools and equipment (£224,465) and motor vehicles (£17,673). These amounts are described in the note as being the 'net book value' of the respective assets, and it can be seen that net book value comes from a comparison of cost and depreciation. Depreciation has been touched on in Part One where it was described as the means by which the cost of a fixed asset is allocated over the various accounting periods that benefit from its use. In so doing the attempt is to match the revenues for a period with the proportion of the cost of fixed assets which is used up in earning them. The amount described as net book value represents the proportion of cost which has not yet been charged against the revenues of past periods, and which is therefore carried forward at the end of 1982 to be allocated against the revenues of future periods.

A closer examination of the note shows that at the beginning of the year Dovetails has tools and equipment, for example, which had cost a total of £391,789. During the year the company bought further tools and equipment at a cost of £43,913, and it disposed of items which had originally cost £18,866. That left £416,836 as the total, accumulated, historic cost of the tools and equipment that Dovetails owned at the end of the year.

The next line reveals that, of the total cost of £391,789 at 1 January 1982, £159,161 (approximately 40 per cent) had already been allocated to previous accounting periods. Of that amount, £17,273 was in respect of assets which had been disposed of during the year, and this amount is eliminated from the depreciation column in the same way as the cost of £18,866 was eliminated from the cost column. (The difference of £1,593 represents the net book value of the tools and equipment disposed of, and would be compared with the proceeds to establish whether a profit or loss was made on disposal.)

The amount of depreciation charged for 1982 is £50,483. This represents Dovetails' estimate of the proportion of the cost of these assets which has been used up in the course of 1982's production. As a result, the total accumulated depreciation at 31 December 1982 amounts to £192,371. In summary, the tools and equipment that Dovetails owned at the end of 1982 originally cost them £416,836, of which £192,371 has been written off and charged as expenses in the years up to and including 1982, leaving unexpired costs, or net book value, to be carried forward at 31 December 1982 of £224,465.

Note 7 provides similar information in respect of Dovetails' two other categories of fixed asset – property and vehicles – and each of these columns can be read in the same way. The relationship between cost and accumulated depreciation can give an indication as to the relative age of the assets in question: the greater the proportion that accumulated depreciation bears to original cost, the older the assets are likely to be (and the sooner they might need replacing). That assessment, however, will also require a reading of the company's depreciation policy.

**DEPRECIATION**

There are a number of alternative methods by which annual depreciation can be estimated, and a company can choose whichever method it believes most appropriate for allocating the cost of a fixed asset against the revenues derived from using it.

Ideally, depreciation would be charged on a usage basis. The cost of a lorry which had an expected life of 100,000 miles would be allocated to accounting periods proportionately to the number of miles travelled each year. Similarly, the cost of a machine which is expected to produce 40,000 units would be charged according to the number of units produced each year. More usually, the assumption is made that from year to year the level of business activity will be reasonably consistent, and depreciation is therefore more often charged on a straightforward time basis.

The simplest and most widely adopted method is to spread the cost of an asset in equal instalments over its expected useful life (the 'straight-line' method of depreciation). Dovetails might expect a wood-turning machine to last 8 years. If it cost £16,000, annual depreciation on a straight-line basis would be £2,000 (1/8th × £16,000) each year. At the end of year one, the machine would be shown in the balance sheet as follows:

| | |
|---|---:|
| Cost | £16,000 |
| *Less:* Accumulated depreciation | 2,000 |
| | £14,000 |

At the end of five years, £2,000 having been written off each year, the machine would be shown in the balance sheet at a net book value of £6,000, as follows:

| | |
|---|---:|
| Cost | £16,000 |
| *Less:* Accumulated depreciation | 10,000 |
| | £6,000 |

Whatever method of depreciation is adopted, it will be based on estimates and expectations, and circumstances can of course change in a way which makes previous estimates and expectations no longer appropriate. For example, heavily carved table legs can go out of fashion, and the wood-turning machine that is used to make them will fall idle. In that case the depreciation policy would have to be revised. The full costs of that machine can no longer be expected to be recovered, and prudence would require that its net book value should immediately be written down – either to its scrap value or to the small proportion of its cost which can reasonably be expected to be recovered from its limited future use.

Depreciation is an expense – often a highly significant one – and, because of the degree of estimation it involves, the method of calculation will usually be found in the notes to the accounts. In Dovetails' case this explanation is given in Note 1(a) – see Frame 8. This note explains that Dovetails do not charge depreciation on freehold land. That is quite usual: land does not depreciate however much it is used – it lasts for ever. On other fixed assets Dovetails charge depreciation on the straight-line basis, i.e. they allocate the cost in equal amounts over the number of years the respective assets are expected to last. The remainder of the note reveals that Dovetails expect their buildings to last 50 years (2 per cent per annum), that they expect their tools and equipment to last, on average, between 6 and 7 years (15 per cent per annum) and that they expect their vehicles to last four years (25 per cent per annum).

We might attempt to confirm this information by referring back to the line in the fixed asset note which shows the depreciation charge for the year.

**Frame 8**

1 (a)    *Depreciation*

Depreciation is not charged in respect of freehold land. On other assets it is charged in equal annual instalments over their anticipated useful lives. The rates of depreciation used are as follows:

| | | |
|---|---|---|
| Freehold buildings | – | 2 per cent per annum |
| Tools and equipment | – | 15 per cent per annum |
| Motor vehicles | – | 25 per cent per annum |

The charge for freehold property (£5,058) represents approximately 1.8 per cent of the total cost at 31 December 1981 of £278,290. The shortfall is due to the element of land included in the cost but which is not depreciated. The charge for tools and equipment (£50,483) represents approximately 12 per cent of the cost of £416,836. This is less than the quoted 15 per cent, and there could be a number of reasons. It may be that Dovetails calculate depreciation on a monthly basis, in which case the additions during the year of £43,913 would have suffered less than a full year's depreciation charge. Or it could be that included in the cost of tools and equipment are items that are more than seven years old, the cost of which would have been wholly written off in previous years and for which there will therefore be no depreciation to charge for the current year. Without knowing this detail we cannot reconcile the depreciation charge exactly, but the fixed asset note will often provide a broad indication of the age of the assets in question. If the charge for the year is considerably less than the quoted rate, the indication is that the assets are relatively old, and have lasted longer than was originally expected.

Depreciation is sometimes referred to, rather misleadingly, as a means of providing for the replacement of the assets in question. It is true that charging depreciation annually against profits will, over the years, ensure that funds are retained in the business equivalent to the original cost of the asset. But a fixed asset can be replaced only if there is sufficient cash – or borrowing power – available to meet the replacement cost. Depreciation can only be said to 'provide' for replacement if the funds that have been retained are kept in liquid form.

More importantly, depreciation only ensures the retention of funds amounting to the *original* cost of the asset and, even if the cash is available, it will often not be enough to buy a replacement. Referring to Dovetails' fixed asset note, it might reasonably – although not necessarily – be presumed that this year's additions to tools and equipment, which cost £43,913, were replacements for the items disposed of during the year which originally cost only £18,866. Even if that cost has been fully written off (which it has not) the accumulated annual depreciation would clearly have fallen very far short of the amount now needed for replacement. For these reasons, the annual depreciation charge is best regarded as no more than one aspect of the general principle of matching – the allocation of the cost of an asset over appropriate accounting periods. Planning for replacement is a matter of quite separate financial policy.

## FIXED ASSET VALUATION

Dovetails have followed normal practice in showing their fixed assets at historic cost, less the proportion of that cost so far written off. However, because fixed assets will usually be several years old, the historic costs will usually be several years out of date. We have seen that this can have important consequences when Dovetails come to make internal plans for plant replacement. It could also have important consequences for any external assessment that might be made of the company's fixed asset position.

Dovetails' buildings, for example, will probably be worth far more – in terms of what they would fetch on the property market – than their book value of £245,923. Buildings usually last a long time; they will often have been acquired many years ago; and their book value, based on original cost, will usually be a considerable understatement of their current worth. Although it is an established principle that accounts do not purport to show disposal values, the inclusion of buildings at original cost can cause a particularly acute distortion in the balance sheet's attempt to describe the current financial position of the business. For this reason it has become a common practice for companies to include property at its current market value.

Although this represents an exception to the general principle of historic cost, it should be noted that there is no corresponding exception to the principle of realisation. If a property is revalued, the surplus that arises is unrealised, and cannot therefore be regarded as a profit. It only becomes realised – and therefore recognisable in the profit and loss account – when it is sold. The surplus does nevertheless represent an increase in asset value and, as such, is properly regarded as an increase – albeit an unrealised increase – in the proprietors' or shareholders' interest in the business. The usual practice is to identify it as a separate element in the reserves section of the balance sheet.

## INVESTMENTS

The next line in Dovetails' balance sheet shows investments of £26,000. There can be any number of reasons why a business might want to hold investments. They may represent money that has been put to one side, ready for when the time comes to replace some fixed assets. Or they may represent no more than a temporary investment of surplus cash. Their purpose will usually dictate the way in which they are disclosed in the balance sheet. In Dovetails' case, they are not shown under the general

**Frame 9**

| 8  Investments | 1982 | 1981 |
|---|---|---|
| | £ | £ |
| Listed investments, at cost | 14,000 | 14,000 |
| Unquoted trade investment, at directors' valuation | 12,000 | 8,000 |
| | 26,000 | 22,000 |

The market value of listed investments at 31 December 1982 was £17,963 (1981 – £15,236).

The trade investment comprises Ordinary shares in Legato Limited, representing 15 per cent of the issued share capital of that company.

heading of current assets – which implies that there is no intention to sell them in the near future.

Investments can also take a variety of forms. In the examples cited, they would usually take the form of marketable securities which could be sold as soon as the funds were needed for the required purpose. Alternatively the investment might be made for purposes connected with the trade. Further details about Dovetails' investments are given in Note 8 – see Frame 9.

Dovetails have two types of investment. Listed investments are investments in companies which have a listing on the Stock Exchange. They cost Dovetails £14,000 but, because they are readily marketable, the note also shows their market value, i.e. the amount that could have been obtained for them if they had been sold on 31 December 1982.

Dovetails also have an unquoted trade investment, which is shown at directors' valuation of £12,000. The note goes on to say that Dovetails have acquired a 15 per cent interest in the business of Legato Limited. There can be a variety of reasons for such trade investments. It might have been to secure benefits for Dovetails' own business operations, e.g. to secure preferential delivery from an important supplier. Or it may be simply an investment in the potential of an unrelated business.

Trade investments should be assessed quite separately from listed securities, for they usually involve a quite different degree of risk. As in Dovetails' case, they are generally shown at directors' valuation for, if the directors do not provide a valuation, there is a legal requirement to disclose somewhat detailed information about the profits and losses of the company in which the investment is held. In any event the valuation is usually based on cost, unless the directors have reason to believe that there has been a permanent diminution in the value of the investment, in which case it would be written down to the lower amount.

**CURRENT ASSETS**

Dovetails have three types of current asset: stock and work-in-progress; debtors; and cash. In Dovetails' case, stock will represent a supply of timber ready to be turned into furniture (raw materials), furniture which is in the course of production at the balance sheet date (work-in-progress), and furniture that is awaiting delivery to customers (finished goods). Debtors represent amounts due from customers in respect of past sales. The distinguishing feature of any asset listed as 'current' is that it is either already in the form of cash or can be expected to be turned into cash in the near future, usually one year.

The transformation into cash may take a number of months – according to the type of current asset in question. Dovetails might expect most of their debtors, for example, to pay within the next month. They might expect to deliver a good proportion of their finished goods stock, and collect payment from customers, over the next two or three months. It will take somewhat longer to process the raw materials, turn them into finished goods, sell them and collect the money. But by grouping these assets all under the heading of 'current', the implication is that, one way or the other, they can all be turned into cash within the next twelve months.

Note that the distinction between fixed and current assets depends not on the type of asset but on the type of business that is buying or selling it. Furniture is Dovetails' trading stock, but the company that buys it might expect to use it as office equipment for several years, and in its own accounts will therefore describe it as a fixed asset. Dovetails describe their delivery trucks as fixed assets, but they would have been a current asset of British Leyland (whose business it is to make and sell lorries) before they sold them to Dovetails. Similarly Dovetails' sawbench – which they hope to use for many years – would have been the trading stock of the manufacturer, Black & Decker.

Note also that the grouping of assets under the general headings of 'fixed' or 'current' is no more than a technique adopted in the preparation of a balance sheet, a technique that provides a helpful means of describing the financial position on a given date. In the days and weeks and months which follow 31 December, Dovetails will continue to make furniture, sell it, and collect money from customers. The debtors at 31 December which are turned into cash will be replaced by other debtors, and the stock which is sold will be replaced by other stock as it is produced. The business cycle continues, and phrases such as 'fixed' and 'current' only arise because of the freeze that is put on a business in order to prepare accounts.

**CASH**

Almost alone amongst the items appearing in a balance sheet, cash is what it appears to be: the amount of cash on the premises or in the bank at 31 December 1982 (see Frame 10). Even here, however, the incidence of uncleared cheques (those which have been issued, and recorded in the company's own records, but which have not yet been cleared through the bank statement) leaves room for some debate as to which is the correct figure to use – the one according to the cash book or the one according to

**Frame 10**

| | 1982 | 1981 |
|---|---|---|
| Current assets: | £ | £ |
| . . . | | |
| Cash | 26,333 | 29,745 |

the bank statement. Usual practice in the UK is to take the former – and to deduct uncleared cheque payments before disclosing both the bank balance and the amount of outstanding creditors.

Dovetails have some £3,000 less cash than they held a year ago, but that is not a figure that should be read in isolation, for as we shall see lower down in the balance sheet they also have a bank overdraft.

**DEBTORS**

Debtors represent the amounts due to Dovetails from customers to whom they have sold goods on credit terms. Dovetails' debtors have increased substantially over the previous year (see Frame 11). That could mean that customers are taking much longer to pay, or it could mean that the volume of sales and number of customers has increased. Once again the figure is not to be read in isolation.

**Frame 11**

| | 1982 | 1981 |
|---|---|---|
| Current assets: | £ | £ |
| . . . | | |
| Debtors | 584,537 | 416,756 |

For the most part, the debtors figure in a balance sheet emerges directly from the accounting records, and is one which is therefore capable of precise calculation. From their supporting records, Dovetails could identify how much of the total of £584,537 was due from each individual customer. The only degree of estimation involved concerns an assessment of whether any debtors will not be able to pay. Where there is evidence of bad or doubtful debts – and this will usually come from knowledge of the financial circumstances of the customers, and depending on how long the debts have been outstanding – prudence requires that they should be written down or provided for.

A provision for such debts (writing down the value of the asset debtors, and recognising an expense or loss in the profit and loss account) can be either 'specific' to the debts in question, or 'general' – in which case it is usually expressed as a percentage of sales or of outstanding debtors, and is based on previous years' experience of the proportion that ultimately are irrecoverable. Either way there are clearly elements of uncertainty and estimation involved in the calculation of the provision, and therefore in the amount at which debtors are stated in the balance sheet.

## PREPAYMENTS

Conventionally, the amount shown for debtors will include any 'prepayments' made by the company. Prepayments represent the amounts of any expenses which have been paid for this year but which are attributable to succeeding years. Although these payments are already reflected in the accounting records, the matching principle requires that, on the preparation of accounts, adjustments should be made to carry forward as an asset that amount which should properly be recognised as an expense of the following year.

The degree of estimation involved in calculating the amount to be carried forward will depend on the type of expense in question. Where it is clearly identifiable with time periods, e.g. rent, the calculation is straightforward. Where it is not, e.g. advertising expenditure or costs in connection with the development of a new product, the estimate may involve a considerable degree of uncertainty. Where the amounts involved are significant, prepayments should usually be identified separately in the balance sheet. Where they are not shown separately it can usually be taken that they will represent only a small proportion of the figure appearing against debtors.

## STOCK AND WORK-IN-PROGRESS

Trading stock is the lifeblood of any business, and it is frequently one of the most significant figures in a balance sheet. It is significant in terms of its size, in the degree of estimation that is often involved in its calculation, and in the critical impact it can have on the story told by the accounts. It is also the figure which is most susceptible to error – or manipulation.

In normal circumstances, the costs of materials, wages and overheads incurred in the course of production during the year will be recorded as expenses. The calculation of stock is no more than an application of the matching principle, requiring an assessment of the proportion of those costs which should properly be regarded as an asset to be carried forward to the following year and matched against the revenues which will be generated when those goods are sold. The significance of stock in accounting terms results primarily from the estimates and assumptions that are involved in these calculations. It becomes doubly important because – as we shall see later – an increase or decrease in the value of closing stock and work-in-progress results in a corresponding increase or decrease in the profit for the year.

Because of its significance, many companies will keep subsidiary records to control the amounts and movement of stock. These records will usually be in terms of both quantities and values: entries will be made whenever raw materials are acquired, whenever they are moved to the production line, and whenever they are issued back to the shelves as finished goods. In their more sophisticated forms, such stock records will also record the labour and overhead costs that go into stock at each stage of the production process. Although they do not play a part in the double entry on which the main financial records are based, stock records do provide a good means of control and, where they exist, they will clearly provide the basis for calculating the amount of stock and work-in-progress on hand at any one time.

Where they do not exist – and Dovetails is a case in point – some other means has to be found of calculating stock and work-in-progress at the balance sheet date, and this is usually done by going into the factory or warehouse and counting what's there. That will give quantities, but the accounts, of course, are based on values, and it is the valuing of stock – the allocation of costs between items sold and items still on hand – that gives rise to the main area of estimation.

**Frame 12**

|  | Note | 1982 | 1981 |
|---|---|---|---|
| Current assets: |  | £ | £ |
| . . . |  |  |  |
| Stock and work-in-progress | 9 | 435,289 | 404,095 |

| Note 9 |  | 1982 | 1981 |
|---|---|---|---|
|  |  | £ | £ |
| *Stock and work-in-progress:* |  |  |  |
| Raw materials |  | 211,579 | 195,026 |
| Work-in-progress |  | 202,993 | 187,792 |
| Finished goods |  | 20,717 | 21,277 |
|  |  | 435,289 | 404,095 |

*Accounting policies*
*(b) Stocks and work-in-progress*
Stocks and work-in-progress are stated at the lower of cost and net realisable value. Cost comprises materials, direct labour and attributable overheads.

Note 9 to the accounts (see Frame 12) shows Dovetails' total stocks of £435,289 to be made up of raw materials £211,579, work-in-progress £202,993 and finished goods £20,717. Because of the principle of historic cost, the stated value of these assets will be based on the costs incurred in acquiring them or, in the case of work-in-progress and finished goods, on the costs that have been incurred into bringing them to their present state. The problem remains of establishing exactly what the 'cost' was.

Suppose that Dovetails had bought 10,000 metres of a certain type of timber evenly during the year. In the first half of the year the timber had cost 95p per metre. By the second half of the year the price had increased to £1.25 per metre. Of the 10,000 metres purchased, Dovetails still had 2,000 metres in stock unused at the end of the year. How should the 2,000 metres be valued?

Dovetails might reasonably proceed on the basis that it will carry its earlier costs forward. In that case, the stock of unused timber at the end of the year would be valued at 95p per metre and would be included in the balance sheet at a value of £1,900. As a result, the profit and loss account would be charged with £9,100 (total cost of timber purchased £11,000, less value of stock carried forward £1,900).

Alternatively, Dovetails might choose to attach the earlier costs to the goods sold during the year and to carry forward the later costs. In that case, the year-end stock of timber would be valued at £1.25 per metre and would be included in the balance sheet at a value of £2,500, and £8,500 would be charged against the current year's sales. The effect of the two alternative bases of valuation is to produce a cost of sales (and therefore a profit) figure which is different by £600 and a stock figure which is different by the same amount – a difference which in this example amounts to 30 per cent of the balance sheet carrying value.

Frame 13 summarises the effect. The difference produced by the alternative bases (£600) arises from only one small element in Dovetails' total stocks of £435,289. If costs had changed similarly during the year on all Dovetails' categories of stock, the magnified effect on the total balance sheet value

**Frame 13**

| Bases of stock valuation | | Balance sheet | Profit and loss account |
|---|---|---|---|
| | | Asset | Cost of sales |
| | | £ | £ |
| A | 2,000 metres at 95p | 1,900 | |
| | 3,000 metres at 95p + 5,000 metres at £1.25 | | 9,100 |
| B | 2,000 metres at £1.25 | 2,500 | |
| | 5,000 metres at 95p + 3,000 metres at £1.25 | | 8,500 |

Basis B produces profits and stock values which are both £600 greater than those resulting from basis A.

could be as much as plus or minus £150,000 – more than Dovetails' total profit for the year!

It should be noted that the attempt to allocate costs between materials that have been consumed and those that remain on hand at the end of the year is not necessarily related to the physical flow of those materials through the business: the alternative assumptions which might be made – and the alternative methods of valuation they lead to – arise only as a result of the need to prepare accounts, and the consequent requirement to allocate costs between different accounting periods.

The allocation of material costs is only one of the problems associated with stock valuations. Dovetails' accounting policy on stocks – which purports to describe the bases adopted in valuing it – states that 'cost' comprises not only the cost of materials but also 'direct labour and attributable production overheads'. This means that the costs at which work-in-progress and finished goods are shown include an allocation of the wages and other expenses that have been incurred in bringing that stock to its present state. Establishing precisely which expenses – and what proportion of them – are directly attributable to stock on hand is a matter requiring judgement and estimation.

For example, it is reasonably clear that the wages of a saw-bench operator for a year could with justification be allocated over the number of lengths of timber sawn up during the year or the number of pieces of furniture produced; and it would be a reasonable allocation of his wages if the amount that was deemed to be attributable to stock on hand at the end of the year was in the same proportion as the quantity of that stock to the total amount produced during the year. However, not all wages are that easily identified directly with production: the factory could not run if it were not supervised or maintained, but it is a matter for debate whether a proportion of the wages of the foremen or cleaners can be said to be directly attributable to the production of closing stock, or whether the whole amount of those costs should be written off on a time basis, as soon as they are incurred. Similar decisions have to be made in respect of the myriad other costs that fall under the heading of 'overheads'. Those decisions will have an immediate effect on both the amount at which stock is stated in the balance sheet and on the amount of profit that is reported for the year.

A third matter to be considered in the valuation of stocks is concerned with the occasions on which it is necessary to show them at a value which is less than cost. This point is also alluded to in Dovetails' accounting policy note, where it is disclosed that stocks and work-in-progress are stated 'at the lower of cost and net realisable value'. This is the prudence concept at work. There will be a number of reasons why the full costs included in stock may not be recoverable on eventual sale. Materials may have been damaged, or finished goods may have proven faulty, or the items in stock may comprise a line which has now gone totally out of fashion. For any of these reasons, stocks will be reduced to the amount, if any, which might reasonably be expected to be recovered from their eventual sale. That amount will be uncertain, and can often only be estimated within wide margins. These matters provide further cause for reflecting that the amount appearing against stock in a balance sheet is very much less than a precisely calculated figure.

In view of the potential variables in the methods of establishing a stock valuation, it is a matter for some regret that the notes which purport to describe the bases which have been adopted are often less than helpful. Dovetails is typical. It should be said, however, that whatever assumptions are made, and whatever methods are adopted, there is a general requirement that they should be applied consistently from year to year.

Unless a change of treatment is announced prominently in the accounts, it can be assumed that if Dovetails, for example, based their stock valuation on latest raw material costs and exclude indirect factory overheads, then those are the procedures which they have followed and will follow from year to year. Despite a variety of possible valuation methods, the requirement for consistency ensures that, after the first year, the adopted treatment should have no significant effect on reported profits. Over the life of a business, profits will always be the same: it is only by virtue of preparing annual accounts, and the need to value stocks at the end of each period, that the accounting policies adopted in that valuation can, if not applied consistently, have the effect of shifting profits from one year to another.

## CURRENT LIABILITIES

In the same way as assets are distinguished in a balance sheet between fixed and current, the liabilities of a business are also grouped together according to whether they are payable in the short term or long term. Current liabilities are those amounts owed by the business which, in general, will fall due for payment within twelve months of the balance sheet date.

Dovetails show four types of current liability: creditors, taxation, bank overdraft and dividend. Some of these will have to be paid in a matter of weeks; others may not fall due for several months. Nevertheless, grouping these various liabilities together under the one heading provides a neat and useful means of presenting an important part of the financial position of a business at a given date.

## CREDITORS

Creditors represent amounts owing to suppliers for goods and services provided to the company which have not yet been paid for. Dovetails owes amounts totalling £461,958 at 31 December 1982, and owed a total of £329,877 at 31 December 1981 (see Frame 14). Of these totals, the largest component will usually be amounts owing to trade creditors, the suppliers who provide Dovetails with their raw materials. In their accounting records, Dovetails will carry details of the amount it owes to each individual supplier and, as was the case with debtors, the amount of trade creditors is a liability which can be calculated quite accurately.

**Frame 14**

|  | 1982 | 1981 |
|---|---|---|
| Current liabilities: | £ | £ |
| . . . | | |
| Creditors | 461,958 | 329,877 |

Although no breakdown is given, creditors will also usually include any 'accrued' expenses. Accrued expenses arise from services that have been provided in the current year – the benefit of which has been used in earning the current year's revenue – but which have not been paid for until the following year. Thus at any given time – including the balance sheet date – money will usually be owing for the recent week's wages, in respect of interest due to the bank, or for the last quarter's electricity or telephone bill. In some cases the amounts owing will have to be estimated in advance of knowing their precise amount although, where the expenses in question are of a recurring nature, that estimate can be made with reasonable accuracy based on past experience of the annual, quarterly or monthly charge.

Creditors may also include provisions for costs which although not yet paid, and even though no benefit may yet have been derived from them, are nevertheless 'provided for' this year on the basis of prudence. This will often be the case, for example, where – either through damage or negligence – machinery breaks down, or buildings fall into disrepair, and it is known that the assets in question can only be restored to their operating level at significant cost. Prudence requires provision for all known losses, even though these provisions can often only be made in round-sum amounts. Thus the pursuit of prudence adds another layer of estimation to the measurements included in accounts.

**TAXATION**

The next in Dovetails' list of current liabilities is taxation (see Frame 15), which amounted to £46,061 at 31 December 1982 and £16,831 at 31 December 1981. Companies pay corporation tax on their taxable profits, currently (1982/83) at a standard rate of 52 per cent (although for smaller companies with lower levels of profit the standard rate is reduced to 40 per cent). For most companies tax is usually payable nine months after the year end, and the amount of £46,061 is the estimated tax that Dovetails will have to pay for 1982.

**Frame 15**

|  | 1982 | 1981 |
|---|---|---|
| Current liabilities: | £ | £ |
| . . . | | |
| Taxation | 46,061 | 16,831 |

**BANK OVERDRAFT**

It was noted under current assets that Dovetails had cash and bank balances totalling £26,333. The balance sheet now shows (see Frame 16) that they also have an overdraft – money owing to the bank – which at 31 December 1982 amounts to £111,966.

**Frame 16**

|  | Note | 1982 | 1981 |
|---|---|---|---|
| Current liabilities: | | £ | £ |
| . . . | | | |
| Bank overdraft | 10 | 111,966 | 85,599 |

*Note '10*
The bank overdraft is secured by a fixed charge on the freehold property of the company.

When a bank grants an overdraft facility, it will usually be made available for a given period of time – often one year and, in normal circumstances, on the understanding that it will be available on a recurring basis thereafter. However, the terms under which it is lent will usually stipulate that an overdraft is repayable on demand; for this reason it is properly regarded as a current liability, even though there is an element of permanence to its recurring availability.

Note 10 reveals that the bank has taken a charge on the company's freehold property as security against the overdraft. If Dovetails defaults in repayment, the charge gives the bank the legal right to sell the property and recover the amount due to them out of the proceeds.

**DIVIDENDS**

Dovetails' remaining current liability (see Frame 17) is described as a dividend of £21,600. A dividend is an amount paid out to the shareholders (the owners) of the company as a return on the funds they have invested by way of share capital.

It was established in Part One that profits accrue to capital. If a business makes profits, the shareholders' capital grows. They will be happy with

**Frame 17**

|  | 1982 | 1981 |
|---|---|---|
| Current liabilities | £ | £ |
| . . . | | |
| Dividend | 21,600 | 20,400 |

that growth for it increases the paper value of their shares but, from time to time, they will also want a more tangible return on their investment. The only way that can normally be provided is by paying them a cash dividend.

The amount of dividend the directors of a company decide to pay is a critical factor in their overall financial policy: as much as profit is distributed to shareholders, that much less profit is retained within the business to finance future growth. For companies listed on the Stock Exchange the pressure to 'maintain (or increase) the dividend' from year to year can be severe; indeed the amount of dividend can act as the primary influence on the price at which shares are quoted, and directors may often feel obliged to maintain dividend payments simply in the – sometimes erroneous – belief that that will keep up the share price, even though the company cannot really withstand the outflow of cash (which might then have to be borrowed elsewhere at high interest rates).

For some family companies the dividend decision will often be less critical. The shareholders are likely to be related, and some of them will usually have a direct interest in the day-by-day running of the company. They will therefore be just as concerned with the long-term growth of the business as they are with any short-term return on their investment.

Note that of the total amount of dividend that the directors of Dovetails have declared during the year the amount shown in the balance sheet represents only that part which remains unpaid at the end of the year. The full dividend story can only be obtained from the profit and loss account.

When a company makes a distribution, it is required to pay tax at the basic income tax rate (presently 30 per cent) on the gross, i.e. before tax, amount distributed. This amount is treated as a payment on account of the company's corporation tax liability for the year in which the dividend is paid. It is described as Advance Corporation Tax (ACT) and, in so far as it is recoverable, is treated as an asset in the balance sheet, usually by way of deduction from the deferred tax liability.

Dovetails' dividend liability of £21,600 represents the net amount payable to shareholders after deducting tax (at 30 per cent) of £9,257; ACT of £9,257 is shown in Note 14 which describes the make-up of the deferred tax balance.

**NET CURRENT ASSETS**    We have now walked through the first half of Dovetails' balance sheet. Only one figure remains and that is the amount of £404,574 which is described as 'net current assets'. It is arrived at by deducting total current liabilities of £641,585 from total current assets of £1,046,159.

The amount of net current assets is a critical figure in any balance sheet. It comprises one measure of the 'working capital' of the business and it is in order to be able to highlight this figure that current liabilities are presented as a deduction from current assets. Current liabilities have been described as amounts which, in general, will fall due for payment within one year.

Current assets have been described as those amounts which are either already in the form of cash or will be turned into cash within one year. It is clear, therefore, that current assets will hopefully provide the funds from which current liabilities will be paid: the comparison of the two provides a useful indication of the short-term financial stability of the business.

Careful control of working capital lies at the heart of efficient business performance. It will form an important part of the analysis of Dovetails' financial strength and profitability, as described in Part Three.

## SHARE CAPITAL

In the case of a company, capital is divided into shares, each representing a stake in the ownership. Company law permits shares to be issued in various types, and in unlimited amount. The type and amount of shares issued by any one company, however, will be governed by its constituting documents (its Memorandum and Articles of Association). As well as representing an interest in the capital of the business, a share will usually carry with it the right to vote – on those occasions when shareholders are asked to decide on some important aspect of the company's affairs – as well as an entitlement to dividends and a share in the proceeds in the event of the company being liquidated.

Dovetails' balance sheet shows share capital of £120,000 (see Frame 18). Note 11 explains that this is made up of Ordinary shares of £1 each. The amount of £1 is the nominal or par value of each share, and it represents the minimum amount that would have been paid in when the shares were first issued. Ordinary shares are the type most commonly issued. Each will usually carry an equal right to vote, an equal right to any profits that are distributed and equal rights in the winding up of the company. The 'authorised' share capital is the maximum amount which the company is presently permitted to issue, although by altering its Memorandum, and on application to the Registrar of Companies, this amount can be

### Frame 18

|  | Note | 1982 | 1981 |
| --- | --- | --- | --- |
|  |  | £ | £ |
| Share capital | 11 | 120,000 | 120,000 |
| *Note 11* |  |  |  |
| *Share capital* |  |  |  |
| Authorised: |  |  |  |
| 150,000 Ordinary shares of £1 each |  | 150,000 | 150,000 |
| Issued and fully paid: |  |  |  |
| 120,000 Ordinary shares of £1 each |  | 120,000 | 120,000 |

increased. Of the 150,000 shares Dovetails has been authorised to issue, Note 11 confirms that it has in fact issued only 120,000.

The holders of Ordinary shares are not guaranteed any dividend. When profits are low they may get no return at all. When profits are high, however, they can usually expect a correspondingly high return on their investment. The strength of entitlement to dividends is the characteristic which distinguishes them from 'preference' shares. Dovetails do not have any preference shares in issue but, where they exist, they carry – as their name implies – preferred rights to any dividends that might be payable and any distributions that might be made on liquidation. Preference shares usually attract a fixed percentage return, which has to be satisfied before any dividend can be paid to the Ordinary shareholders. They therefore carry less risk than Ordinary shares and as a result will often be issued without voting rights. It is the Ordinary shareholders who provide the risk capital of the company and it is they who will reap the rewards if the company is successful.

**RESERVES**

Where reserves are shown as one figure in a balance sheet they will often comprise the aggregate of a number of quite separate balances. Note 12 to Dovetails' accounts (see Frame 19) shows that their reserves contain two distinct elements: a share premium account amounting to £243,336 and revenue reserves which, at 31 December 1982, totalled £316,192. These two amounts are quite different in their characteristics.

The share premium account represents money paid in by shareholders over and above the nominal value of the shares that they hold. The existence of a

**Frame 19**

|  | Note | 1982 £ | 1981 £ |
|---|---|---|---|
| *Reserves* | 12 | 559,528 | 519,373 |
| *Note 12* | | | |
| *Reserves* | | | |
| Non-distributable: share premium account | | 243,336 | 243,336 |
| Distributable: revenue reserves | | | |
| At 1 Jan 1982 | | 212,037 | 233,627 |
| Retained profit for the year | | 40,155 | 42,410 |
| At 31 Dec 1982 | | 316,192 | 276,037 |
| Total reserves | | 559,528 | 519,373 |

share premium account indicates that at some stage in the company's past a block of shares has been issued at a price in excess of their nominal value.

One of the primary functions of company law is to provide protection for the interests of creditors and other third parties who might enter into financial dealings with the company. One of the ways in which the law can do this is to provide safeguards to ensure that the capital subscribed by the shareholders is not subsequently and wilfully reduced, impaired or otherwise repaid to them – by way of dividend or otherwise – except in specified circumstances. Because it represents money subscribed by the shareholders, the same legal safeguards apply to the share premium account. The essential characteristic of a share premium account is, therefore, that it is non-distributable.

In that respect it is totally different from revenue reserves, which are fully distributable. Revenue reserves are sometimes alternatively described as retained profits. They represent the accumulation of profits made by a company during its lifetime, subject to the extent to which in the past those profits have been distributed by way of dividend. Thus a company which in its first year makes profits of £10,000, and pays a dividend of £2,000, will have revenue reserves or retained profits at the end of that year amounting to £8,000. If in the second year it makes profits of £12,000, and pays a dividend of £3,000, its revenue reserves at the end of Year 2 will amount to £17,000.

Dovetails' revenue reserves at the beginning of 1982 amounted to £276,037. Of the profit made during 1982, £40,155 was retained, leaving accumulated retained profits at 31 December 1982 of £316,192.

It is important to recognise that the full amount of retained profits shown in a balance sheet is not necessarily immediately available for distribution to shareholders. A dividend can only be paid out of profits, but the dividend decision will depend just as much on whether there is sufficient cash available to pay it. It is rare that the full amount of a company's retained profits will be available in the form of cash. The purpose of retaining profits will usually have been to finance the further growth of the company, and those profits will usually have been re-invested or 'ploughed back' into other assets. Past profitability does not necessarily go hand in hand with present liquidity. To assess the amount of retained profits that are potentially available for distribution, we need to look also at the assets side of the balance sheet to see how much cash the company has available.

Although it does not figure in Dovetails' accounts, a third source of reserves will often arise as the result of a revaluation of assets. By way of exception to the general principle of historic cost, it is increasingly becoming the case that companies will obtain independent professional revaluations of certain of their assets (particularly property) which will then be included in their accounts at the higher revalued amount. In so far as profit, in its broadest sense, results from increases in net asset values, the surplus that arises on the revaluation of property can be regarded as a profit, and can therefore properly be regarded as part of the company's reserves. The essential difference, of course, is that as long as the company continues to use the property and does not sell it, that profit remains unrealised. Where it appears, therefore, it should usually be described as non-distributable.

**LONG-TERM LOANS**

Given the earlier definition of current liabilities, long-term liabilities will comprise amounts owed by the company which are repayable in more than a year's time.

Note 13 to Dovetails' accounts (see Frame 20) states that the long-term loan of £140,000 comprises 9 per cent unsecured loan stock 1990/95. This means that the company has borrowed money on which it has to pay a fixed rate of interest at 9 per cent per annum. The lenders have not been provided with any security for their loan. The note goes on to say that the loan is repayable at the company's discretion sometime between 1990 and 1995, but not later than 31 December 1995.

**Frame 20**

|  | Note | 1982 £ | 1981 £ |
|---|---|---|---|
| Long-term loan | 13 | 140,000 | 140,000 |
|  |  |  |  |
| *Note 13* |  |  |  |
| *Long-term loan* |  |  |  |
| 9% Unsecured loan stock 1990/95 |  | 140,000 | 140,000 |

The 9% unsecured loan stock is repayable at the company's option between 1990 and 1995 with a final redemption date of 31 December 1995.

Long-term loans of this sort can take a variety of forms. In Dovetails' case, each separate part of the loan will be supported by a certificate issued to the lender in acknowledgement of the debt due to him. Alternatively, these loans can take the form of debentures, which is really no more than a different way of describing the piece of paper that acknowledges the debt. They can be secured (implying that the lenders have taken a charge over some of the company's assets as security for their debt), or unsecured. They are sometimes described as convertible, which means that at some time in the future the lender has the right to convert them into Ordinary shares in the company. They can be either redeemable, as with Dovetails, or irredeemable – in which case the company has no obligation to repay them (except in liquidation). There may even be a premium payable on final redemption, i.e. repayment, by the company. Their one essential characteristic is that they will always carry a fixed rate of interest.

There are similarities here with preference shares. Preference shares will also carry a fixed return and they can be issued under terms which describe them as convertible or non-convertible, redeemable (at par or at a premium) or irredeemable. The critical difference is that interest on borrowings is an annual commitment which has to be met each year, regardless of whether the company has made any profits and before any of the shareholders – preference or otherwise – become entitled to any dividends. Interest is an expense which has to be paid and accounted for before calculating profit. Dividends to shareholders are dependent upon profitability.

The distinction between debt and equity capital is an important one. Each can provide a source of long-term finance for the company. From the point of view of the lender or the investor, the choice between a fixed rate of return or a return linked to profitability will depend very largely on the degree of risk inherent in the company's operations.

The same assessment of risk will also affect the choice from the company's point of view. Any preference for debt as a source of finance will depend very much on the required rate of interest. But it will also depend on the expected pattern of profitability. If profits are consistent from year to year, debt can provide an attractive source of long-term funds. If profits are volatile, the annual interest burden of debt could, in unprofitable years, prove terminal. For these reasons most companies will seek to achieve a careful balance between the two and it is this balance which is referred to as a company's 'gearing'. The choice between debt and equity lies at the heart of a company's long-term financing policy and an assessment of its gearing plays an important part in any examination of a company's financial stability. This matter is re-examined as a feature of the analysis in Part Three.

## DEFERRED TAXATION

During the review of Dovetails' current liabilities it was observed that the amount appearing against taxation represented corporation tax payable at 52 per cent on the taxable profit for the year. A glance at Dovetails' profit and loss account will show that the tax liability of £46,061 is very much less than 52 per cent on Dovetails' profit for 1982. The difference arises because the rules by which the Inland Revenue calculate 'taxable profit' differ in certain respects from the principles that apply in the measurement of accounting profit.

The first – and major – difference concerns the capital allowances which are granted in respect of fixed assets. The accounting treatment of fixed assets is to depreciate them over their useful lives, resulting in an annual charge for depreciation in the profit and loss account. For tax purposes, however, the full cost of plant and machinery acquired during the year is allowed as a deduction against profits: the depreciation charge is consequently disallowed. Thus in computing the amount of profits on which tax is payable, the amount of any depreciation has to be added back to the profit shown in the accounts and the full cost of any plant and machinery acquired during the year has to be deducted. For this reason taxable profits will often be significantly less than accounting profit.

Note, however, that the capital allowance is granted only once – in the year of acquisition – and the tax advantage therefore arises only in that first year. In all subsequent years for which the plant is depreciated in the accounts, the disallowance of the depreciation charge will result in taxable profits which are higher than accounting profits.

Consider a machine which costs £1,000 and which is depreciated over 10 years. In Year 1, the depreciation charge in the accounts would be £100, whereas the deduction allowed for tax purposes will be the full cost of £1,000. As a result, the tax bill for the year will be less than it would otherwise have been by an amount of 52% × £900. In each of the nine subsequent years, the tax bill will be more (by an amount of 52% × £100) than a straight 52 per cent on the profit for the year. The incidence of capital allowances, therefore, is not to reduce the amount of tax payable in the long run but merely to defer its payment to later years. It is in order to retain the relationship between profits shown in the accounts and the full amount of tax payable in respect of those profits that it has become standard practice to provide not only for the amount of tax immediately payable but also for any tax in respect of those profits the payment of which has been deferred.

The second respect in which tax rules differ from accounting rules is in the relief that is granted in respect of appreciating stock values. In recognition of the potentially distorting effect of inflation on a company's profits, the Inland Revenue has in recent years allowed a deduction from profit to the extent that any increase in the carrying value of stock has arisen solely as the result of changing price levels.

Until November 1980, stock appreciation relief was available only as long as a company's stock and work-in-progress levels continued to increase in value; as soon as they started to decrease, the relief granted in past years was liable to be 'clawed-back' by the Revenue. The effect of stock appreciation relief was therefore similar to that of capital allowances: it postponed tax, but did not reduce the amount payable in the long term. The Government introduced new rules for stock relief in the 1981 Finance Act, by which the relief is related to the rate of inflation rather than the actual increase (or decrease) in stocks and work-in-progress. Under the new rules stock appreciation relief, once granted, will only be liable to claw-back in extreme circumstances and will therefore comprise not merely a postponement of tax but a permanent reduction in the amount of tax payable. For the future, therefore, stock relief will result in a continuing difference between taxable profit and accounting profit. Future provisions for deferred tax will usually only be necessary in respect of capital allowances.

The need to provide for deferred tax in respect of capital allowances is clear if we consider it only in terms of a single allowance on a single piece of plant or machinery. It is the habit of most companies, however, to replace their fixed assets from year to year as part of a continuous programme. In the earlier example we assumed that the company did not buy any further fixed assets after Year 1. If it had bought more plant in Year 2, further capital allowances would then have been available, and that year would therefore have been one of tax advantage rather than disadvantage. The same would apply to any plant that was acquired – and any allowance that were thereby obtained – in Years 3 and 4 and 5, and onwards. In each year there would be a tax advantage as long as the amount of capital allowances available exceeded the total amount of depreciation that was disallowed. To this extent an element of tax is deferred not temporarily but permanently. The permanence of the deferral will depend on the company's future capital investment programme: if the plans are for a steady, annual re-investment in fixed assets, there is the prospect of the attributable taxation not merely being deferred but never becoming payable at all. And this raises the question of whether it really needs to be provided for in the first place.

The assessment of future tax liabilities is a matter of some concern for accountants. In recent years there have been a number of different attempts at establishing standard accounting practice in this area. The latest version requires that provision should be made for all deferred taxation, except where it is unlikely that any liability will arise in the

**Frame 21**

|  | 1982 | 1981 |
|---|---|---|
|  | £ | £ |
| Deferred taxation | 99,107 | 94,900 |

Note 1(c)
Deferred taxation
Provision is made for taxation deferred because of timing differences in the treatment of certain items for accounting and taxation purposes, but only where there is reasonable probability of payment.

| Note 14 | 1982 | 1981 |
|---|---|---|
|  | £ | £ |
| Accelerated capital allowances | 108,364 | 103,643 |
| Advance corporation tax | (9,257) | (8,743) |
|  | 99,107 | 94,900 |
| If full provision were made, the potential liability would be as follows: |  |  |
| Accelerated capital allowances | 147,500 | 138,000 |

'foreseeable future'. We might well ponder how much of the future is foreseeable and therefore question the practicalities of this standard treatment. Nevertheless, it is the one adopted by Dovetails, as described in their accounting policy.

Dovetails have estimated that in addition to the amount of tax that will be payable within nine months of the year end (and shown under current liabilities), there will be a probable further liability to taxation amounting to £99,107 (see Frame 21). [The net amount of £99,107 is made up of future estimated liabilities (arising from accelerated capital allowances) of £108,364, less recoverable ACT of £9,257.] That is really no more than the best guess that can be made at the end of December 1982 of the proportion of the full potential liability (£147,500) which is likely to crystallise. The amount that will eventually prove to be payable over the next few years will depend on Dovetails' future capital expenditure programme; and it really cannot be said whether any amount that might fall due will be payable in two years' or in ten years' time.

Companies vary widely in their attitudes to deferred tax, and the uncertainty that surrounds any future liability – whether or not it is

**Frame 22**

| Dovetails Limited | | |
|---|---|---|
| *Where does the business stand at the end of 1982?* | | |
| *Where is the money now?* | | |
| | £ | £ |
| Fixed assets | | 488,061 |
| Investments: | | 26,000 |
|    Current assets | 1,046,159 | |
|    Current liabilities | 641,585 | |
| Working capital | | 404,574 |
| | | 918,635 |
| *Where did it come from?* | | |
| Capital and reserves | | 679,528 |
| Long-term liabilities | | 239,107 |
| | | 918,635 |

provided for in the accounts – is a matter which can cause some difficulty when it comes to assessing a particular company's financial position. The policy on deferred tax will also have a profound effect on the profit and loss account, where the extent to which it is or is not provided will have a direct and immediate impact on the amount of profits that are reported to be available for distribution to shareholders.

**SUMMARY**

We have now completed our 'walk through' Dovetails' balance sheet at 31 December 1982. Before concluding, we might revert to the description of the balance sheet that was used in Part One and summarise where Dovetails now stands (see Frame 22).

At the end of 1982 Dovetails has funds totalling £918,635. Of that amount, £679,528 came from capital introduced by the shareholders and from profits retained within the business; £239,107 has been borrowed long term.

Of the total funds available, £488,061 is invested in fixed assets and £26,000 in investments; £404,574 has been used to finance the company's working capital.

Dovetails' gross current assets have been financed as to £641,585 by short-term liabilities. To support the level of stock, debtors and cash they need to carry, totalling £1,046,159, Dovetails have 'borrowed' money from trade creditors, from the bank, from the tax authorities and, to the extent that they have not yet paid the dividend due to them, from shareholders.

# 5 The profit and loss account

If the balance sheet attempts to answer the financial question 'Where does the business stand?', the profit and loss account seeks to explain 'How well has the business done?'. Its function is to compare all the revenues earned by selling goods with all the expenses that have been incurred in earning them. This comparison will show whether the company has made a profit or a loss on trading. Note that whereas the balance sheet describes the financial position on a particular day, the profit and loss account summarises the results of trading over a given period, usually one year.

It has been established that all costs have to be described either as assets in the balance sheet or as expenses in the profit and loss account. Their inclusion in the balance sheet as an asset will depend on whether there is any benefit to be derived from them in future periods. It has also been established that the amount at which certain assets are stated in the balance sheet will often be a matter requiring a good deal of estimation, and it will now be clear that the converse effect of those estimates is reflected in the amount of expense that is recorded in the profit and loss account. It is also clear that the expenses that have to be incurred in the earning of revenue are great in their number and variety, including all the costs of converting raw materials into finished goods, as well as the costs of selling them, and the whole range of administration expenses that arise in the general course of running a business.

In view of all this, the relatively simple format of Dovetails' profit and loss account may come as something of a surprise. In its published form, the profit and loss account is a highly condensed and summarised statement, giving the briefest possible answer to the question 'How well did the business do?'. A limited amount of supporting information is given in the notes – particularly notes 2 and 3 to the accounts – but it is highly selective. By its nature (How much did the directors pay themselves? How much did the audit cost?) it can be seen to be the sort of information that is required to be disclosed by law. For the most part, it arises from the function which accounts serve in reporting to shareholders on how the directors have conducted their stewardship of the company's affairs.

As far as the businessman is concerned, the published form of profit and loss account tells him very little about how well he did and even less about why he did not do better. If the businessman wants to use his accounts to plan and control his business, he will need more detailed information than is given here. Part Five provides a description of how changes in company law will in future require greater disclosure from companies as to their costs and profit margins. For the time being, however, we can examine the limited story as it is told by Dovetails' profit and loss account in its presently published form.

**TURNOVER**

The first line in Dovetails' profit and loss account shows turnover for 1982 of £2,424,900 (see Frame 23). Turnover represents the total amount of revenue earned during the year from the company's normal trading

**Frame 23**

|  | 1982 | 1981 |
|---|---|---|
|  | £ | £ |
| Turnover | 2,424,900 | 1,993,400 |

operations. In Dovetails' case, it would be made up of the total sales value (excluding VAT) of furniture delivered and invoiced to customers during 1982. Note that Dovetails' turnover is greater this year than it was last. That could mean that the volume of their sales has increased; or it could mean that they have sold the same amount of furniture at higher prices.

**OPERATING PROFIT**

The figure for turnover does not form part of the addition within the profit and loss account; it stands on its own as a piece of separate disclosure. The arithmetic of the profit and loss account begins with the figure for operating profit (see Frame 24).

**Frame 24**

|  | Note | 1982 | 1981 |
|---|---|---|---|
|  |  | £ | £ |
| Operating profit, before taxation | 2 | 129,833 | 134,218 |

Operating profit is the key figure in the profit and loss account. It represents the net result of trading for the year and is arrived at by comparing total sales revenue with total expenses incurred in earning that revenue. Note that the profit and loss account only reveals the net result: it says nothing about the make-up of the various expenses that have been incurred. All we can deduce is that if sales have totalled £2,424,900 and have resulted in a profit of £129,833, then expenses must, in total, have amounted to the difference, £2,295,067.

It will be noted that Dovetails' trading profit has fallen compared with the previous year, despite the increase in turnover. Without further information about expenses we cannot analyse why that has happened. It may be that the increased level of sales has only been achieved by reducing selling prices. Or it may be that increased costs have eroded Dovetails' trading margin. The additional information we need, and which the businessman needs in order to monitor his trading performance properly, is more typically found in the sort of management accounts which are included and analysed in Part Three.

**TAXATION**

Most of what needs to be said about taxation has been covered in the discussion of the taxation amounts appearing in the balance sheet. As far as the profit and loss account is concerned (see Frame 25), it is notable that,

**Frame 25**

|  | Note | 1982 | 1981 |
|---|---|---|---|
|  |  | £ | £ |
| Taxation | 4 | 49,736 | 71,408 |
|  |  |  |  |
| *Note 4* |  |  |  |
| *Taxation* |  |  |  |
| Corporation tax at 52% |  | 45,015 | 15,538 |
| Transfer to deferred taxation |  | 4,721 | 55,870 |
|  |  |  |  |
|  |  | 49,736 | 71,408 |

on a trading profit of £129,833, Dovetails estimate that the corporation tax payable will amount to £49,736. Note 4 shows how this figure is broken down into the amount that is payable in the near future (and which will therefore be shown as a current liability) and the amount by which the liability is expected to be deferred.

**EXTRAORDINARY ITEMS**

The next line in Dovetails' profit and loss account (see Frame 26) describes an extraordinary item of £18,342. 'Extraordinary' items are costs or revenues which are so unusual in the context of the business that they require separate disclosure.

Three conditions will normally have to be met for an item to be described

**Frame 26**

| | Note | 1982 | 1981 |
|---|---|---|---|
| | | £ | £ |
| Extraordinary item | 5 | 18,342 | – |

*Note 5*
Redundancy and other costs relating to the closure of the Scunthorpe factory (less related taxation of £19,012).

as extraordinary: it has to be large in amount; it has to arise from an event or transaction which is not expected to recur frequently or regularly; and it has to result from an activity which is outside the normal routine of business operations.

Current accounting practice attempts to distinguish between items which are extraordinary (as defined) and those which are merely 'exceptional' by way of their abnormal size or incidence. The difference is that while an amount or transaction may be regarded as exceptional because it is unusually large, or because it doesn't happen very often, it should only be described as extraordinary if it arises from an event or activity which the business would not normally be expected to engage in. For example a large customer might go bankrupt, and the business might incur a very large bad debt. The amount involved will be significant, and the business might hope that it is something which won't arise very often, but it should not be regarded as extraordinary because it is in the nature of most businesses that from time to time debts do go bad. On the other hand, a factory might be destroyed by fire, and the company suffer heavy loss. This loss might reasonably be regarded as extraordinary, on the basis that it is not one of the normal expectations of business life that property should be burned down.

The line between exceptional and extraordinary items is sometimes thinly drawn, and what is extraordinary to one business may not be extraordinary to another. If a business moves premises, for example, and makes a windfall profit on the sale of the old building, it will be a matter for careful consideration whether that profit is extraordinary or merely exceptional.

This distinction is more than a matter of mere terminology; it can have a critical impact on the story told in the profit and loss account. Standard accounting practice is to treat exceptional items 'above the line', i.e. to account for them *before* arriving at the amount disclosed as operating profit for the year. Extraordinary items, on the other hand, are added or deducted 'below the line' and, as we can see in Dovetails' case, have their impact lower in the body of the profit and loss account. In so far as the top line operating profit is used as an important indicator of business performance, the distinction between extraordinary and exceptional items, and their alternative treatment, will often be critical.

Note 5 explains that Dovetails' extraordinary item is in respect of redundancy and other costs connected with the closure of one of their factories. These costs relate to the discontinuance of a part of the business and are not associated with continuing business operations. It is therefore appropriate to disclose them below the line and thereby exclude them from the calculation of operating profit.

**DIVIDENDS**

After accounting for taxation and extraordinary items, £61,755 of the profits Dovetails have made in 1982 remain available for distribution to shareholders. Of this amount, Dovetails' directors have decided to distribute £21,600 and to retain £40,155 in the business. The 1982 dividend amounts to a return of 18p on each of the 120,000 Ordinary shares of £1 each (see Frame 27): Note that Dovetails' dividend is bigger this year than it was last, even though last year's profits were higher.

**Frame 27**

|  | Note | 1982 £ | 1981 £ |
|---|---|---|---|
| Dividend | 6 | 21,600 | 20,400 |
| Note 6 Dividend Proposed Ordinary dividend of 18p (1981 – 17p) per share |  | 21,600 | 20,400 |

It is preferable – although not necessary – that the amount of dividend declared should be seen to be covered by the current year's profit. However dividends can also be paid out of profits which have been retained in earlier years, even if the current year has resulted in a trading loss. Dovetails' directors would be legally entitled to declare a dividend of up to £316,192 (the full amount of their retained revenue reserves at December 1982 – see Note 12). But this would be impossible in the short term (because the cash is not available) and would be a dubious policy even in the long term (because the company's net assets would be reduced by about half).

Dividend policy is therefore something which needs to be assessed in terms of both current and past profits, as well as in terms of current liquid resources and the requirements for the future. Of their profit for 1982, Dovetails' directors are retaining £40,155 in the business. From their point of view, that retention will provide a further basis for the company's continuing growth. From the shareholders' point of view, that retention represents a growth of capital, an increase in the value of their interest in the business. The balance sheet shows the shareholders' interest to have increased from £639,373 to £679,528. The profit and loss account shows how that increase came about.

# 6 The funds statement

The purpose of the funds statement – the third and concluding chapter in the story told by the accounts – is to explain how far the business has managed to generate additional funds during the year, where they have come from, and how they have been used.

It should be noted that the information contained in the funds statement does not emerge directly from the accounting process in the same way as do the figures which appear in the balance sheet and profit and loss account. Indeed the function of the funds statement is to provide no more than further analysis and re-presentation of information which, for the most part, is already contained in those other two main statements.

That is not to say that the funds statement does not provide a further valuable insight into the operation of a business. Thus, a balance sheet will describe, at a given date, where the total funds presently available to a business have come from and how they are presently deployed; and a profit and loss account will show whether funds have been increased (a profit) or decreased (a loss) by the results of trading. The funds statement, however, explains the changes in the financial strength and standing of the business that have arisen as the result not only of trading but also of any other major business transactions which have taken place during the year.

The particular value of the funds statement is that it focuses on the cash flow generated by a business, on the extent to which working capital has grown or contracted, and on the consequent improvement or deterioration in business liquidity.

**THE PARTS OF A FUNDS STATEMENT**

There are three parts to a funds statement: a statement of sources (where the new funds have come from); a statement of applications (what the funds have been used for); and an analysis of how the net inflow or outflow of funds is reflected in the change in the net liquid position of the business and other elements of its working capital.

**SOURCES**

Looking at Dovetails' statement for the year ended 31 December 1982 (see Frame 28), the first source of funds is described as the operating profit before tax of £129,833 (£134,218 for the previous year) less the costs associated with the factory closure (£18,342) which have been treated as an extraordinary item. These figures are drawn directly from the profit and loss account. They are followed by two amounts which are described as 'items not involving the movement of funds'.

**Frame 28**

| Where they came from | | | |
|---|---|---:|---:|
| | | *1982* | *1981* |
| | | £ | £ |
| Source of funds: | | | |
| Operating profit before taxation | | 129,833 | 134,218 |
| Extraordinary item | | (18,342) | – |
| Adjustment for items not involving the movement of funds: | | | |
| Depreciation | 65,404 | | 59,926 |
| Profit on sale of fixed assets | (3,907) | | 1,320 |
| | | 61,497 | 58,606 |
| Funds generated from operations | | 172,988 | 192,824 |
| Other sources: | | | |
| Sale of fixed assets | | 5,500 | 3,250 |
| | | 178,488 | 196,074 |

The first of these is in respect of depreciation of £65,404. The point here is that the annual charge for depreciation is an accounting adjustment: it did not give rise to an outflow of £65,404 during 1982. The outflows occured when the related fixed assets were variously acquired, and amounted to the full costs of acquisition. For the purpose of assessing the flow of funds in 1982 the amount of depreciation expense can be ingnored: as a source of funds the trading operations for the year generated more than is shown in the profit and loss account – and depreciation is 'added back' in recognition of this fact.

The same reasoning applies to the adjustment which is made in Dovetails' statement for the profit on sale of fixed assets (£3,907)*. The inflow of funds that results from those disposals amounts not just to the profit but to the full amount of the proceeds. For the purposes of the funds statement, therefore, the profit on disposal is eliminated and the proceeds of £5,500* are included in full lower down in the statement as a source.

*The profit of £3,907 arises from a comparison of the net book value of the assets sold with the proceeds of selling them. Note 7, which describes movements on Dovetails' fixed assets, shows that during the year Dovetails dispose of assets which had originally cost £18,866 and on which the accumulated depreciation amounted to £17,273. Their net book value at the time of disposal was therefore £1,593 and, if the proceeds obtained from selling them resulted in a profit of £3,907, we can deduce that those proceeds must have amounted to £5,500.

In Dovetails' case, that concludes the company's only two sources of funds during the year – the amount of profit generated from its trading activities (before charging depreciation or tax) and the inflow resulting from the sale of fixed assets. There are of course other sources from which funds can arise: for example, if the company had borrowed money, or asked the shareholders to inject more capital during the year. In Dovetails' case, however, no new money came from either of these two sources during 1982.

**APPLICATIONS**

Having summarised the sources from which funds have been increased during the year the next part of the statement describes how they have been used – see Frame 29.

**Frame 29**

| Where they went to | | |
|---|---|---|
| | *1982* | *1981* |
| | £ | £ |
| Application of funds: | | |
| Purchase of fixed assets | 100,674 | 83,499 |
| Taxation paid | 16,299 | 12,101 |
| Purchase of trade investments | 4,000 | – |
| Dividend paid | 20,400 | 18,000 |
| | 141,373 | 113,600 |
| Increase in working capital | 37,115 | 82,474 |

This section of the statement shows that Dovetails spent £100,674 on fixed assets during the year (whereas it had only spent £83,499 during the previous year). During 1982, the company also paid tax amounting to £16,299, put a further £4,000 into its trade investment, and paid a dividend of £20,400. Note that the dividend paid during 1982 was in respect of the dividend declared on the 1981 profits, and is the amount which appears in the comparative column of the profit and loss account. [The dividend proposed for 1982 (£21,600) remains unpaid at the end of the year and is therefore not shown in the statement. It would presumably have been paid in the early months of 1983.]

**CHANGE IN WORKING CAPITAL**

Comparing Dovetails' sources with its application of funds during 1982 shows that the company has generated a surplus of £37,115 during the year, which has served to increase working capital by that amount – see Frame 30.

**Frame 30**

|                              | 1982<br>£  | 1981<br>£  |
|------------------------------|-----------:|-----------:|
| Increase in working capital  | 37,155     | 82,474     |
|                              |            |            |
| Comprising changes in:       |            |            |
| Stock                        | 31,194     | 28,967     |
| Debtors                      | 167,781    | 52,390     |
| Creditors                    | (132,081)  | (33,523)   |
| Net liquid funds             | (29,779)   | 34,640     |
|                              | 37,115     | 82,474     |

This final section shows how the various component parts of Dovetails' working capital have increased or decreased during the year. Probably as a result of their increased level of business, Dovetails have had to invest more money in stocks (£31,194) and they now have more money tied up in debtors (£167,781). However, part of this increased investment has been financed by creditors: Dovetails now owes £132,081 more to its suppliers.

The final, key figure in the statement shows whether the net liquid position of the business has improved or worsened as a result of the year's operations. Liquid funds represent the net aggregate of cash balances and bank overdraft. In Dovetails' case, net liquid resources have decreased by £29,779 during the year. (Sometimes this movement is shown separately from the other working capital items because of its significance and because it is often truly the 'remainder' when all the transactions of the year are completed.)

The funds statement therefore provides a convenient way of showing whether the working capital of the business is growing or shrinking. We should note, however, that the change in the working capital position is something which can also be assessed from the face of the balance sheet. Indeed we can check the derivation of the figures appearing in the funds statement by comparing Dovetails' current assets and liabilities at 31 December 1981 and 31 December 1982 – see Frame 31.

For the most part, therefore, the funds statement provides little that is new: it merely re-analyses information which is already contained in the balance sheet and the profit and loss account. But in re-presenting the information in this way, the statement does provide a useful description of the ways in which the business generated funds during the year, and how they were used. If the balance sheet shows where a business stands and the profit and loss account provides a brief statement as to how it got there, the funds statement reveals something about what happened on the way.

The story in Dovetails' statement is that working capital has grown by £37,115. That will usually reflect well on the company, but we should be

**Frame 31**

|  | 1982 | 1981 | Change |
|---|---|---|---|
|  | £ | £ | £ |
| Current assets: |  |  |  |
| Stock | 435,289 | 404,095 | + 31,194 |
| Debtors | 584,537 | 416,756 | +167,781 |
| Cash | 26,333 | 29,745 | – 3,412 |
| Increase in current assets |  |  | 195,563 |
| Current liabilities: |  |  |  |
| Creditors | 461,958 | 329,877 | +132,081 |
| Bank overdraft | 111,966 | 85,599 | + 26,367 |
| Increase in current liabilities |  |  | 158,448 |
| Net increase in working capital |  |  | 37,115 |

In the funds statement, the decrease in cash is added to the increase in bank overdraft to reveal the total change in net liquid resources of £29,779.

careful not to draw any firm conclusions from this fact alone. When assessing working capital the businessman should consider not only how much it has grown by but also the amount to which it has now increased. In other words, he should also have regard for the working capital position as disclosed in the balance sheet. A healthy surplus of working capital is desirable, but too much of it can become a leadstone. It is too easy to have too much money tied up in stock, or debtors, and too little readily available in the form of cash. The control of working capital will form a major section of Part Three.

# Part Three

# ANALYSIS OF ACCOUNTS: HOW TO USE THEM

# 7 Outline

The first two parts of this book have examined the content of accounts in terms of how they are made, i.e. the principles that are adopted in preparing them, and what they say, i.e. what the words mean and how the figures are arrived at. Part Three describes how accounts can be analysed and how careful analysis can provide valuable insights into the state of a business. In particular, we shall be concerned to examine how a businessman can use his accounts to:

*Control* the current performance of his business

*Plan* for improved performance in the future.

For the most part, the tools of analysis take the form of ratios and comparisons. There are of course a great number of ratios that can be extracted from a set of accounts. The following chapters concentrate only on the most important ones. Most are designed to help the businessman in managing his business, and can be conveniently grouped under the general heading of management ratios. Each is designed to address one of the two basic questions which lie at the heart of business performance:

*Profitability* – how well has the business done, and how might it do better?

*Liquidity* – what is its financial state of health, and how can it be made stronger?

In the case of medium-sized companies such as Dovetails, the businessman will often have an interest in his business not only as a manager but also as an investor. Under the general heading of proprietary ratios, later chapters therefore describe some of the ways in which business proprietors and shareholders generally can use their accounts to assess the value and security of their private investment.

# 8 Methods of analysis

Accounts provide a great deal of information. We can learn very quickly from reading Dovetails' accounts, for example, that the company made a profit of £129,833 in 1982, or that it spent £100,674 on fixed assets, or that it had stocks of £435,289 at the end of the year . . . and so on. All that is informative, but it is not necessarily useful. Before we put the question 'How can that information be used?' we might first consider some of the factors which cause us to regard information in general as being useful or otherwise.

Consider the statement: 'A young man weighs 14 stone'. Of itself, it is difficult to know what to make of that piece of information. We might conclude differently according to whether we were told that he was 18 or 8 years old; and our assessment would vary according to whether he was 6 feet or 4 feet tall. We might take a more favourable view if we knew that twelve months ago he weighed 19 stone, whereas the same information would cause concern if his weight last year was 10 stone. And if we are to make any judgement of his condition, it would also be useful to know the average weight for men of his height and age.

So it is with accounts. Taken line by line, or item by item, individual pieces of information taken from accounts will be of limited value if they are read in isolation. If we are to make use of that information, we need to assess it against other pieces of related information. Identifying relationships between items in accounts and expressing that relationship in a useable form is the first step in unlocking the full potential value of accounting information.

**RATIOS**

Consider the statement included in a balance sheet that debtors at the end of the year amounted to, say, £1,000. Of itself, that is not a statement which can be used to any great purpose. We know, however, that debtors arise from sales. If sales for the year were also £1,000, the amount of outstanding debtors would be viewed with concern: the inference would be that no money had been collected from any customers throughout the year. If sales were £10,000, our view of debtors would be more favourable. Debtors would then represent only 10 per cent of sales for the year. The other 90 per cent would have been realised in cash, and that statistic clearly reflects better on the ability of the company to collect money from its customers.

**COMPARISONS**

We cannot say, however, whether that debtor/sales ratio is good or bad, better or worse than it might have been. To do that we need a point of reference by which to compare and assess it. There are three primary sources of comparison for accounting information.

If accounts show what has happened this year, the first useful point of comparison is with what happened last year. If, last year, debtors represented 12 per cent of sales then 10 per cent this year would indicate an improvement; if the debtors/sales ratio last year was 6 per cent, the position has worsened, indicating that the company's collection performance has deteriorated.

The assessment of trends is one of the most important uses which a businessman can make of his accounts. The accounts themselves provide comparative information for the previous year, but there is no reason why the assessment should be limited to two years. The longer the period over which a trend can be observed, the better the basis from which to predict its course in the future. Five years would certainly not be too long a period. If the pattern is improving, those features of business performance are to be developed and encouraged. If the trend is deteriorating, corrective action is needed. Either way, an assessment of the trend of past and present performance is a most valuable tool in charting the path to better performance in the future.

The second potential source of comparison is with budgets: to compare what has happened with what was expected to happen. A full discussion of standard-setting and the techniques of variance analysis falls outside the scope of this book. It should be noted, however, that the preparation of budgets is an important feature of business planning; and regularly monitoring actual against budgeted or expected performance is one of the most useful means by which management can exercise day-to-day control over the affairs of the business.

The third potential source of comparison is with similar businesses in the same industry. There are a number of publications that summarise and compare business performance in various sectors of industry. They do, however, derive the bulk of their information from larger public companies and the private businessman should take care not to compare his own performance too closely with others who might be operating in different conditions and under different circumstances. A better source of comparative statistics might be those available from the appropriate trade association. Appendix 2 provides a summary of the sort of information that trade assosications – and other sources – make available.

A direct source of comparison – for companies – is from the accounts that are required to be put on public record. In the same way as the businessman uses his accounts to assess his own business performance, one of the best ways for him to evaluate that performance is by analysing the published accounts of his immediate competitors.

A final source – and one which is probably not tapped as much as it should be – is the use the businessman can make of his accountant who, in his professional capacity, will often act for a number of clients in the same trade. While his dealings with each will of course be confidential to the particular client, the professional accountant does, in the nature of his work, obtain a global view of trends within particular trades and his knowledge of average performance between a number of similar clients could provide a useful benchmark against which he can measure each result.

**EVALUATION**

Whatever the ratios, and whatever the means of comparison, a third and critical element in the use of accounts is the interpretation that is placed on the results of the analysis. Accounts can reveal what has happened, but not why. Ratios provide the tools, but to use them effectively the businessman needs to evaluate the movements and changes in them against his knowledge of the business and its trading circumstances.

If it was known that the young man, who had reduced his weight from 19 to 14 stone, had been dieting for the past 12 months, we would say that it was to be expected that he would lose weight. Similarly with business performance. If, for example, the price of timber has increased dramatically during the year, that factor would, on the face of it, be expected to affect the profitability of a furniture manufacturer. Similarly, a 5 per cent increase in sales might be interpreted as a creditable achievement in a declining market; less so in a buoyant one. Or if recent policy has been to offer substantial discounts to customers for prompt payment, an improvement in the ratio of debtors to sales would be expected, and would be a cause for investigation if it did not arise. It is against this sort of background knowledge of his business, the factors that have affected it and the circumstances in which it has had to trade, that the businessman should interpret the information which comes out of his accounts and evaluate his relative business performance.

One final point on the matter of interpretation: care should be taken not to place too much emphasis on any one ratio or percentage in isolation. A healthy increase in sales, for example, will usually be a good sign – but not if those increased sales have only been achieved at a price which offers little or no profit. Similarly, the offer of discounts for prompt payment might work to the advantage of cashflow, but it might also work to the disadvantage of business profitability.

**SUMMARY**

In summary, accounts can be used to plan and control business performance by:

● Identifying inter-relationships between individual items within the accounts, and expressing those relationships in the useable form of ratios or percentages.

● Comparing amounts or ratios for the current year
   a   with those for previous years, so as to establish trends;
   b   with budgets or expectations, to identify unusual or unexpected variations (or expected or anticipated variations which fail to occur);
   c   similar businesses, to assess relative performance.

- Evaluating the results of this analysis against a background knowledge of the business, its recent policy, and the circumstances of trading .

- Taking appropriate action – to encourage favourable trends and correct unfavourable ones.

In this last respect, the action that is taken will of course depend to some extent on the wider business plan – whether, for example, the present objective is growth or survival; whether the present strategy is expansion or containment; whether the immediate need is for more profits, or a greater share of the market, or more ready cash. Whatever the policy, a careful analysis of accounts will reveal its success or failure, and will indicate those parts of the business or areas of activity to which management needs to direct its attention if the objectives are to be achieved.

These principles of analysis will now be applied to the accounts of Dovetails. Of necessity, the focus of comparison in these pages will be to assess the current year's performance against that for the previous year (rather than against budget, or that of other businesses). The purpose throughout, however, will be to address the two basic themes which lie at the heart of business performance: profitability and liquidity.

# 9 Analysis for business managers – profitability

**PROFIT**

How much profit did Dovetails make in 1982? Their profit and loss account for the year shows four levels of profit:

|  | £ |
|---|---|
| Operating *profit* before tax | 129,833 |
| *Profit* after tax | 80,097 |
| *Profit* after tax and extraordinary item | 61,755 |
| Retained *profit* | 40,155 |

Each of these measures of profit will have their uses – according to the particular aspect of the business that is being assessed. The level of retained profit, for example, will indicate the extent to which management has sought to retain funds within the business to support its future growth. The figure for profit after tax and extraordinary items will be of particular interest to shareholders: it shows the amount of profit earned in the year which is available for dividends. For the purposes of assessing overall business performance, however, and particularly for the purpose of assessing relative performance year by year, the most appropriate indicator will be the amount of operating profit before tax.

**PROFITABILITY**

Dovetails' operating profit for 1982 was £129,833 but, of itself, that does not provide a sufficient basis from which to assess the company's performance. It is the same with any form of income: if an investor had earned £1,000 in a year, we could not say whether he had done well or badly without knowing the amount he had invested; £1,000 earned on investments of £5,000 would be a better achievement than earning the same income from £50,000 of investments. Similarly with income generated by a business: two companies earning the same profit are not equally profitable if one has to use twice as much capital. In order to measure business performance, profits have to be related to the resources that are used in earning them: the information contained in the profit and loss account has to be related to that contained in the balance sheet.

**CAPITAL EMPLOYED**

In the same way as the profit and loss account gives several different levels of profit, so the balance sheet can give several readings for capital. For the purposes of assessing profitability, however, the measure of capital employed should reflect the full value of resources available to management during the year. All sources of capital should be included, whether loan or equity, and including the funds which are available as the result of retaining profits within the business.

Dovetails' balance sheet shows that the funds available at the start of the year totalled £874,273, and came from:

|  | £ |
|---|---|
| Share capital | 120,000 |
| Retained profits and reserves | 519,373 |
| Long-term loan | 140,000 |
| Deferred taxation | 94,900 |
|  | 874,273 |

Viewed from the other side of the balance sheet, these funds were represented by:

|  |  | £ |
|---|---|---|
| Fixed assets |  | 454,384 |
| Investments |  | 22,000 |
| Current assets | 850,596 |  |
| *Less:* current liabilities | 452,707 |  |
|  |  | 397,889 |
|  |  | 874,273 |

Note that current liabilities are excluded from the calculation of capital employed. Although representing a source of finance, they are by definition only available on a short-term basis and they are, for the most part, closely identifiable with the current assets which they support. The amount of capital employed is therefore represented by the aggregate of fixed assets, investments, and the net investment in working capital (current assets less current liabilities).

These definitions should not be regarded as inviolable. The reference here for example has been to resources available at the *start* of the year: if Dovetails had received a substantial injection of new capital during 1982, that fact should be taken into account (by averaging) when calculating the amount of capital employed. Similarly, there may be circumstances in which a bank overdraft is better regarded as a permanent source of long-term funds – and therefore as part of capital employed – rather than as a deduction from net working capital. The important point is that the figures for profit and capital employed should be extracted on a consistent basis. In Dovetails' case, this leads to one further refinement: operating profit of £129,833 is stated after deducting interest but, in terms of management performance, the purpose is to assess the full amount of profits earned from capital employed *before* accounting for any return on that capital (whether that return be in the form of dividends on shares or interest on loans). Interest payable on the long-term loan (given in Note 2 to the accounts as £12,600) should therefore be added back in order to arrive at a full measure of the profit generated by operating the business.

## RETURN ON CAPITAL EMPLOYED

Expressed in the form of a percentage, this relationship is usually referred to as the return on capital employed. It is the primary indicator of business performance. For Dovetails, the figures are as shown in Frame 32.

**Frame 32**

|  | 1982 | 1981 |
|---|---|---|
| Operating profit* | 142,433 | 146,818 |
| Capital employed | 874,273 | 757,651† |
| Return on capital employed | 16.3% | 19.4% |

*Operating profit per the accounts, plus interest added back of £12,600 for both years.

†Representing the amount of capital employed at the start of 1981. This figure is taken from Dovetails' previous balance sheet and is not readily available from the accounts reproduced in this book.

Dovetails' achieved a return of 16.3 per cent in 1982. It should be noted however, before too much is read into that single statistic, that it is only as good as the figures on which it is based. Earlier discussion in this book has underlined the degree of estimation and judgement involved in preparing accounts. Thus a different method of stock valuation, or a different depreciation policy, would have produced different figures in both the profit and loss account and the balance sheet. They would have produced a different amount of profit and a different amount of capital employed - and would therefore have given the appearance of different profitability.

In particular, the principle of historic cost serves in times of inflation to understate the value of assets employed. A return of 16.3 per cent would show a dramatic decline if Dovetails had, for example, to replace their old plant and machinery (stated at old historic cost) with new equipment (stated at much higher replacement cost). The possible disparity between the age (and therefore the cost) of their fixed assets is one reason why comparisons between the returns on capital employed of two apparently similar businesses should only be made with care. For any one business however, the principle of consistency ensures that accounts will be drawn up on a comparable basis from year to year, and the percentage return on capital employed will therefore provide a reliable basis for comparing relative profitability from one year to the next.

Dovetails have been less profitable in 1982 (a return of 16.3 per cent) than they were in 1981 (19.4 per cent). A first answer to the question 'How well did they do? is therefore 'Not as well as last year'. Comparing these returns with those for the previous, say, five years would reveal whether the fall in 1982 was exceptional or whether it represented a continuation of a steadily declining trend.

A second answer to the question 'How well did they do?' might come from comparing Dovetails' profitability with that of other similar businesses. That comparison would show whether Dovetails' experience was unusual or whether it was typical of the general decline in the industry.

Whatever the case, further analysis can indicate why the company has been less profitable, and where corrective action is needed.

**ELEMENTS OF PROFITABILITY**

Profits come from sales. Sales arise from the productive use of assets. The key to profitability is to recognise that it arises not only from the profit margin on sales, but also from the effective use of capital.

The principle can be simplified by analogy. Jack and Jill both have identical capital of £20,000, represented by a villa in Spain. Each time they let their property, the rental income less the costs involved provides each of them with the same profit margin of £350 per month. Jack manages to let his for three months in the summer, and therefore makes a profit of £1,050 for the year – which represents a return of approximately 5 per cent. Jill lets hers for six months. Her return of 11 per cent is better not because she charges a higher rent but because she puts her villa to better use – she makes her capital work harder.

In the case of a business, profitability results from both

• The ability to generate profit from a given volume of sales; and

• The ability to generate sales from a given volume of capital.

The formula for return on capital employed can therefore be expressed as:

$$\frac{\text{Profit}}{\text{Capital employed}} = \frac{\text{Profit}}{\text{Sales}} \times \frac{\text{Sales}}{\text{Capital employed}}$$

Thus a 16 per cent overall return on capital employed might alternatively result, for example, from a profit margin on sales of 8 per cent multiplied by a ratio of sales to capital employed (referred to as turnover of capital employed) of 2, or from a profit to sales percentage of 1 multiplied by a capital turnover rate of 16. The first example would be more appropriate to heavy manufacturing industry. The second might be typical of supermarkets, who traditionally operate on low margins and high turnover. The figures which result from applying this analysis to Dovetails are summarised in Frame 33.

They show that the company's return on capital employed has fallen (from 19.4 to 16.3 per cent) despite a more efficient use of capital (the ratio of sales to capital employed has increased from 2.6 to 2.8). The main

**Frame 33**

| | Return on capital employed | = | $\dfrac{\text{Profit}}{\text{Sales}}$ | $\times$ | $\dfrac{\text{Sales}}{\text{Capital}}$ |
|---|---|---|---|---|---|
| | £000s | | £000s | | £000s |
| 1982 | $\dfrac{142}{874}$ | | $\dfrac{142}{2,424}$ | $\times$ | $\dfrac{2,424}{874}$ |
| | 16.3 | | 5.9 | $\times$ | 2.8 |
| 1981 | $\dfrac{147}{758}$ | | $\dfrac{147}{1,993}$ | $\times$ | $\dfrac{1,993}{758}$ |
| | 19.4 | | 7.4 | $\times$ | 2.6 |

problem appears to be that increased sales have not resulted in a proportionate increase in profit: the net profit percentage has fallen from 7.4 to 5.9 per cent. In other words, the company generated £2.8 worth of sales for every £1 of capital employed in 1982 (whereas it only generated £2.6 in 1981), but each £1 of sales generated only 5.9p of profit – compared with 7.4p in 1981.

The sections that follow illustrate how the analysis of Dovetails performance can be extended in more detail. It should be clearly established, however, that each step in the analysis flows from one or other of the twin roots of profitability: the margin on sales on the one hand and the efficient use of capital on the other.

**PROFIT: SALES**

There are two ways in which the ratio of profit to sales can be improved increase selling prices or reduce costs. The first is a marketing decision and accounts cannot help – except by indicating how far past selling prices have or have not been sufficient to recover past costs. In the second respect – the control of costs – accounts provide not only a useful but an essential management tool.

**CONTROLLING COSTS: GROSS PROFIT MARGINS**

Costs can of course be analysed in a variety of different ways – by product by department, by month – and costing records can be introduced into the accounting system according to the particular requirements of management.

So far in this book we have been concerned only with annual, financial accounts, and the point has already been made that in its published form the annual profit and loss account is a document of very limited usefulness

**Frame 34**

## DOVETAILS LIMITED

### Detailed profit and loss account
### for the year ended 31 December 1982

| | 1982 £ | 1982 % | 1981 £ | 1981 % |
|---|---|---|---|---|
| Sales | 2,424,900 | 100 | 1,993,400 | 100 |
| Cost of sales: | | | | |
| Materials | 1,335,217 | 55.1 | 1,105,190 | 55.4 |
| Wages | 451,257 | 18.6 | 330,666 | 16.6 |
| | 1,786,474 | 73.7 | 1,435,856 | 72.0 |
| Gross profit | 638,426 | 26.3 | 557,544 | 28.0 |
| Overhead expenses: | | | | |
| Production | 290,819 | 11.9 | 232,643 | 11.7 |
| Distribution | 98,637 | 4.1 | 72,005 | 3.6 |
| Administrative | 106,537 | 4.4 | 106,078 | 5.3 |
| | 495,993 | 20.4 | 410,726 | 20.6 |
| Net operating profit, before interest and taxation | 142,433 | 5.9 | 146,818 | 7.4 |

to pursue the analysis of profitability we need more information than it presently contains.

Frame 34 therefore reproduces Dovetails' profit and loss account in more detail. The additional information does not imply the existence of any detailed costing system. It should all be readily available to the businessman from his primary accounting records. It is, anyway, similar in many aspects to the sort of profit and loss account which most companies will soon have to produce (see Part Five).

The more detailed statement shows how the various broad categories of costs have reduced sales of £2,424,900 in 1982 to a profit of £142,433*. The first half of the statement compares the revenue from goods sold during the year with the direct costs of producing those goods – in Dovetails' case the

*The difference with the profit shown in Dovetails' profit and loss account on page xvi is £12,600, which is, of course, the interest on the long-term loan. The total shown for administration and finance expenses in the more detailed statement has been adjusted for this amount in order to arrive at the same operating profit as was used in the earlier calculation of return on capital employed.

costs of timber and labour that go into the making of furniture. The second half of the statement summarises, by type of expenditure, the various overhead expenses that are incurred in running the business.

Comparisons with the previous year are made much easier if the figures are expressed in the form of percentages – in this case as a percentage of sales. Immediately the picture becomes clearer: the key percentages in Frame 34 show that for every £1 generated from sales, Dovetails spent:

|  | 1982, p | 1981, p |
|---|---|---|
| On materials | 55.1 | 55.4 |
| On wages | 18.6 | 16.6 |
| On overheads | 20.4 | 20.6 |
| Leaving, as profit | 5.9 | 7.4 |
|  | 100.00 | 100.00 |

Increased wage costs (from 16.6 to 18.6 per cent of sales) can now be seen to be the main cause of Dovetails' declining profitability. Management can investigate (if they do not already know) how far those increased costs are due to wage rate increases, or how far they are attributable to lower productivity. Whatever the cause, Dovetails have been unable to pass the full impact of the increased costs on to their customers: they have instead eroded profit margins, and action will be needed to correct the trend of wage costs if they are not to erode those margins still further.

Increased wage costs have caused Dovetails' gross profit margin to fall from 28 to 26.3 per cent. In other respects, Dovetails have done well to restrict the fall in profits to this level. The average price of timber increased during 1982 by some 4 per cent over the previous year. All other things being equal, a 4 per cent increase in material costs would, based on their 1981 results, have wiped out 30 per cent of Dovetails' profit (4 per cent of £1,105,190 equals 30 per cent of £146,818). Clearly, the company has managed to pass on the bulk of this price increase to its customers. Alternatively they may have improved production methods, or reduced wastage. Their success may in part have been due to astute buying in anticipation of sharp price increases. One way or the other Dovetails have, against this sort of background, done well to limit their fall in profitability to the extent that they have.

**CONTROLLING COSTS: OVERHEADS**

The use of accounts to identify cost changes (and then to investigate and control them) can, of course, be extended in greater detail. Dovetails' overheads have increased over the year from £410,726 to £495,993. Expressed as a percentage of sales, however, these amounts represent a reduction from 20.6 to 20.4 per cent.

To a certain extent, that is to be expected – according to how far the overheads in question are fixed (in the sense that they would not normally be expected to vary with the level of sales or production) or variable (in so far as they would be expected so to vary). Material and direct wage costs will vary directly with the level of production. (Strictly, therefore, these costs should be expressed as percentages of the value of production, not sales. However if it can be assumed that the pattern of sales and production levels are similar – which it often can – sales figures will usually provide an acceptable and more readily available surrogate). Production and distribution overheads will similarly contain variable cost elements. Some administrative overheads on the other hand – such as office rent – would be expected to remain unchanged regardless of the level of production – at least in the short term and until such time as a threshold is reached at which the increased level of business activity demands, for example, more office space.

An understanding of the nature of overheads – how far they are fixed and how far they are variable – will help in the interpretation of any changes in them which are revealed in the accounts. Frame 35 shows Dovetails' production overheads broken down in more detail. Most of these cost

**Frame 35**

### Production overheads

| | 1982 £ | 1981 £ | Percentage increase | 1982, % of sales | 1981, % of sales |
|---|---|---|---|---|---|
| Consumable tools and stores | 49,636 | 36,697 | 35.3 | 2.0 | 1.9 |
| Hire of plant | 16,416 | 12,210 | 34.4 | 0.7 | 0.6 |
| Depreciation: factory buildings and equipment | 41,632 | 36,092 | 15.3 | 1.7 | 1.8 |
| Repairs and maintenance | 25,001 | 7,464 | 234.9 | 1.0 | 0.4 |
| Supervisory wages | 136,021 | 125,923 | 8.0 | 5.6 | 6.3 |
| Sundry works expenses | 22,113 | 14,257 | 55.0 | 0.9 | 0.7 |
| | 290,819 | 232,643 | | 11.9 | 11.7 |

headings will contain both fixed and variable elements and the comparisons are therefore expressed in two ways: first (column 3) as an increase over the same costs for the previous year and second (columns 4 and 5) as percentages of sales for each of the two years.

The two largest increases in Dovetails' production overheads have been in repairs and maintenance (234.9 per cent) and sundry works expenses (55 per cent). While both these costs might to some extent be expected to vary with the level of activity, the increases are wholly disproportionate to the increase in sales (which was 21.6 per cent). As a result, for every £1 generated from sales in 1982, 1.0p went on repairs and maintenance, whereas only 0.4p was absorbed by these costs in 1981.

In their attempt to control costs, management should focus not only on percentage increases but also on the size of the overhead in question. Profits are highly sensitive to even a relatively small increase in a large cost: a 1 per cent increase on an overhead of £500,000 will be more damaging to profit than a 20 per cent increase on an overhead of £20,000.

The biggest cost amongst Dovetails' production overheads is supervisory wages. Here management have done well to restrict the increase to 8 per cent. As sales have increased by 26.1 per cent the proportion of the supervisory wage costs to sales has dropped from 6.3 to 5.6 per cent. The figures imply that more or less the same level of supervisory staff have been deployed to oversee an increased level of activity. If Dovetails had allowed their supervisory costs to increase proportionately with sales, the 1982 operating profit would have been some £17,000, or 13 per cent, less than it was.

By this sort of analysis, management can use their accounts to identify cost changes, assess the causes, evaluate the consequences, and seek to control them in the interests of greater future profitability. For a given level of sales, each £1 of cost saved is £1 extra profit.

Effective cost control needs to be timely. The discussion here is based on Dovetails' annual accounts, but by the time the year-end accounts are ready it may be too late to correct unfavourable cost trends that should beneficially have been recognised much earlier. Astute management will therefore seek to examine their costs regularly and will design their accounting records to provide them with cost information in as much detail as they require. They may arrange that their recording methods provide them with information about the costs and profitability not only of the business as a whole but also of each product or activity that the business is engaged in. Most importantly, management will ask for reports or accounts on a regular – probably monthly – basis. The quicker the information is available, the quicker management can respond.

## SALES: CAPITAL EMPLOYED

The attempt to generate more profit from a given volume of sales is one of the two routes to improved profitability. The second route lies in the attempt to generate more sales from a given volume of capital resources.

The discussion here assumes that the *potential* for increasing sales does in fact exist. That potential will depend upon the demand for the product, the company's marketing ability, its sales drive, advertising techniques and all those other aspects of business acumen which would enable Dovetails, for example, to take a greater share of the market for furniture. All of that is outside the province of accounts. What accounts can do is indicate how effectively management are using the resources available to them; they can point to the areas where a more efficient use of capital would lead to greater profitability. In the general attempt to improve the ratio of sales to capital employed, the use of accounts is to focus not so on increasing the level of sales but on the means of minimising the amount of capital that is tied up in generating those sales.

Dovetails' ratio of sales to capital employed was 2.8 for 1982 and 2.6 for 1981 (see Frame 33). Each £1 of capital produced £2.6 of sales in 1981 and £2.8 of sales in 1982. Expressed alternatively, Dovetails have had to invest less capital in order to generate the same amount of sales revenue. How has this been achieved, and how can Dovetails encourage the trend? A careful analysis of accounts will help steer management's attention in the right direction. In the same way as sales have been expressed as a ratio of total capital employed, so the various components of that total capital – that is, the various classes of Dovetails' operating assets – can be expressed and compared in the same terms.

Of the total capital employed by Dovetails during 1981 and 1982, the bulk of the money was tied up in fixed assets, stocks and debtors. To assess the efficiency with which the company has used its resources we should, therefore, focus on these three major asset categories. The relevant figures from Dovetails' accounts are summarised in Frame 36.

**Frame 36**

|  | 1982 | 1981 |
|---|---|---|
|  | £000 | £000 |
| Fixed assets | 488 | 454 |
| Stocks: |  |  |
| Raw materials | 212 | 195 |
| Work-in-progress | 203 | 188 |
| Finished goods | 20 | 21 |
|  | 435 | 404 |
| Debtors | 585 | 417 |
| Sales | 2,425 | 1,993 |

**FIXED ASSET PRODUCTIVITY**

The aim of every business should be to make the fullest use of its fixed assets, and particularly to maximise the proportion of time that plant and machinery is in productive use, rather than lying idle. The ratio of sales to fixed assets provides an indication of how effectively fixed assets have been utilised during the year. Dovetails have achieved an improvement (Frame 37): each £1 invested in fixed assets produced £5.0 of sales revenue in 1982, compared with £4.4 for the previous year.

**Frame 37**

|  | 1982 | | 1981 | |
|---|---|---|---|---|
|  | £000 | | £000 | |
| Sales / Fixed assets | $\frac{2,425}{488}$ | = 5.0 | $\frac{1,993}{454}$ | = 4.4 |

The aim should be to push this ratio as high as possible (without of course exceeding the operating capacity of the machinery in question). It should also be remembered that this statistic is based on the historic cost of fixed assets: a ratio based on *current* costs will usually reveal a much less satisfactory return. On the other hand, new machinery would normally be expected to have greater productive capacity, and would therefore generate more output – as long as the demand existed to translate output into sales.

When management make a decision to increase the company's investment in productive fixed assets, they may not expect that investment to show an immediate payoff: the benefits might only be expected to flow after a number of years. In this circumstance the ratio of sales: fixed assets should be assessed over a run of years, rather than merely from one year to the next. More immediately controllable in the short term, and an area which should attract management's continuous attention, is the amount of their investment in working capital.

## STOCK TURNOVER

The ratio of sales to stock, sometimes referred to as the rate of stock turnover, is a primary measure of the company's operating efficiency. It also provides a good guide to the liquidity of the company's stock.

The optimum level of stockholding is a matter that requires very careful assessment which can only be decided in the light of the trading circumstances of each individual company. Nevertheless, the *general* aim should be to minimise the amount of money tied up in stocks at any one time, and thereby maximise the rate of stock turnover. A low rate of stock-turn hints at slow-moving stocks, over-buying, or possible obsolesence. On the other hand, an extremely high stock-turn may indicate that the production floor is over stretched, continually flat out, unable to meet demand. The general message bears repetition: ratios or analysis drawn from accounts can indicate changes or trends; it is then up to management to interpret that information, investigate the causes, and evaluate the position in the light of their knowledge of the trading circumstances of the business.

Dovetails' rate of stock turnover has increased from 4.9 to 5.6 (Frame 38) they turned their stock round 4.9 times in 1981, and 5.6 times in 1982 – a healthy improvement. This ratio can be adapted to give an indication of the

**Frame 38**

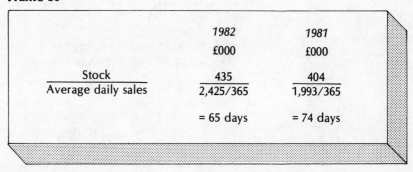

|  | 1982 | 1981 |
|---|---|---|
|  | £000 | £000 |
| $\dfrac{\text{Sales}}{\text{Total stocks}}$ | $\dfrac{2,425}{435} = 5.6$ | $\dfrac{1,993}{404} = 4.9$ |

**Frame 39**

|  | 1982 | 1981 |
|---|---|---|
|  | £000 | £000 |
| $\dfrac{\text{Stock}}{\text{Average daily sales}}$ | $\dfrac{435}{2,425/365}$ | $\dfrac{404}{1,993/365}$ |
|  | = 65 days | = 74 days |

length of time stocks are held on the shelves – see Frame 39. Here it is easier to see that Dovetails are moving their stocks more quickly.

There are two approximations which should be mentioned in this form of stock-turn analysis. First, it is assumed that the level of the stocks held at the year end (and included in the balance sheet) are reasonably reflective of the average value of stock that the company carries day by day during the year. If the level of year-end stock is unrepresentative, management will know the reasons and should take those factors into account in their analysis. The second approximation is that stocks are compared with the revenue from sales: a truer rate of stock-turn will emerge from comparing stocks with the *cost* of sales for the year.

The analysis can be developed – and management can exercise their control with greater precision – by examining the raw material, work-in-progress, and finished goods components of Dovetails' total stock.

**RAW MATERIAL STOCKS**

Frame 40 compares raw material stocks with the total costs of raw materials consumed in sales during the year (for which see Frame 34).

The result of this comparison shows that Dovetails turned their raw material stock round approximately 5.7 times in 1981 and 6.3 times in 1982. Dividing the rate of stock-turn into 365 gives an indication of the number of days' supply of raw material stock that is available on the shelves. At the

**Frame 40**

|  | 1982 | 1981 |
|---|---|---|
|  | £000 | £000 |
| $\dfrac{\text{Raw materials consumed in sales}}{\text{Stock of raw materials}} =$ | $\dfrac{1{,}335}{212}$ | $\dfrac{1{,}105}{195}$ |
| Rate of turnover | = 6.3 | 5.7 |
| Into 365 | = 58 days | 64 days |

end of 1981 Dovetails had raw material stock sufficient for 64 days' usage. At the end of 1982, they had the equivalent of 58 days' usage in stock.

It is of course possible to use alternative bases for these calculations. Dovetails could, for example, use the number of working days in the year instead of the full 365 in the calendar. They could compare stocks with the cost of goods produced (rather than sold) during the year. Each basis would produce different statistics. Whatever basis is used, the important point is that it will give a genuine indication of the *trend* of stockholding from year to year (or month to month) and it is the improvement or otherwise in the trend that is of first importance to management.

In general terms, it can be said that the trend of Dovetails' raw material stockholding policy is improving: the rate of stock turn is increasing. It is less easy to generalise about what is the 'right' amount of raw material for a business to hold. Management will want to hold sufficient at all times to feed an uninterrupted production line. Most importantly, therefore, they will have regard for the expected levels of activity. They will also have regard for the time it takes suppliers to deliver, as well as the possible cash advantages of bulk orders. Good management will usually establish different holding policies for different lines of stock and set minimum reorder levels (and maximum holding levels) for each. Different and sometimes conflicting factors will have to be weighed. The general aim, however, should be quite clear: to minimise the amount of money tied up in raw material stocks at any one time.

**WORK-IN-PROGRESS**

In Frame 41 the same form of analysis is applied to Dovetails' work-in-progress. Here again the rate of turnover is increasing (from 7.6 times to 8.8 times) and Dovetails are therefore showing an improvement. Under normal conditions (where the pattern of production and sales are consistent over the year) this statistic can give a broad indication of the efficiency of production: the number of days that the average level of work-in-progress takes to pass through the factory. The aim should be to maximise the efficiency of the production process, to minimise production

**Frame 41**

|  | | 1982 | 1981 |
|---|---|---|---|
|  | | £000 | £000 |
| Cost of sales | | 1,786 | 1,436 |
| Work-in-progress | | 203 | 188 |
| Rate of turnover | = | 8.8 | 7.6 |
| Into 365 | = | 41 days | 48 days |

time and thereby minimise the amount of money tied up at any one time in work-in-progress.

**FINISHED GOODS**

Frame 42 shows that at the end of 1982 Dovetails had finished goods in stock which were only sufficient to meet just over four days' sales. Goods are being delivered to customers almost as soon as they come off the production line. Generally, that is an ideal position for a business to be in, although one might harbour some reservations. Dovetails' management

**Frame 42**

|  | | 1982 | 1981 |
|---|---|---|---|
|  | | £000 | £000 |
| Cost of sales | = | 1,786 | 1,436 |
| Stock of finished goods | | 20 | 21 |
| Rate of turnover | = | 89.3 | 68.4 |
| Into 365 | = | 4.1 days | 5.4 days |

will, for example, have presumably assessed the risk of being unable to meet a sudden, unforeseen demand for their furniture. They should also be aware that any future labour or production difficulties – amounting to no more than a few days' lost production – would very quickly put them out of stock, unable to deliver, with the potential loss of customer goodwill.

**DEBTORS: SALES**

A comparison between sales and stock gives an insight into a company's operating efficiency. The comparison between sales (strictly, credit sales)

**Frame 43**

|  | | 1982 | 1981 |
| --- | --- | --- | --- |
|  | | £000 | £000 |
| $\dfrac{\text{Debtors}}{\text{Average daily sales}}$ | = | $\dfrac{585}{2{,}425/365}$ | $\dfrac{417}{1{,}993/365}$ |
| Collection period | = | 88 days | 76 days |

and debtors provides an indication of the efficiency of a company's credit-control procedures.

Frame 43 illustrates how the amount of debtors carried by a company can be expressed as a number of days' sales. The statistic can be interpreted as the average number of days' credit allowed to customers, or the length of time it takes the company to collect its debts. Dovetails' performance in this respect has deteriorated: by the end of 1982 the company was, on average, taking 12 days longer to collect its money than it was a year earlier.

Taking, £6,643 (£2,425,000/365) as an average day's sales, that is a further £79,700 (£6,643 × 12) of additional and presumably free credit that the company is providing for its customers; and Dovetails are of course having to finance it – by increasing their investment in working capital, for no return.

The company should review its collection procedures, and the terms of credit it presently offers. Management should review the procedures by which debts are reported as soon as they become overdue, so that they can take quick and appropriate action. The aim should be to reverse the recent trend in collection periods, to minimise the average number of days that debts remain outstanding, and thereby minimise the amount of money tied up in debtors.

**CONTROL OF WORKING CAPITAL**

In analysing Dovetails' profitability, and in using their accounts to pinpoint trends that need to be encouraged or corrected, the emphasis has been on the need to minimise the amount of capital employed, particularly the amount of working capital employed. Control of working capital lies at the heart of profitable performance. It is an area which any businessman ignores at his peril.

In order to illustrate this point, suppose Dovetails have a local competitor, Mortise and Tenon Limited. A year ago, Dovetails looked at the accounts published by M&T and found them to be identical in every respect: the same line of business, the same sales, the same fixed assets, the same amounts of working capital, the same profits and the same profitability.

**Frame 44**

|  | Dovetails | Mortise & Tenon |
|---|---|---|
|  | £000 | £000 |
| Sales | 2,424 | 2,424 |
|  |  |  |
| Cost of sales | 1,786 | 1,786 |
| Cost of raw materials for year | 1,335 | 1,335 |
|  |  |  |
| Stock, 31 December: |  |  |
|   Raw materials | 212 | 105 |
|   Work-in-progress | 203 | 102 |
|   Finished goods | 20 | 10 |
|  | 435 | 217 |
| Debtors | 584 | 292 |
| Gross working capital | 1,019 | 509 |
|  |  |  |
| Rate of stockturn: |  |  |
|   Cost of RM for year: raw materials | 6.3 (58 days) | 12.7 (29 days) |
|   Cost of sales: work-in-progress | 8.8 (41 days) | 17.5 (21 days) |
|   Cost of sales: finished goods | 89.3 (4 days) | 178.6 (2 days) |
|  |  |  |
| Collection period: |  |  |
|   Debtors ÷ sales/365 | 88 days | 44 days |

A year later Dovetails take a further look at M&T's accounts. They extract information which is summarised in Frame 44 and set against Dovetails' own figures. Once again the two companies are found to be identical in most respects. They have achieved the same level of sales in 1982 and the same profit margins. The one essential difference is that M&T now have only half the working capital that Dovetails are carrying. Dovetails may think that makes them twice as strong as their competitor. The truth is quite the opposite: they have been only half as efficient.

Dovetails pursue their analysis. They assume the absence of seasonal factors, so that the year end can be taken as being representative of the position at any time during the year. At any one time M&T are carrying half the amount of timber stocks that Dovetails carry. But they are achieving the same level of production and sales, so the timber they do buy they must be using twice as quickly.

Dovetails' calculations support that conclusion: their own timber lies on the shelves, on average, for 58 days before it is used; on the same basis, however, they calculate that M&T's stock waits only 29 days before it is put into production. Similarly with work-in-progress: both companies

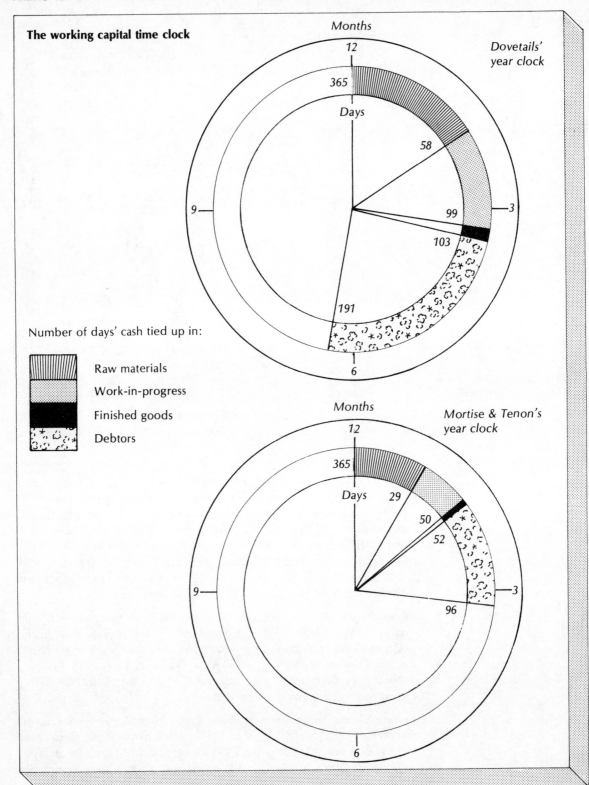

The working capital time clock

Months
12
365
Days
58
99
103
191
6
9
3

Dovetails'
year clock

Number of days' cash tied up in:

Raw materials
Work-in-progress
Finished goods
Debtors

Months
12
365
Days
29
50
52
96
6
9
3

Mortise & Tenon's
year clock

produce the same amount each year, but at any one time Dovetails have twice as much furniture in the factory awaiting completion; it takes them twice as long to complete the manufacturing process (41 days compared with 21 for M&T). And once it is finished, M&T deliver and sell it twice as quickly – so they only have half the amount tied up in finished goods in the warehouse. M&T also only have half the amount of debtors, because it takes them half the time to collect their money (M&T 44 days; Dovetails 88 days).

To outward appearances the two companies may well look the same. Both will take in the same amount of timber each month and each month both will produce and sell the same amount of furniture. They will have the same level of monthly cash outgoings and both will collect the same amount of money each month from their customers. The difference is simply one of timing.

Frame 45 illustrates the difference diagrammatically. Based on the analysis of their accounts, the money Dovetails pay out for timber remains tied up as raw materials on the shelves for about 58 days. It is then tied up in work-in-progress for the further 41 days it takes to turn it into furniture. It spends four days in the warehouse as finished goods, and a further 88 days locked up in the amounts due from customers. Only then – 191 days later – does it come back to Dovetails in the form of cash.

In contrast, it takes M&T only 96 days to convert cash outflow into cash inflow. M&T can use the cash that flows in on day 96 to buy their next supply of timber; and because it takes them half the time to put the timber into production, and half the time to make the furniture, sell it and collect from their customers, they can go through the whole cycle twice in the time it takes Dovetails to go through it once.

The essence of working capital is that it should be made to work: the harder it is made to work the better for the business. M&T make theirs work twice as hard as Dovetails, and they therefore only need to use half as much of it. There is no better illustration of the saying that time is money.

The extra time they are taking, and their unnecessarily large working capital, is indeed costing Dovetails money – in at least three ways. First, they are having to devote time and resources to the extra paperwork that is needed to control the movements on twice as much stock, and to chase up twice the number of outstanding debtors.

Second, their inefficiency is costing the company money in terms of lost income. Every £1 unlocked from working capital is an extra £1 of cash available for other purposes. Dovetails started the year with a gross working capital base (stock and debtors) of some £800,000. If it had made the same effort as M&T to reduce that by 50 per cent, the benefit would have been reflected in their balance sheet at the end of the year – in the shape of some £400,000 additional cash. With interest rates upwards of 15 per cent, that money in a full year could earn the company £60,000 additional income.

Third, and most important, the cash that is released can alternatively be used to finance expansion. By the same token, as half the amount of working capital might be used to support a given volume of sales, so the same amount of working capital might be used to support double the amount of sales. With tighter control of working capital, and by halving the time they take to convert cash outflow into cash inflow, Dovetails have the potential for doubling their level of business and doubling their level of profits.

As they presently stand, therefore, M&T's efforts to reduce working capital have put them in a much stronger position than Dovetails. If fashions change, M&T can respond much more quickly: they only have half as much work to clear in the production pipeline and they can get their new styles on the market twice as fast as Dovetails. M&T are therefore more adaptable. They are also less vulnerable: if fashions do change, M&T will be carrying only half the amount of old stock and are therefore exposed to only half the amount of stock write-offs and losses that Dovetails could suffer.

If demand increases, M&T can statisfy it more quickly, and with less strain. At present levels, M&T support sales of £2,424 from a working capital base of £509. If demand goes up by 50 per cent, M&T will need to increase their investment in working capital by some £250 in order to finance their share of the new market. They could probably do that from their own resources.

Dovetails currently need £1,019 working capital to support the same level of sales. They will need to find another £500 – twice as much as M&T – if they are to expand output and take their share of the new business. Because they already have so much money tied up in working capital, they will probably have to borrow the extra they need. That may prove difficult: banks may be reluctant to lend to a business which has already let its working capital run to such high levels. It will certainly be costly in terms of interest, and costs reduce profits.

All that goes to underline one message: tight control of working capital is essential to business profitability. The aim of every business should be to minimise the amount of working capital needed to support a given level of activity. There is no better example, in current political terms, of what is meant by the merits of a leaner and fitter industry. The best way of keeping constant control of working capital is for the businessman to analyse his accounts – and to listen to what they are telling him.

## EMPLOYEE RATIOS

One of the most valuable resources available to a business, but one which is given no value at all in the balance sheet, is its employees. Business performance depends very much on staff performance, particularly on the performance of those involved in production on the shop floor and those engaged in selling to the market.

The behavioural aspects of management are, of course, a very significant element in labour relations, and an increasingly large body of theory is now devoted to the effectiveness of different forms of incentive, the motivating influence (or otherwise) of budgeted targets, and the benefits of employee participation. The purpose here is not to discuss the general question of motivation, but to suggest some of the ways in which accounts might be used to assess how effectively management are using the employee resources at their disposal.

The ratio of value of production to direct factory wages, for example, offers a measure of the value produced for each £1 wage cost, and will provide an indicator of whether shop floor productivity is improving or declining. Caution is needed when interpreting the figures. A falling trend does not necessarily imply an inefficient workforce; a decline in productivity might equally result from poor-quality materials, or from machinery breakdowns. Nevertheless, with proper evaluation, the productivity ratio is a useful measure, and one which could be of potential interest, for example, to the parties on both sides of a wage negotiation.

Similarly, the ratio of sales to salesmen's wages gives a measure of the amount of sales generated by each £1 spent on the wages of those employed to sell. Here again, the trend in the ratio reflects not only on the efficiency of salesmen but also on the effectiveness of management in motivating salesmen to higher levels of performance, thereby generating higher levels of sales from a given wage bill.

Employee ratios can of course be expressed in terms of numbers of employees rather than wage costs. In either case, comparison of the ratios with those for other businesses should only be made with great care. Productivity ratios will fluctuate significantly according to whether the business is capital- or labour-intensive. For comparable businesses the statistics will be influenced by the conditions in which the workforce are expected to work, and the quality of the plant and machinery they are expected to work with. For businesses in the same trade, the ratio of total payroll to number of employees can, however, provide a useful comparison of average wage levels. Carefully and sensibly used, employee ratios have an important part to play in the control of business performance.

**SUMMARY**

The profitability of a business depends on both the amount of profit derived from a given volume of sales and the amount of sales generated from a given volume of capital. To improve profitability management's objectives should be to maximise profit (and sales) and to minimise capital employed. Analysis of accounting information provides indicators by which management can assess how far their objectives are being achieved – see Frame 46.

**Frame 46**

The profit achieved on a given volume of sales can be improved by increasing selling prices (subject to competition and elasticity of demand) or by reducing costs:

The relationship between sales and capital employed can be improved by increasing sales (if demand and productive capacity exists, and profit margins can be maintained) or by reducing capital employed:

The calculation and interpretation of these and other indicators has been explained in the preceding text. The final two objectives listed – to minimise stockholding levels and to improve collection performance – will also be relevant to an assessment of business liquidity, as described in the following chapters.

# 10 Analysis for business managers – liquidity

**TRADE CREDIT**

For most businesses, the amount locked up in working capital can be reduced by taking credit from suppliers. Ideally a business would work off zero working capital – by taking extended credit from suppliers and using the cash collected from customers to pay for the materials.

The investment in working capital can also be reduced by working off a bank overdraft, but whereas credit from a supplier is usually free, money borrowed from a bank is costly in terms of interest.

Once a business starts taking credit, the need to monitor and control working capital becomes even more acute. The use of trade creditors and even bank overdrafts to support working capital may be sound business strategy but it does of course also create liabilities. Liabilities have to be paid, and for the business manager they bring the further task of ensuring at all times that the business has sufficient liquid funds to meet its debts as they fall due.

The potential conflict between minimising working capital and maintaining sufficient liquidity is illustrated in Frame 47.

Assuming an even pattern of buying, throughput and selling, a comparison between trade creditors and average daily raw material usage will give a bearing on the degree to which a business is extending or reducing the period of credit it takes from suppliers. On this basis, Dovetails are now taking some two weeks' additional credit: they presently wait 126 days before making payment, whereas a year ago they were paying within 109 days. That may be good in terms of minimising working capital: as Dovetails take more credit from suppliers, so less of its own money is needed to finance a given level of stock. But with the company now taking upwards of four months to settle its accounts, suppliers themselves will be concerned to assess Dovetails' liquidity position, and management will have to be vigilant in ensuring that there is always sufficient cash to satisfy those creditors who are pressing for payment. The higher the level of creditors, the greater the risk of the company over-extending itself, defaulting on payment, and losing its credit rating. Once suppliers start to lose confidence a business can very quickly find itself in severe difficulties – with creditors all pressing for payment at the same time and not enough money to satisfy them.

It is important to recognise that a profitable business will not necessarily be a liquid one: profits can be represented by, or be invested in, assets other than cash. Profitability is important, but liquidity is critical. In the long

**Frame 47**

|  | | 1982 | 1981 |
|---|---|---|---|
|  | | £000 | £000 |
| $\dfrac{\text{Trade creditors}}{\text{Cost of raw materials/365}}$ | = | $\dfrac{462}{1{,}335/365}$ | $\dfrac{330}{1{,}105/365}$ |
| Credit taken | = | 126 days | 109 days |

term, a business cannot survive if it is unprofitable; but problems of liquidity do not have a long term – they are usually immediate. A great number of businesses may have the potential for making large profits, but only the liquid ones survive to make them.

A number of the ratios and analyses described in earlier sections have a bearing on liquidity and will help the businessman in his control of it. The average collection period for debtors and the rate of stock turnover tell as much about the relative liquidity of stocks and debts as they do about the efficient use of resources. The emphasis in preceding pages, however, has been on minimising the amount of funds tied up in working capital – converting cash outflow into cash inflow as quickly as possible – and constantly reinvesting it in the working capital cycle. In terms of liquidity, the emphasis is on the sufficiency of liquid funds *at any one point in time,* and for that purpose the main indicators will come from the balance sheet.

**CURRENT RATIO**

The current ratio results from a simple comparison between current assets and current liabilities. On the basis that the cash to pay current liabilities (by definition payable within one year) will come from the funds generated by current assets (by definition convertible into cash within one year), the ratio provides a broad measure of the ability of a business to meet its short-term obligations.

The ratios for Dovetails are shown in Frame 48. The trend is worsening: at

**Frame 48**

|  | | End of 1982 | End of 1981 |
|---|---|---|---|
|  | | £000 | £000 |
| $\dfrac{\text{Current assets}}{\text{Current liabilities}}$ | = | $\dfrac{1{,}046}{641}$ | $\dfrac{850}{452}$ |
| Current ratio | = | 1.63 | 1.88 |

31 December 1981, Dovetails had £1.84 of current assets to cover each £1 of current liabilities; at the end of 1982 they had £1.63 to cover each £1 owed.

The current ratio is, however, only a very arbitrary measure of liquidity. It does not take into account the different degrees of liquidity of the various types of current asset. The cash tied up in Dovetails' raw material stocks, for example, may not be available for another six months, but that may not be soon enough if suppliers are pressing for payment.

Neither is it the case that a high current ratio is necessarily a sign of good business health. A surplus of current assets is a good and necessary thing, but an excessive surplus – particularly if it is represented by old stock and ageing debtors – merely suggests that the control of working capital has been neglected.

**QUICK RATIO**

A better measure of current liquidity is the quick ratio, which excludes stock from the comparison of current assets and liabilities. By expressing the cover for current liabilities only in terms of cash or near-cash (debtors), the quick ratio provides a more immediate indication of short-term liquidity.

The figures for Dovetails are shown in Frame 49. In these terms the company is almost as liquid as it was a year ago. Traditional benchmarks

**Frame 49**

|  |  | End of 1982 | End of 1981 |
|---|---|---|---|
|  |  | £000 | £000 |
| $\dfrac{\text{Current assets, less stocks}}{\text{Current liabilities}}$ | = | $\dfrac{611}{642}$ | $\dfrac{446}{453}$ |
| Quick ratio | = | 0.95 | 0.98 |

were that a company should seek to maintain a current ratio of 2.0 and a quick ratio of 1.0. By that standard, Dovetails' quick ratio of 0.95 compares very reasonably.

Here again, however, the business manager should beware of placing too much reliance on a single statistic. A quick ratio of even 10.0 will give no indication of continuing liquidity if all available cash is needed urgently to replace plant, or if large long-term borrowings are known to fall due for repayment in a year's time. The quick and current ratios calculated from accounts give a first indication of financial health, but good management will assess these statistics in the round of information they can glean from other parts of the balance sheet, in their knowledge of the forthcoming transactions and requirements of the business, and in terms of their ability or otherwise to turn stock and debtors into cash as quickly as possible.

At best, therefore, ratios extracted from annual accounts provide no more than a broad indication of the general trend of liquidity. Unfortunately, the liquidity sickness – when it strikes – strikes very quickly, and the business manager who looks to no more than his year-end accounts will usually find that they tell him too little too late. The cure is to inject more cash, but sufficient cash cannot always be found in time. Even if it can be found, it will usually prove to be very costly medicine. The best form of cure is prevention, and the best way of preventing a liquidity crisis is to prepare cash-flow forecasts.

## CASH-FLOW FORECASTS

A cash-flow forecast is the most effective means by which a businessman can plan to ensure that his business will always have sufficient funds to meet its debts. It is a technique which no businessman can ignore. Cash-flow problems are not unique to unprofitable businesses; indeed the very danger of the liquidity crisis is that it can strike at the most successful businesses, particularly those which are expanding.

At their 1982 levels of operation, Dovetails presently incur the following amounts of monthly cash payments (the figures are based on their 1982 accounts and are rounded for simplicity): £110,000 to suppliers for materials; £40,000 on direct wages; £42,000 on overheads. Each month they collect approximately £202,000 from customers. The company is generating a healthy cash surplus each month of £10,000.

They have a good order book, so that they plan to operate at the same levels for at least the first six months of 1983. They start the year with £26,000 in cash and, because they are overdrawn £112,000 against a bank facility of £200,000, further funds of £88,000 are available from the bank should they be needed. The company is profitable and financially sound.

On 1 January 1983, a new customer makes a large order. The first delivery – for goods worth £60,000 – is for the end of June. The customer will pay cash on delivery, and the price will give a better than average profit margin. It will mean increasing their monthly output by 25 per cent from February onwards, but management assess that they can rearrange the shifts and keep the factory running for 10 hours a day instead of 8. The order is accepted: 25 per cent more business means 25 per cent more profit. The directors are delighted. The truth is that by accepting the order they run a great risk of going out of business before the end of May.

Frame 50 shows the cash-flow forecast that Dovetails should have prepared at the beginning of the year. If they had done so, they would have seen that they would use up their bank overdraft facility in less than five months' time.

Increasing production by 25 per cent will mean spending 25 per cent more

**Frame 50**

| Dovetails' cash-flow forecast 1983 | | | | | | | |
|---|---|---|---|---|---|---|---|
| £000 | Jan | Feb | Mar | Apr | May | Jun | Jul |
| Opening balance | – 86* | – 76 | –110 | –144 | –178 | –212 | –186 |
| Cash receipts | +202 | +202 | +202 | +202 | +202 | +262† | +262 |
| Cash payments | –192 | –236 | –236 | –236 | –236 | –236 | –236 |
| Closing balance | – 76 | –110 | –144 | –178 | –212 | –186 | –160 |

\* Overdraft £112 less cash £26
† Including £60,000 from first delivery of new order

**Frame 51**

| Monthly cash outgoings | On existing level of business | On increasing production by 25% |
|---|---|---|
| | £ | £ |
| Materials | 110,000 | 137,500 |
| Wages | 40,000 | 50,000 |
| Overheads | 42,000 | 48,500 |
| Total | 192,000 | 236,000 |

on materials each month (suppliers demanded COD for the additional deliveries) and 25 per cent more on wages. Because some overheads are fixed, total overheads should not increase proportionally (the new work is therefore even more profitable). In fact, Dovetails expect overheads to increase by £6,500. In total, accepting the new order will cause the company's monthly cash outgoings from February onwards to increase from £192,000 to £236,000 (Frame 51). However the higher level of receipts will only start to flow in from the end of June. In the meantime, the old level of business is only generating a monthly surplus of £10,000, and existing resources soon expire. The company will exceed its overdraft limit in May. Unless it acts quickly there will be no money to pay creditors, or to pay the wages.

As a result of accepting the new order Dovetails have had to increase their investment in working capital by £176,000 (£44,000 for each of the four months February–May) before any of the extra cash begins to flow back in June. Dovetails then start to reap the benefits, and from then onwards the liquidity position becomes increasingly better. The problem is that the company may not survive until June.

With proper planning, Dovetails would have no difficulty in arranging for a temporary increase in their bank overdraft, or for a payment on account from their new customer. Alternatively, they could seek ways of generating the needed funds internally – by improving their stock turn-round or the collection performance from their debtors – in order to be able to finance the increased level of business from their own resources. With no planning, and no cash forecast, the shortfall in May remains hidden. The irony then is that the company should not take on the new order: they simply cannot afford to be so successful.

**SUMMARY**

See Frame 52.

**Frame 52**

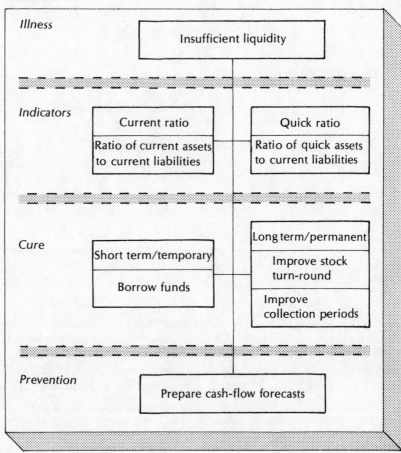

# 11 Analysis for business proprietors

For the sort of company of which Dovetails is typical, the directors will usually be shareholders in the business as well as managers of it. As well as using accounting information for management purposes, they will also want to use accounts as a basis for examining the worth of their personal investment. The following sections describe methods by which proprietors can analyse their accounts in order to assess the relative profitability of their investment and the degree of risk that attaches to it.

**RETURN ON EQUITY**

In the same way as the return on capital employed has been used as the primary measure of overall business performance, so the return on their equity provides the first basis from which proprietors can assess the relative profitability of their investment.

When calculating the overall return on capital employed, the comparison was between the full amount of resources available to management (from whatever source they were provided) and the full amount earned from the use of those resources (before accounting for any return on them – whether by way of dividends to shareholders or interest on debt).

For present purposes, however, the definition of capital is limited to the funds provided by Ordinary shareholders and excludes those provided from long-term borrowing. The relevant measure of profit is the amount available for Ordinary shareholders, after interest on borrowings and any other prior claims have been satisfied.

At the beginning of 1982, the shareholders' funds (share capital plus reserves) included in Dovetails' balance sheet amounted to £639,373. The return earned on those funds during the year – represented by profit after tax and interest, and after extraordinary items – was £61,755. Dovetails return on equity for 1982 is therefore:

$$(£61,755/£639,373) \times 100 = 9.7\%$$

On every £1 of equity, Dovetails have earned 9.7p. By comparing that return with market interest rates, or with the returns available from other forms of investment, proprietory shareholders can assess how effectively the company has used the equity funds available to it, which itself provides a measure of the relative profitability of their investment.

**EARNINGS PER SHARE**

A further measure of equity investors' earning potential is provided by the amount of earnings per share. The calculation is based on profit after tax and interest, but before extraordinary items, divided by the number of Ordinary shares in issue. Extraordinary items are excluded because of the distorting effect they have on year-by-year comparisons. The figures for Dovetails are shown in Frame 53. The 1982 earnings are a considerable improvement on those for 1981.

**Frame 53**

|  | | 1982 | 1981 |
|---|---|---|---|
|  | | £ | £ |
| Profit after tax and interest, and before extraordinary items | = | 80,097 | 62,810 |
| Number of Ordinary shares in issue | | 120,000 | 120,000 |
| Earnings per share | = | 67p | 52p |

For companies listed on the Stock Exchange, earnings per share serve as a major indicator of performance, and have a direct bearing on the market's assessment of those shares. Dividing the earnings per share into the quoted market price provides what is known as the price/earnings or P/E ratio. If Dovetails were listed and their shares were quoted, say, at £5, their 1982 earnings per share of 67p would indicate a P/E ratio of 7.5 (£5 divided by 67p). If the share price went up to £8 the P/E ratio would be 11.9: the shares would be said to be selling at 11.9 times earnings. Market prices are of course influenced by a great many different factors, some of them totally unrelated to the company's performance. Nevertheless the P/E ratio provides the primary indicator of the level of risk which the market attaches to the investment in question.

**DIVIDEND COVER**

In many respects, therefore, the trend of a company's earnings per share over a number of years – and the estimates which might then be made from that trend as to its likely earning power in the future – act as a major influence on the current price of the shares, and therefore on the value of an investor's shareholding.

A second influence, and one which is regarded by many analysts as being equally important, is the company's dividend record. Regardless of the level of profits that have been generated for equity shareholders, an investor will be concerned also to receive some form of immediate distribution of those earnings as a tangible return on his investment. In particular, he will want to assess the likely level of dividends to come in the future. The relationship between the amount of the company's earnings

**Frame 54**

|  | 1982 | 1981 |
|---|---|---|
|  | £ | £ |
| Earnings available for Ordinary shareholders | 61,755 | 62,810 |
| Dividend paid | 21,600 | 20,400 |
| Dividend cover = | 2.9 times | 3.0 times |

and the amount distributed is usually expressed as the level of dividend cover.

Frame 54 shows the calculations for Dovetails. The 1982 dividend is covered almost three times, as was the dividend for 1981.

The extent of the cover provides an indication to shareholders both of the company's ability to pay out a dividend from current earnings and their willingness to do so. A high level of cover implies that the company can maintain its present dividend with comfort and at the same time provide a supporting cushion from which dividends might be more comfortably maintained in the future. Low cover suggests the company is straining to provide a tangible return to investors and casts greater doubt on the ability to maintain dividend levels in the future. The likely future level of dividends should not, of course, be assessed simply on the basis of one year's payout ratio. Profits accumulated and retained from previous years remain available for subsequent distribution and the amount of reserves shown in the balance sheet will be very relevant to any assessment of future dividend streams. A company's dividend policy will usually be evident from the pattern of dividends over a number of years, and particularly from the relationship between the dividends paid and the earnings available each year. It is notable, for example, that in the last two years Dovetails have paid out only about one-third of their available earnings – implying that they were not concerned to maximise the immediate return to shareholders but preferred to retain a substantial proportion of profits within the business to finance its future expansion. That of course is also to the advantage of shareholders, who may sacrifice income in the present but who then have the prospect of income in the future which is enhanced by the growth of the business.

## INTEREST COVER

A matter of major concern to the investor is the degree of risk that attaches to his investment. That risk comes from two main sources: business risk and financial risk. Businesses within the same trade may vary in the general volatility of their profits but that element of risk – the predictability or otherwise of the future flow of profits – will apply to some extent to all businesses which operate in the same sector.

The degree of financial risk, on the other hand, is something which is specific to a particular company. It arises from management's financing policy: the choice between equity and debt as a source of funds.

One measure of the degree of financial risk is given by the calculation of interest cover: a comparison between the interest charges payable on debt and the level of profit from which that interest is funded. In Frame 55, Dovetails' profit before interest and tax is divided by the £12,600 interest paid on long-term borrowings (which is 9 per cent on the unsecured loan stock of £140,000). The interest charge is covered 11.3 times. In 1981 it was covered 11.7 times. That indicates a very low level of risk to the equity investor: at its present levels of profit, the company is easily able to meet the prior charges on debt and still have a very healthy surplus available for retention or for distribution to shareholders.

**Frame 55**

|  | | 1982 | 1981 |
|---|---|---|---|
|  | | £ | £ |
| $\dfrac{\text{Profits before interest and tax}}{\text{Interest on long-term borrowings}}$ | = | $\dfrac{142{,}433}{12{,}600}$ | $\dfrac{146{,}818}{12{,}600}$ |
| Interest cover | = | 11.3 times | 11.7 times |

The number of times interest is covered is a statistic which is also very relevant to business managers. As the level of profits becomes low in comparison with fixed interest charges, so proportionately less profits are available from which to provide a return on equity. In the longer run, a low and deteriorating level of interest cover implies that the company is increasingly exposed to the risk of defaulting on interest payment – with the consequent threat of foreclosure.

For these reasons the level of interest cover will also be a matter of first importance to existing lenders – whether they be banks, debenture holders or, as in Dovetails' case, unsecured loan stock holders. Just as importantly, it will be the first point of reference for potential lenders. A company with already low levels of interest cover will find it increasingly difficult to borrow more money; if they do succeed in attracting funds, they will certainly have to pay higher rates of interest on them – in order to compensate lenders for the higher level of risk that attaches to their loan.

**GEARING**

The comparison between interest costs and the available return on equity i
one measure of a company's gearing. Gearing is more usually expressed a
the ratio of debt to equity, as measured by the amounts of long-term
borrowings and shareholders' funds in the company's balance sheet. I
provides an indicator of the company's financing policy: the extent t
which management have preferred to finance their long-term requirement
from borrowings rather than shareholders' funds.

Dovetails' gearing is calculated in Frame 56. The ratio has fallen from 3
per cent in 1981 to 35 per cent in 1982. Note, however, that the figures use
for borrowings include amounts representing deferred taxation (£99,10
for 1982 and £94,900 for 1981) in addition to the £140,000 unsecured loa
stock. Dovetails have not in fact increased their fixed-interest borrowin
during the year, and for a profitable company (with growing reserves) tha
should result in a declining gearing ratio.

**Frame 56**

|  |  | 1982 | 1981 |
|---|---|---|---|
|  |  | £ | £ |
| $\dfrac{\text{Long-term borrowings}}{\text{Shareholders' funds}}$ | = | 239,107 / 679,528 | 234,900 / 639,373 |
| Gearing | = | 35% | 37% |

The inclusion of deferred tax may not rest easily in this context: there is a
least some doubt that it will ever have to be paid, and it is certainly
liability which is very different in nature from loan stock. Nevertheless, it i
included in the sense that it represents medium-term borrowing from th
Inland Revenue, albeit interest-free.

Other bases, apart from the quirk of deferred tax, are sometimes used t
define gearing: for example the ratio can alternatively be expressed as th
proportion of borrowings to the total of shareholders' funds *plu*
borrowings (which will of course give lower percentages); and overdraft
can, if appropriate, be included in the amount of borrowings (which wi
increase the percentages). The important point, whatever basis is used, i
the trend which emerges from year to year.

Once again the key word is risk. High gearing means high risk – for bot
lenders and equity investors. Potential lenders will demand a relativel
higher rate of interest from a company which is already highly geared. A
the gearing and the interest burden increases, so the risk attached to equit
earnings also increases: with a higher interest burden, a company will hav
to make larger profits before any money is available to pay dividends t

investors. In return for the higher risk they carry, equity investors will expect a higher than average return when the profits start to flow.

The question of gearing is therefore a matter of the greatest importance to management. Their aim should be to achieve the best mix of capital at the minimum cost. That in turn will require a careful assessment of the expected rates of return on both debt and equity and an awareness of how, for example, an increase in the cost of debt can cause corresponding increases in the expected return on equity.

Nevertheless, any difficulty there might be in establishing the optimum capital mix for a company should not be allowed to blur the basic advantage of gearing. If a business can earn a better return than the rate it has to pay, then every £1 borrowed will increase profitability.

Suppose Dovetails can earn a return of 16 per cent on the capital they employ in the business, and that they presently have equity totalling, say, £5 million, and borrowings of £1 million on which they pay 15 per cent interest. On a total capital employed of £6 million, 16 per cent gives an overall return of £960,000; £150,000 goes on interest, leaving £810,000 for ordinary shareholders – a return on equity of 16.2 per cent. The 1 per cent turn on borrowed money serves to 'gear up' (the North American phrase is 'leverage') the return on equity.

In that example Dovetails have only a modest level of borrowing, and are therefore only moderately geared. Nevertheless a 4 per cent increase in overall return (20 per cent on £6 million = £1,200,000) would result in a 30 per cent increase in earnings for equity (a return of £1,050,000, instead of £810,000, on £5 million). That is the benefit of gearing.

The effect is even more dramatic as the gearing increases. Suppose Dovetails restructure their capital to a gearing ratio of 5:1, £1 million equity and £5 million debt. The overall return of 16 per cent is the same, but a far higher proportion – £750,000 – now goes on interest. That still leaves £210,000 for shareholders on an investment of £1 million – a return of 21 per cent. If overall profitability now goes up by 4 per cent, profits available to shareholders increase to £450,000 – a 115 per cent increase in return on equity! High gearing means high risk, and high risk sometimes brings high reward.

Of course it can also bring disaster. If profits had fallen instead of increasing by as little as 4 per cent (to £720,000), the company would be unable to meet its interest payments out of current earnings. They may be able to draw on reserves for one year, but if the lower rate of profitability continues for any time the company will soon be insolvent. A highly geared company is highly sensitive to even relatively small fluctuations in profit. It is also highly vulnerable to changes in interest rates. A 4 per cent increase in the borrowing rate would wipe out Dovetails' profit.

Gearing is therefore critically important to the businessman – both as a business manager in his search for the most appropriate sources of finance, and as a proprietory shareholder who is concerned with the security of his investment.

## VALUE OF A BUSINESS

Gearing also has an immediate and direct bearing on the question of how much a business is worth. An immediate response to that question might be to go to the latest set of accounts. Dovetails' balance sheet at the end of 1982 shows total assets of £918,635, financed by £679,528 shareholders' funds and £239,107 borrowings.

The first question that arises is therefore whether we are concerned with the total value of the business or only the value of its equity. An assessment of the total worth of the business might start from £918,635 total assets. An assessment of equity value starts from £679,528, i.e. the amount of assets that remain after all borrowings have been repaid. Dividing the amount of shareholders' funds by the number of shares in issue (120,000) gives a figure of £5.65, which could be described as the net asset value per share.

It must be said, however, that for the purposes of valuing a business a set of accounts is not very helpful. Total value or equity value is one question; the next is whether the business is to be valued as a going concern, or whether its worth is to be based on break-up values. The book value of Dovetails' work-in-progress, for example, is based on costs incurred to date. It may well be appropriate to use that figure in a sale as a going concern but, if the business is to be broken up, the half-finished furniture represented by work-in-progress would probably be worthless.

Even in terms of a sale as a going concern, it is very doubtful whether balance sheet values will add up to a reasonable assessment of the worth of the business. The purpose in Part One of this book was to emphasise the fact that although accounting principles provide a useful and valuable framework in which to draw up a set of accounts, they do also act as limiting factors on the type of information that accounts are intended to convey, and they do therefore impose limitations on the alternative uses to which accounts can be put – including the question of the worth of a business. Dovetails' property, for example, is included in the balance sheet at a value of £245,923. That value is based on original cost. The value of the property now could be several times that figure. Similarly with plant, which is included at a residual cost based on an annual depreciation rate of 15 per cent. On the occasion of sale, there may be good cause for reassessing the remaining useful life of plant and machinery, which in turn would lead to revised assessments of their present worth to a potential buyer.

The valuation of a business is therefore fraught with uncertainty. It is even more fraught if we begin to consider the range of intangible factors that can have a bearing on the price at which a buyer and a seller might agree. They include the reputation of the product, the state of the order book and the share of the market the business commands. Those sort of considerations will help build up a picture of the likely future flow of profits – just as much as will the figures reported in any past sets of accounts. And all of that will go to support any figure for goodwill – over and above the values recorded in a balance sheet – which a seller might want to ask and for which a buyer might be willing to pay.

Other influences on the value of a business will include the quality of management, the level of their expertise, the industrial relations record of the business, and the extent to which any development programmes have laid the ground for future commercial growth. And of course there is the question of gearing: a highly geared business is more risky, and will be a less favourable proposition for a potential buyer.

For these sorts of reasons the valuation of the business is one of the more creative financial arts. For companies listed on the Stock Exchange, an alternative method of valuation – but one which is no less influenced by the whole range of imponderables – is through the quoted market price. 200,000 shares in issue, for example, at a current market price of £3 per share gives a market capitalisation for the company of £600,000. But of course this only represents the summation of numerous small holdings: the value of control of the whole business may be worth 50 to 100 per cent more than that figure, as 'takeover' bids have so often demonstrated.

**Frame 57**

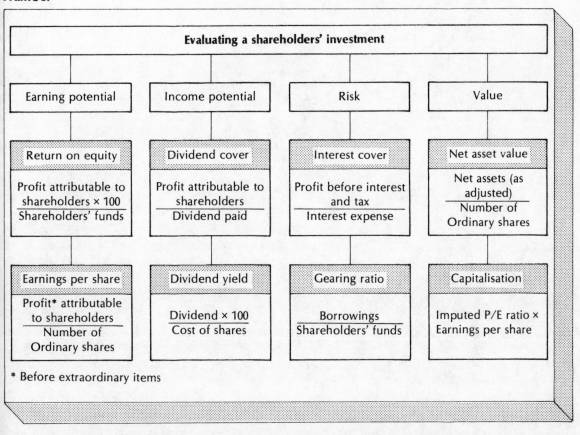

| Evaluating a shareholders' investment | | | |
|---|---|---|---|
| Earning potential | Income potential | Risk | Value |
| Return on equity | Dividend cover | Interest cover | Net asset value |
| $\dfrac{\text{Profit attributable to shareholders} \times 100}{\text{Shareholders' funds}}$ | $\dfrac{\text{Profit attributable to shareholders}}{\text{Dividend paid}}$ | $\dfrac{\text{Profit before interest and tax}}{\text{Interest expense}}$ | $\dfrac{\text{Net assets (as adjusted)}}{\text{Number of Ordinary shares}}$ |
| Earnings per share | Dividend yield | Gearing ratio | Capitalisation |
| $\dfrac{\text{Profit* attributable to shareholders}}{\text{Number of Ordinary shares}}$ | $\dfrac{\text{Dividend} \times 100}{\text{Cost of shares}}$ | $\dfrac{\text{Borrowings}}{\text{Shareholders' funds}}$ | $\text{Imputed P/E ratio} \times \text{Earnings per share}$ |

\* Before extraordinary items

A variation on this method of valuation is frequently used to value the equity in a company like Dovetails. Dovetails' earnings per share in 1982 were 67p. Reference to the P/E ratios of listed companies in the same business sector might produce an average P/E ratio of say 10. That average would then be (somewhat arbitrarily) adjusted to reflect the lesser marketability of shares in a non-listed company. Further adjustments would be made according to the size of the holding that is being acquired: substantial mark-downs for small, minority holdings; less so as the percentage acquired increases towards a controlling interest, i.e. more than 50 per cent. Whatever the case, applying an adjusted P/E of, say, 7.5 to Dovetails' current earnings per share would give a value for each share of £5.02. That compares with a net asset value per share of £5.65. (In times of high interest rates and yields it is not unusual for a business to sell at less than its so-called 'net asset value'.) The point around those two figures at which a deal might be struck is then a matter for informed guesswork, and clever bargaining.

**SUMMARY**   See Frame 57 (page 101).

# Part Four

# ACCOUNTS AND INFLATION: HOW TO ADJUST FOR IT

# 12 Inflation and current cost accounting

**THE EFFECTS OF INFLATION**

Prices change. Usually they go upwards. In recent years the rate at which prices have increased has had a major impact on the profitability and performance of all types of business. Some, unable to pass cost increases on to customers, have suffered more than others. None have been immune, and businessmen have become increasingly used to the idea of having to retain increasingly large amounts of their apparent profits in order to 'provide for the effects of inflation'.

How much they need to retain, and why they need to retain it, is not always apparent. Conventional accounts offer no guidance: built on the principle of historic cost, they are not designed to measure the effects of inflation. Instead, businessmen have to rely heavily on their instinct and general business acumen when assessing how much they can really afford to pay out as dividends and how much they need to keep in order to finance their existing level of business at increased levels of cost. In fact the effects of price changes on a business can be measured quite easily. This chapter will show how.

**THE HISTORIC COST ILLUSION**

Historic cost accounting records the amount of money that was exchanged in business transactions, whenever they took place (see Chapter 1). Assets shown in a balance sheet at a cost of £100 might therefore be made up of £40 of 1982 cost, £50 of 1975 cost and £10 of 1950 cost. The aggregate of £100 in the historic cost balance sheet is deceptive: it does not account for the fact that the 1950 pound was worth several times more than the 1982 pound.

The deception is greater in the profit and loss account: 1982 revenues are matched against costs of 1981 and earlier years, which are expressed in 1980 and earlier pounds. Because like is not matched with like, historic cost accounting produces misleadingly high profits in times of inflation. (In times of deflation it would produce misleadingly low profits.)

The main purpose of inflation-adjusted accounting systems is therefore to restore the principle of matching to the profit and loss account, and thereby to remove the inflationary element from historic cost profit.

**INFLATION AND PRICE CHANGES**

Before attempting to dispel the illusion we should establish precisely what it is that we are trying to adjust for. In this respect a clear distinction needs to be drawn between general inflation and specific price changes. General inflation arises from an increase in the general level of prices, usually expressed and measured by changes in the Retail Price Index (RPI). The consequence of general inflation is a fall in the general purchasing power of money.

In times of inflation the price of most things will go up, but it will only be by coincidence that the prices of particular types of assets, goods or services increase exactly in line with the RPI. In the last decade the price of oil-based products, for example, has increased faster than the general rate of inflation; the price of some things (calculators, video equipment, airfares) has fallen. Very rarely will the change in a specific price exactly match the change in the RPI over the same period.

This distinction is central to the question of what is meant by 'accounting for inflation'. It leads to two alternative methods of adjustment: to account for changes in the value of money, referred to as current purchasing power accounting (CPP); or to account for changes in the prices of the particular types of asset that a particular business is concerned with, referred to as current cost accounting (CCA). Each method seeks to make different corrections to the historic cost figures. Each can provide the businessman with useful information – according to the viewpoint from which he may wish to assess the performance of his business.

Suppose a trader buys for £100 an item of stock that retails then for £140. Suppose he holds it during a period when the RPI increases by 5 per cent but when prices in his particular trade increase by 10 per cent. When he sells the item for £154, historic cost accounting would match against revenue the original cost of £100. The historic cost profit would be £54. CPP accounting would update the original cost by the movement in the RPI: revenue would be matched against a cost (£100 × 1.05 = £105) expressed in pounds of equivalent purchasing power. The CPP profit would be £49. The CCA method would match revenue with the current cost of the stock sold (£110); the CCA profit would be £44.

## CAPITAL MAINTENANCE

These different measurements of 'profit' derive from the general relationship between profit and capital, and from alternative perceptions of what capital itself represents. An economic view of profit is the maximum amount which an individual can consume during a period and still remain as well off at the end of it as he was at the beginning. The equivalent accounting view is of profit as the maximum amount which a business can distribute during a period and still maintain its capital intact. Different measures of profit will arise according to the different views of what it is that needs to be maintained.

Historic cost accounting is a system that seeks to maintain no more than the original money amount of the capital invested by the shareholders. Any surplus realised over and above that amount is profit. The trader makes an historic cost profit of £54 because that is the amount which can be distributed without reducing his original money investment below £100.

CPP accounting seeks to preserve the original purchasing power of the capital invested. Because of 5 per cent inflation it now takes £105 to achieve the same level of purchasing power as was originally acquired from £100; the trader needs to attain a 5 per cent growth in his original investment merely in order to stand still. Of his historic cost profit, £5 must be retained in order to maintain his capital in these terms. His CPP profit is only £49 because any distribution above that amount would erode the purchasing power of his capital.

## CURRENT PURCHASING POWER ACCOUNTING

The CPP system operates by adjusting all accounting figures for changes in the RPI between the date of the original transaction and the accounting date. By this means it provides a comprehensive method of adjusting accounts for the effects of inflation. It assumes a 'proprietary' view of the capital to be maintained, and its interest to businessmen will therefore rest primarily in their capacity as proprietors who are concerned to preserve the value of their investment and who look to accounts to assess its growth. Part of the historic cost illusion is that, over a number of years, a business (and the value of the equity interest in it) may appear to have grown in size, whereas the 'growth' in figures is attributable to no more than the fall in the value of money. CPP adjustments correct that illusion.

The main shortcoming of the CPP system is that by adjusting all figures for changes in the RPI it fails to account for the very different ways in which inflation affects different businesses. In the earlier example, the price of the particular item of stock increased faster than the RPI. If the trader wants to stay in business he will need to replace his stock: the critical figure is not the historic cost of stock adjusted by the change in the RPI, but its replacement cost of £110. It is not sufficient for the trader to maintain his equity by retaining £105 in the business: he will want to maintain the business itself, and that needs £110.

## CURRENT COST ACCOUNTING

This is the principle of current cost accounting. In this system the focus is on the assets side of the balance sheet: the capital to be maintained is not the value of the proprietary investment but the physical resources of the business itself. In this respect CCA merely extends the principle of the going concern: it assumes that a business will not only continue in the foreseeable future but that it will continue at the same level of operations.

The CCA objective is achieved by matching revenues with the current cost of resources which are consumed in earning it. Historic cost figures are adjusted for changes in those prices which are specific to the particular business. The trader's current cost profit of £44 is freely distributable because the funds retained (£110) are sufficient to enable the replacement of stock and the continuation of business at the same level.

Because it seeks to preserve the operating capacity of the firm, the CCA method of adjusting for changing price levels will be of particular relevance to business managers. For this reason it is the method of 'adjusting for inflation' which is developed further in the rest of this chapter. It is also the method which has found most recent favour with the accounting bodies, as promulgated in their Statement of Standard Accounting Practice No. 16 (issued March 1980).

## CCA TECHNIQUES

Techniques for adjusting historic cost to current cost can feasibly be built into the accounting system, in which case the periodic accounts which are produced from the accounting records will already be adjusted for the impact of price changes. Many large companies use CCA for internal reporting purposes, both to establish pricing policies and, because it provides a more reliable measure of the return on capital employed, to assess the comparative performance of different divisions within a diversified group.

There are, of course, costs involved: the price information fed into the system needs to be constantly updated. These systems costs may be prohibitive for companies without computerised records (although the increasing availability of relatively cheap micro facilities will bring the potential for in-built CCA systems within the reach of more and more firms).

Prohibitive or otherwise, these costs need not deprive other companies of the benefits of CCA. At present, most companies who wish to prepare current cost figures still do so by making annual adjustments to their year-end historic cost accounts. The calculations are straightforward and the insight they offer into the performance of a business can be revealing. The result of applying them to Dovetails' accounts are set out in Frame 58 which displays that company's current cost profit and loss account and balance sheet for 1982. For those who wish to follow the calculations in detail the step by step workings are set out in Chapter 13.

## CURRENT COST PROFIT

The current cost (CC) profit and loss account starts with the profit figure reported in the historic cost (HC) accounts. CC profit is arrived at by adjusting this figure for the difference between the historic and current cost of resources consumed during the year. The adjustments fall into three categories:

- *Depreciation* – to account for the difference between the historic and current cost of fixed asset resources used up during the year.

- *Cost of sales* – to account for the difference between the historic and current cost of stock consumed during the year.

- *Monetary working capital* – to account for the impact of price changes on the amount of net trade credit given or received by the business.

**Frame 58**

### DOVETAILS LIMITED

**Current cost profit and loss account
for the year ended 31 December 1982**

|  |  | £000 |
|---|---:|---:|
| Operating profit, as reported in historic cost accounts |  | 129 |
| CURRENT COST OPERATING ADJUSTMENTS: |  |  |
| Depreciation | 33 |  |
| Cost of sales | 15 |  |
| Monetary working capital | 5 |  |
|  |  | 53 |
| CURRENT COST OPERATING PROFIT |  | 76 |
| Gearing adjustment |  | 13 |
|  |  | 89 |
| Taxation |  | 49 |
|  |  | 40 |
| Extraordinary item |  | 18 |
| CURRENT COST PROFIT ATTRIBUTABLE TO SHAREHOLDERS |  | 22 |
| Dividend |  | 21 |
| Current cost profit |  | 1 |

**Current cost balance sheet
at 31 December 1982**

|  | £000 |
|---|---:|
| Fixed assets | 953 |
| Investments | 30 |
| Stocks | 436 |
| Monetary working capital | 123 |
| NET OPERATING ASSETS | 1,542 |
| Share capital and reserves | 1,171 |
| NET BORROWINGS | 371 |
|  | 1,542 |

## DEPRECIATION ADJUSTMENT

Suppose a manufacturer acquired an item of plant in 1970 for £100, and expects it to last for 10 years. His annual charge for depreciation would be £10. When he scraps the plant in 1980, the accumulated depreciation will be £100, which we may assume (but only for the purposes of this example) is represented by a separate cash balance, £10 having been set aside in each of the last ten years. To stay in business he must buy a replacement item of plant, but at 1980 prices it may now cost £200. Historic cost depreciation has provided him with only half this amount; the other half he must find out of his apparent 'profits' – assuming they have not already been distributed.

On a current cost basis the manufacturer would adjust his annual depreciation charge as soon as the replacement price of the plant in question was seen to increase. In this example, the depreciation adjustment would be £10 – the difference between the £10 already charged for depreciation in the HC accounts and the CC depreciation of £20. CC depreciation represents the consumption of one year out of a 10-year life for an asset whose current cost is £200.

In practice the calculation of the depreciation adjustment involves a calculation of the current replacement cost of the fixed assets in question (the £200 in the manufacturer example). The businessman may have current replacement prices readily to hand, in which case he has all the information he needs. Alternatively, and this is more usually the case in practice, current costs can be calculated by reference to price indices published by the Department of Industry. Their booklet, *Price Index Numbers for Current Cost Accounting,* is compiled specifically for this purpose. It includes price indices for a large range of plant, machinery and vehicles used by specified industries and for most businesses it will provide a sufficiently reliable basis from which to calculate approximate replacement costs. The application of the indices, and the detailed workings that lead up to the current cost of Dovetails' fixed assets at 31 December 1982, are set out in Chapter 13, pages 117-120.

Dovetails' total depreciation adjustment for 1982 is £33,000 which is the amount by which the company's apparent HC profits are reduced as the result of charging depreciation on the basis of 1982 costs, rather than on the basis of the costs which applied when the fixed assets were variously acquired.

The depreciation adjustment is a measure of the additional amount which Dovetails need to provide from their 1982 profits in order to maintain their fixed asset resources on a continuing basis at current price levels.

In Dovetails' case the bulk of the adjustment is in respect of tools and equipment. A lot of this equipment was bought over the last three years, and none of it is more than six years old (see page 118). Even so the incidence of price increases over that period has been such that the adjustment increases by some 60% the depreciation charge shown in the HC accounts (see page 120).

In so far as it reflects the difference between current and historic costs, the amount of a company's depreciation adjustment provides an indicator of the relative age of the fixed assets employed in the business. In times of rising prices the age of an asset will determine the relative amount of the 'uplift' required to restate it from historic to current cost: the older an asset the greater the uplift, and the greater will be the difference between HC and CC depreciation. Companies with old plant can expect to suffer bigger depreciation adjustments than companies with new plant.

## COST OF SALES ADJUSTMENT

The cost of sales adjustment is the additional amount that needs to be provided in order to match revenues with the current rather than the historic cost of stock consumed during the year. Referring back to the simple trader example, the cost of sales adjustment is £10 – the difference between the historic cost (£100) of the item of stock and the amount it costs to replace it once it has been sold.

In Dovetails' case the cost of sales adjustment for 1982 amounts to £15,000. In principle, this amount represents the aggregate of the differences between the historic and current cost of each item of stock sold during the year. If details of price changes are incorporated into the accounting system as they arise, that is how it would be calculated in practice: stock would automatically be charged at current cost as it was consumed. More often, the cost of sales adjustment is calculated as a one-off exercise based on the year-end accounts.

Chapter 13 illustrates the calculation of Dovetails' cost of sales adjustment by what is known as the 'averaging' method. Essentially, the averaging method converts the prices at which opening and closing stock are shown in the historic cost accounts to the average replacement prices that apply during the year. The method is more arbitrary than the specific 'item-by-item' basis and, to produce reasonably accurate results, it does require that purchases, any changes in stock levels, and the incidence of any price changes all occur evenly over the year.

Given these conditions, however, the averaging method effectively achieves a restatement of the whole of the cost of sales to average current cost for the year. The workings set out in the appendix can be confirmed by comparing Dovetails' historic and restated trading account for 1982 (see Frame 59).

The cost of sales adjustment of £15,000 appearing in Dovetails' current cost profit and loss account is the difference between the historic (£1,786,000) and current (£1,801,000) cost of stock consumed during the year. The company needs to retain the additional amount of £15,000 in the business in order to be able continually to replace stock from its own resources. Distributing the £15,000 would impair the capacity of the company to continue in the future at the same level of trading.

**Frame 59**

|  | Historic cost | Restated to average current cost |
|---|---|---|
|  | £000 | £000 |
| Sales | 2,425 | 2,425 |
| Opening stock | 404 | 410* |
| Purchases | 1,817 | 1,817 |
|  | 2,221 | 2,227 |
| Closing stock | 435 | 426* |
| Cost of sales | 1,786 | 1,801 |
| Gross profit | 639 | 624 |

*See workings on page 121.

An alternative way of looking at the cost of sales adjustment is that it represents stock profits – the 'holding gains' which accrue from holding stock over a period during which its price increases. This perception of the effect of price changes on the results of trading provides, for those who want it, a rough and ready method of assessing the effect of price changes on their business: at the start of the year Dovetails carried stock of £404,000; during 1982 the price index for timber and furniture stocks rose from 189.1 to 197.7, an increase of approximately 4 per cent. A 4 per cent price increase on stock-carrying values of £404,000 means that the company has to find an additional £16,000 in order to finance the same volume of stock at the end of the year as it did at the beginning; £16,000 is an approximation to the cost of sales adjustment of £15,000 as it was calculated by the averaging method.

**MONETARY WORKING CAPITAL ADJUSTMENT**

In the simple trader example it was assumed that stock was bought and sold for cash. Immediately the item was sold, cash was available with which to replace it at the higher cost of £110; and charging sales with the current cost of stock consumed ensured that sufficient funds were retained for replacement.

If, however, the trader had given one month's credit to his customer, he would have had to wait that further month before receiving the cash with which to re-stock, and if its price had increased further during that month the £110 retained in the business would prove insufficient for replacement.

The converse applies to trade credit received: a trader who receives credit terms from his supplier may be able to replenish his stocks regardless of the incidence of any price increase.

The monetary working capital adjustment accounts for these timing differences in the receipt or payment of cash. It applies to trade credit in the same way as the cost of sales adjustment applies to stocks. It recognises that if a business is to be a going concern it must maintain not only its physical stock levels but also its net involvement in trade credit.

Most businesses offer credit terms to customers. Dovetails do: almost three months (see Frame 43). A price increase in the items in which Dovetails trade will increase the amount of money committed to a given volume of debtors just as surely as it increases the amount of money committed to financing a given volume of stock. The monetary working capital adjustment provides for the additional amount required to finance debtors at current price levels.

Most businesses also buy on credit. Some, like supermarkets, take credit terms from their suppliers but sell only for cash. They have no debtors to finance and they use suppliers' money to finance part, or sometimes all, of their physical stocks. In these cases the burden of replacing stock at increased price levels shifts from the trader to the supplier. How far it shifts will depend on the relation between the trader's stockholding period and the extent of credit received. If the trader can sell the goods before he has to pay for them the whole of the financing burden rests with the supplier. The monetary working capital adjustment takes this into account by reducing the cost of sales adjustment to the extent that stocks are financed by trade creditors.

Stock, creditors and debtors make up the net working capital of a business, and the cost of sales and monetary working capital adjustments belong together as part of an overall working capital adjustment. In practice the two adjustments are calculated by the same averaging method (see page 123) which, in the case of the monetary working capital adjustment, is usually based on the net amount of monetary working capital.

Dovetails is a net giver of trade credit (debtors exceed creditors). The result of price increases in the trade is that the amount of money needed to finance their involvement in trade credit has correspondingly increased. The monetary working capital adjustment of £5,000 quantifies the additional amount needed at current price levels.

For many companies the current cost adjustments in respect of working capital can be very substantial. In Dovetails' case the adjustments are relatively small. They reflect the fact that the price of furniture materials during 1982 increased (by approximately 4 per cent) at a much slower rate than the general level of inflation (approximately 12 per cent over the same period). The impact of price changes in other business sectors during 1982 will have been much more severe.

**CURRENT COST OPERATING PROFIT**

The amount which remains after the current cost adjustments (for depreciation, cost of sales and monetary working capital) have been deducted is described as current cost operating profit. It represents the surplus arising from ordinary trading operations after accounting for the impact of price changes on the funds needed to maintain the operating capability of the business. In Dovetails' case the additional funding requirements which result from price changes during 1982 absorb £53,000 of the company's apparent profit: operating profit on a current cost basis (£76,000) amounts to less than 60 per cent of the profit reported in the historic cost accounts.

**GEARING ADJUSTMENT**

Those CCA principles which have so far been described cover all except one of the adjustments propounded in SSAP16. The exception is the gearing adjustment. It is included here for the sake of completeness, and for those who may wish or need to prepare current cost accounts in accordance with standard accounting practice, but the business reader should beware that the gearing adjustment is of a very different order from the 'operating' adjustments which precede it.

It has been said that the capital to be maintained in CCA is represented by the operating resources of the business. The CC operating adjustments provide a measure of the additional amounts that need to be retained in order to maintain those resources. Because these adjustments are charged against profits the implication is that each year the additional funding requirements will be found wholly from that source: there is no regard thus far in the CCA methodology for the fact that business resources will usually also be financed, at least in part, by borrowings. The purpose of the gearing adjustment is to recognise this alternative financing arrangement.

The rationale for the gearing adjustment is based on a further extension of the going concern principle. It assumes that if in the past a business has used both debt and equity to finance its resources then it will continue to do so in the future – and in the same proportions. If the need for extra financing arises because of price increases, it is assumed that the additional resources required will be financed in part by increased borrowings.

The accounting effect is that the burden of the current cost adjustments is assumed to be shared, in the gearing proportion, between the providers of outside finance (debt) and the business shareholders (equity). The business can therefore account to its shareholders on the basis that not all of the extra money needed to maintain business resources needs to be found from shareholders' profit. The gearing adjustment accounts for this benefit by reducing the current cost adjustments in the gearing proportion. The gearing adjustment introduces a 'proprietary' view into the CC profit and loss account: it leads to a measure of profit which is described as 'profit attributable to shareholders'.

In Dovetails' case the gearing effect reduces the current cost adjustments by 24 per cent (see page 124), thereby adding £13,000 to the current cost profit attributable to shareholders. It should be said, however, that the gearing adjustment is one that does not rest easily on a concept of capital which seeks to preserve the operating assets of the business: if the amount of this 'benefit' is distributed, the operating capacity of the firm will be impaired unless borrowings are correspondingly increased.

**CURRENT COST BALANCE SHEET**

The workings which lead to the figures in Dovetails' CC balance sheet are described in Chapter 13. Most of them are implicit in the methods used to calculate the CC operating adjustments. The overall purpose in the balance sheet is to show Dovetails' existing operating resources at their net current replacement cost at December 1982. The layout of the balance sheet reflects the general principles on which CCA is based: the line drawn at 'net operating assets' (£1,542) represents the CCA capital to be maintained; the financing analysis between shareholders' funds (£1,171) and net borrowings' (£371) provides the proportion which forms the basis for the gearing adjustment (see page 124).

**DOVETAILS: HC AND CC COMPARISON**

Frame 60 compares Dovetails' performance in HC and CC terms. (For the purposes of this comparison the figures have been taken directly from the respective December 1982 HC and CC accounts.) Putting operating profit on a current cost basis reduces it substantially (HC £129; CC £76). Dovetails' management may wish to reflect on the implications of this comparison when they next come to assess their pricing policy.

Putting capital employed on a current cost basis casts further light on the 1982 performance. What seemed to be a healthy return of 14 per cent (HC operating profit £129; HC capital employed £918) becomes a far less

**Frame 60**

|  | 1982 | |
|---|---|---|
|  | HC | CC |
|  | £000 | £000 |
| Operating profit | 129 | 76 |
| Profit attributable to shareholders | 61 | 22 |
| Dividend | 21 | 21 |
| Retained profit | 40 | 1 |
| Capital employed | 918 | 1,542 |
| Return on capital employed | 14% | 5% |

satisfactory return of 5 per cent when CC profit is assessed against the current cost of resources employed in earning it.

Most importantly, the CC figures restore the comparison between the amount the company can afford to distribute and the amount it has distributed. On the basis of its HC accounts, Dovetails' 1982 dividend is covered three times. On a current cost basis the company is shown to have paid to shareholders almost all it earned for them during the year.

# 13 Appendix: adjusting Dovetails' accounts to current cost basis

The following pages set out the workings which lead up to the restatement of Dovetails' 1982 accounts on a current cost basis. The resultant figures are explained and interpreted in the preceding text.

## 1 DEPRECIATION AND FIXED ASSETS

The purpose is to restate Dovetails' fixed assets to their current replacement cost as at December 1982, and to charge depreciation on that basis. The figures are restated by using price indices. All references are to the Government Statistical Services publication *Price Index Numbers for Current Cost Accounting*.

Index numbers update a cost from the date of acquisition to the accounting date. In order to use indices, the historic cost total for each category of fixed asset must be broken down according to the respective years of acquisition. Note, however, that this fully aged analysis and the volume of calculation it involves only arises in the first year for which current cost accounts are prepared: thereafter, the current costs calculated at the previous year end need only to be updated in total for each category by the rate of price increase during the current year.

*1.1 Tools and equipment*   Details are given in Frame 61. The analysis in Column 3 totals to the gross historic cost (£416,836) for tools and equipment shown in Note 7 to Dovetails' 1982 accounts.

To ease the calculations, fixed assets are assumed to have been purchased in the middle of any year, and the indices shown in Column 2 are those which applied at the mid-point of each year of acquisition.

The gross current cost in Column 4 is found by dividing historic cost by the price index at the acquisition date and multiplying by the price index at the accounting date, December 1982. Thus the current cost of replacing plant acquired for £82,000 in 1977 would now be:

$$(£82,000 \times 203.9)/118.9 = £141,000$$

Dovetails depreciate tools and equipment at a rate of 15 per cent p.a., i.e. they expect them to last approximately seven years. Accumulated current cost depreciation in Column 5 is calculated pro rata according to the

**Frame 61**

**Tools and equipment**
**Price index reference: 11100**

Index at December 1982 = 203.9

| (1) | (2) | (3) | (4) | (5) |
|-----|-----|-----|-----|-----|
| Year of purchase | Price Index | Gross HC, £000 | Gross CC, £000 | Acc. CC depreciation, £000 |
| 1977 | 118.9 | 82 | 141 | 127 |
| 1978 | 141.6 | 51 | 73 | 55 |
| 1979 | 155.3 | 35 | 46 | 28 |
| 1980 | 167.4 | 112 | 136 | 61 |
| 1981 | 189.0 | 93 | 100 | 30 |
| 1982 | 198.0 | 44 | 45 | 7 |
| | | 417 | 541 | 308 |

proportion of expected life that has already been used up. By the end of 1982 plant acquired in 1977, for example, will have been in use for six years. The accumulated depreciation on that plant is therefore:

$$6 \times 15\% \times £141,000 = £127,000$$

The current cost depreciation charge for 1982 is found by applying the adopted rate of depreciation to the gross current cost at December 1982:

$$15\% \times £541,000 = £81,000$$

The depreciation adjustment in respect of tools and equipment is the difference between this amount and the amount of depreciation charged in the HC accounts – see Section 1.5.

For balance sheet purposes, the current cost net book value of tools and equipment at December 1982 is:

$$£541,000 - £308,000 = £233,000$$

*1.2  Motor vehicles*  The workings (see Frame 62) are the same as for tools and equipment, and the ageing analysis is extracted in the same way from the company's records. Motor vehicles are depreciated over four years.

Current cost depreciation charge for 1982
$$= 25\% \times £48,000 = £12,000$$

Current cost net book value at December 1982
$$= £48,000 - £28,000 = £20,000$$

**Frame 62**

|  | | Motor vehicles | | |
| --- | --- | --- | --- | --- |
|  | | Index at December 1982 = 236.4 | | |
| Price index reference: 17,600 | | | | |
| Year of purchase | Price Index | Gross HC, £000 | Gross CC, £000 | Acc. CC depreciation, £000 |
| 1980 | 187.3 | 15 | 19 | 14 |
| 1981 | 212.6 | 21 | 23 | 12 |
| 1982 | 226.8 | 6 | 6 | 2 |
|  | | 42 | 48 | 28 |

*1.3 Property*   Indices are available for property (for example, the price index for the 'cost of new construction') but, because the costs and values of buildings will vary according to region and location, index numbers can produce estimates of replacement cost which are unreliable.

The more usual method is to obtain an up-to-date valuation of the property in question, based on its open market value for existing use. That will usually provide a better estimate of what it would cost to replace it. Alternatively, with a knowledge of the local property market, directors can make their own valuation. Dovetails estimate that the current existing use value of their property is £700,000. This figure is an estimate of net current replacement cost (the amount that would have to be paid out at December 1982 in order to acquire the property in its existing condition and location) and no analysis between gross cost and accumulated depreciation is therefore necessary.

In Dovetails' case, the bulk of the appreciation is attributable to an increase in land values. The current cost of the buildings themselves is assessed to be not materially different from their historic cost. Current cost and historic cost depreciation are equivalent, and no depreciation adjustment is therefore necessary in respect of buildings.

Current cost depreciation charge for 1982 (equivalent to HC) = £5,000

Current cost net book value at December 1982 = £700,000

*1.4 Investments*   Note 8 to Dovetails' historic cost accounts contains all the information necessary to restate investments to a current cost basis. Listed investments have market value of £18,000. The directors estimate that their valuation of the trade investment has not changed. It therefore remains at £12,000. The current cost of investments at December 1982 is, therefore,

£18,000 + £12,000 = £30,000

**Frame 63**

|  | HC deprec- iation | CC deprec- iation | HC net book value | CC net book value |
|---|---|---|---|---|
|  | £000 | £000 | £000 | £000 |
| Tools and equipment (1.1) | 50 | 92 | 224 | 307 |
| Motor vehicles (1.2) | 10 | 12 | 18 | 20 |
| Property (1.3) | 5 | 5 | 246 | 700 |
|  | 65 | 109 | 488 | 1,027 |
| Investments (1.4) | – | – | 26 | 30 |
|  | 65 | 109 | 514 | 1,057 |
|  |  | 65 |  | 514 |
|  |  | 44 |  | 543 |

*1.5 Summary* Dovetails' total depreciation adjustment for 1982 is, therefore, £33,000 (see Frame 63). This is the amount shown in the CC profit and loss account. The £469,000 is the revaluation surplus which arises from restating fixed assets shown in the historic cost balance sheet at £514,000 to their net current cost (as shown in the current cost balance sheet) of £983,000. The credit entry for this surplus goes to the current cost reserve (see Section 6.1).

## 2 COST OF SALES AND STOCK

*2.1 Cost of sales* The purpose is to charge profits with the current cost of stock consumed. By converting opening and closing stock to average prices for the year, the 'averaging method' isolates the volume change and exposes the part of the change in stock values wholly attributable to price increases. Note that although the method is based on adjustments to the opening and closing values of stock on hand, the purpose is to calculate the current cost of stock consumed.

The usual rules apply for the use of indices: stock must be aged so that the price index numbers appropriate to those dates can be applied. The 'average' cost to be calculated is the average for the 12 months of the accounting period, which is the period over which stock was consumed. The calculation is shown in Frame 64.

For greater accuracy, stock should be broken down into its categories (raw materials, work-in-progress, finished goods) and a separate cost calculated for each category. Note that the costs for wages and overheads included in work-in-progress and finished goods, for example, may not increase in line with the cost of materials, and it may be necessary to calculate and apply a separate index for each category (weighted according to the

**Frame 64**

### Cost of sales
### Index number reference: 25400

Dovetails' stocks are assumed to represent four months' purchases at the start of the year, and three months' purchases at the end of it. The average age of stock is therefore two months and one and a half months, respectively. The relevant price indices are those applying at:

| | |
|---|---|
| 31 October 1981 | 190.8 |
| Mid-November 1982 | 197.7 |
| Average for year to December 1982 | 193.4 |

|  | £000 |
|---|---|
| Historic cost of closing stock | 435 |
| Historic cost of opening stock | 404 |
| Total increase | 31 |
| Closing stock at average 1982 prices: | |
| £435,000 × (193.4/197.7) = | 426 |
| Opening stock at average 1982 prices: | |
| £404,000 × (193.4/190.8) = | 410 |
| Volume increase | 16 |

The cost of sales adjustment (price increase) is £15,000 – the total increase (£31,000) less the volume increase (£16,000) – and this is the amount which appears in the current cost profit and loss account.

**Frame 65**

### Balance sheet stock
### Index number reference: 25400

The average age of closing stock is one and a half months. The appropriate price indices are therefore:

| | |
|---|---|
| Mid November 1982 | 197.7 |
| 31 December 1982 | 198.1 |

HC closing stocks
= £435,000 × (198.1/197.7) = £436,000

The current replacement cost of stock at 31 December 1982 is £436,000. This amount appears in the current cost balance sheet. The revaluation surplus (£1,000) goes to current cost reserve.

material/wage/overhead content of that category). In addition, assuming that historic costs have been attributed on a FIFO basis, the ageing of raw materials, work-in-progress and finished goods will be different, and the price indices used in each calculation should be chosen according to these different dates.

*2.2 Balance sheet stock*   The purpose is to restate unconsumed stock shown in the balance sheet from historic costs to the current replacement cost at the accounting date. The calculations are shown in Frame 65 (page 121).

## 3   MONETARY WORKING CAPITAL

The purpose is to provide for the funds needed to finance the extra monetary working capital required as the result of increased prices. The same averaging method is used, and it will usually be appropriate to apply the same price index or indices as are used in the cost of sales adjustment. The calculations are shown in Frame 66.

The treatment of cash and overdraft balances in these calculations is a moot point. Where cash balances are used in the conduct of day-by-day trading operations it will be appropriate to include them as monetary working capital. Where overdraft balances fluctuate with the levels of stock, debtors and creditors (so that the overdraft would normally be extended, for example, where price increases necessitate additional borrowing to finance the same volume of trade), it may be appropriate to treat them as being analagous to trade credit received, and to include them also in the monetary working capital calculations.

Where some part or all of an overdraft balance does not fluctuate with the level of trading, so that it is more in the nature of permanent long-term finance, it should be excluded from monetary working capital and included instead in 'borrowings' for the purpose of the gearing adjustment (see Section 5).

In practice, this distinction may be difficult to draw. One way or the other, however, overdrafts will be brought into the current cost calculations and the alternative treatments – either through gearing or through monetary working capital – will often lead to adjustments which, in total, are not significantly different from one another.

Note that, for monetary amounts, no adjustment is needed to the balance sheet figures.

## 4   SUMMARY

*4.1   Current cost operating adjustments*   These are detailed in Frame 67. The sum of £53,000 is a measure of the total amount of additional funds the company needs to retain within the business in order to maintain its resources (its operating capacity) at current price levels.

*4.2   Net operating assets*   These are detailed in Frame 68 from which it

**Frame 66**

### Monetary working capital

Dovetails' monetary working capital comprises:

|  | 1982 | 1981 |
|---|---|---|
|  | £000 | £000 |
| Trade debtors | 585 | 417 |
| Less: Trade creditors | 462 | 330 |
|  | 123 | 87 |

Debtors and creditors are taken to represent three months' sales and purchases, respectively. (Where their average age is different, the monetary working capital adjustment should be calculated in the two separate parts.) The appropriate indices are therefore:

| Mid-November 1981 | 189.1 |
|---|---|
| Mid-November 1982 | 197.7 |
| Average 1982 | 193.4 |

|  | £000 |
|---|---|
| Closing monetary working capital | 123 |
| Opening monetary working capital | 87 |
|  | 36 |
| Closing monetary working capital at average prices = 123 × (193.4/197.7) | 120 |
| Opening monetary working capital at average prices = 87 × (193.4/189.1) | 89 |
| Volume change | 31 |

The effect of price changes during the year is therefore £5,000 (£36,000 less £31,000), which is the amount of the extra funds needed to finance monetary working capital at current price levels.

**Frame 67**

### Current cost operating adjustments

|  | £ |
|---|---|
| Depreciation adjustment (Section 1.5) | 33,000 |
| Cost of sales adjustment (Section 2.1) | 15,000 |
| Monetary working capital adjustment (Section 3) | 5,000 |
|  | 53,000 |

**Frame 68**

## Net operating assets

|  | HC | CC |
|---|---|---|
|  | £000 | £000 |
| Fixed assets (Section 1.5) | 488 | 953 |
| Investments (Section 1.5) | 26 | 30 |
| Stock (Section 2.2) | 435 | 436 |
| Monetary working capital (Section 3) | 123 | 123 |
|  | 1,072 | 1,542 |
|  |  | 1,072 |
| Revaluation surplus |  | 470 |

**Frame 69**

## Gearing adjustment

|  | £000 |
|---|---|
| Net borrowings: |  |
| Long-term loans | 140 |
| Deferred taxation | 99 |
| Bank overdraft | 112 |
| Taxation | 46 |
|  | 397 |
| *Less:* Cash | 26 |
|  | 371 |
| Shareholders' equity: |  |
| Per HC balance sheet | 680 |
| Dividend | 21 |
| Revaluation surpluses (Section 4.2) | 470 |
|  | 1,171 |

Gearing proportion
$$= 371/1,171 + 371) = 0.24 \text{ or } 24\%$$

The gearing adjustment is found by applying the gearing proportion, 23%, to the total current cost operating adjustments of £53,000 (Section 4.1), i.e.

$$24\% \times 53,000 = £13,000$$

Which is the amount added back in the CC profit and loss account.

can be seen that the current replacement cost, at December 1982, of the company's unconsumed operating resources amounts to £1,542,000. If prices remained at their December 1982 level, these costs would flow through future years' current cost profit and loss accounts as the resources are used up.

The unrealised surplus of £470,000, which results from the restatement of operating assets from historic to net current cost, is included in the current cost reserve (see Section 6.1).

**5    GEARING ADJUSTMENT**

The purpose is to measure the benefit that accrues to shareholders from the assumption that part of the burden of increased prices will be financed from increased borrowings.

The rationale for this adjustment rests on the assumption that as the total amount of resources to be financed increases (because of price increases), the proportion that is financed from borrowings will remain constant, i.e. as resources increase, so borrowings increase pro rata. On this basis, not all of the additional financing requirement (represented by the total of the current cost operating adjustments) needs to be found from profits. The gearing adjustment accounts for this expectation by reducing the current cost adjustments in the gearing proportion.

For the purposes of this calculation (detailed in Frame 69), net borrowings is normally taken to include all liabilities except those included in monetary working capital; shareholders' equity is usually taken from the current cost balance sheet, i.e. including the current cost reserve.

**6    SHARE CAPITAL AND RESERVES**

*6.1   Current cost reserve*   The current cost reserve houses the double entry for all the adjustments that have been made in order to prepare current cost accounts. It is made up as shown in Frame 70.

**Frame 70**

| Current cost reserve | £000 | £000 |
|---|---|---|
| Revaluation surpluses on fixed assets, investments and stocks (Section 4.2) | | 470 |
| Current cost operating adjustment (Section 4.1) | 53 | |
| *Less:* Gearing adjustment (Section 5) | 13 | |
| | | 40 |
| As included in current cost balance sheet (see Frame 71) | | 510 |

6.2 *Current cost balance sheet*   The amount for share capital and reserves included in the current cost balance sheet is made up as shown in Frame 71.

**Frame 71**

| Share capital and reserves | | |
|---|---:|---:|
| | £000 | £000 |
| Share capital (per HC balance sheet) | | 120 |
| Share premium account (per Note 12 to the HC accounts) | | 243 |
| Revenue reserves brought forward (per Note 12) | 276 | |
| Current cost profit for the year (per CC profit and loss account) | 1 | |
| | | 277 |
| Current cost reserve (Section 6.1) | | 510 |
| Proposed dividend | | 21 |
| | | 1,171 |

# Part Five

# ACCOUNTS IN THE FUTURE: THE 1981 COMPANIES ACT

# 14  Legislation and accounts

**EEC FOURTH DIRECTIVE**

The United Kingdom has been a member of the European Economic Community since 1973. In 1978, as part of its general programme of 'harmonisation', the EEC Commission in Brussels issued its Fourth Directive on Company Law. The purpose of this Directive was to establish common standards for the preparation and presentation of company accounts within the Community, and thereby to achieve a level of comparability between the accounts of companies prepared in different member states. The Fourth Directive applies only to the accounts of individual companies: the harmonisation of group accounts is the subject of a further Directive, the Seventh, which is still in the course of drafting.

Work on the Fourth Directive started in 1967, and the 11 years it took to produce reflects the difficulties which confront any attempt to harmonise the widely discordant accounting practices of nine (now ten) different countries. In the event, the document that emerged from Brussels contained a good degree of compromise, particularly in the level of choice it provides from a permitted range of alternative accounting principles. The level of comparability achieved is therefore likely to be cosmetic rather than substantial. For the future, accounts prepared in different EEC countries may well have a similar appearance, but the bases on which they have been prepared are likely to be as diverse as they have been in the past.

Nevertheless the Fourth Directive will result in substantial changes in accounting practice throughout the Community. The terms of EEC membership require each member state to incorporate directives into their own national law. In the UK the provisions of the Fourth Directive have been implemented in the 1981 Companies Act.

**1981 COMPANIES ACT**

The 1981 Companies Act was enacted in November 1981. Those parts concerned with accounting matters cover more than 70 pages, and they replace large sections of the previous law on company accounts as it was contained in the 1948 and 1967 Acts. The major impact of the new law on UK accounting practice is likely to be felt in three main areas.

First, companies will have to present their accounts in accordance with prescribed formats, and new disclosure and presentation rules will require significantly greater disclosure than has been given in the past.

Second, companies will have to prepare their accounts on bases that are in accordance not only with professional standards but also with what are now statutory requirements as to how certain of the figures are to be arrived at. This is new ground: in the past, statutory accounting requirements in the UK have been concerned exclusively with matters of disclosure; the 1981 Companies Act extends the scope of accounting law over the boundaries of disclosure and into the field of accounting principle. As a result, the historic cost principle, for example, is now given legal backing as the general basis on which accounts should be prepared (although the Act does permit alternative bases, which allow for revaluations as well as for current cost accounting). In addition, new legal definitions are introduced for such things as 'turnover', 'related companies' and 'production cost', and there are now specific statutory rules dealing with fixed asset accounting and revaluation surpluses. The treatment of goodwill, stock, investments, research and development costs and formation expenses are other areas where accounting practice will now be subject to legal requirements.

The third major area of change introduced by the new Companies Act is in the distinction which it draws between the publicity and filing requirements of different companies according to their size. In the past, all companies have been subject to the same disclosure requirements and were under the same obligations regarding the filing of their accounts. For the future, small and medium-sized companies will have the option of omitting certain disclosures from the accounts they put on public record by filing with the Registrar.

The provisions of the new Act will have a major impact on the future shape of company accounts. The following paragraphs provide an outline of the main provisions, with particular reference to the areas of significant change. Marginal references to the appropriate section numbers are provided for those who wish to refer to the detail of the Act itself (S = Section number; 1/- = Schedule 1, Paragraph -).

## EFFECTIVE DATES

S. 17(2)   The new accounting requirements come into effect for financial years beginning on or after 15 June 1982. (Accounts for periods beginning before that date may also be drawn up under the new rules, or they may be drawn up under the old rules – in which case they must include a statement of that fact.) The first accounts prepared under the new rules – whether voluntary or compulsory – will have to contain information on a comparable basis in respect of the preceding year.

## TRUE AND FAIR VIEW

S1   The general requirements under the new law are that accounts should both comply with the provisions of the Act and give a true and fair view. Where these twin objectives are incompatible

S.1(3)   the requirement for a true and fair view overrides all other provisions. (Thus for example a company must depart from a detailed requirement of the Act if, due to the special circumstances of the business, compliance with that requirement would result in the accounts not showing a true and fair view. In this case details of the departure and the reasons for it must be disclosed.)

## ACCOUNTING PRINCIPLES

For the most part the accounting principles now written into the law merely give statutory backing to matters which are already recognised to be professional best practice: most of the principles described below will already be well known to those who are familiar with Statements of Standard Accounting Practice: a good number of them have featured in the earlier parts of this book. Nevertheless it can be expected that the legal strength now given to certain of these principles will give companies greater cause to reflect on the accounting policies which they adopt in their own accounts: in the past, departures from certain principles have been in conflict with no more than professional best practice; in the future a departure from these principles will be illegal. The following paragraphs summarise the new statutory rules.

## BASIC RULES

1/10-13   Accounts must be prepared in accordance with the fundamental principles of going concern, consistency, prudence and accruals (see Part One).

1/15   Departures are only permitted for special reasons, and those reasons and the effects of the departure must be disclosed. The
1/36   usual practice of disclosing accounting policies is also now a statutory requirement.

1/12   Only realised profits may be recognised. The Act does not define 'realised', but a late insertion makes it clear that for statutory purposes the recognition of profit should follow
1/90   generally accepted accounting principles. The inclusion of long-term contracts at cost plus attributable profit, for example, is an approved method of accounting and would therefore not be prohibited, even though it could strictly be regarded as a departure from the principle of realisation.

1/16   The primary method of valuation of assets is the historic cost of purchase or production. Purchase price is defined to include expenses incidental to the acquisition. Production cost is defined to include all costs directly attributable to the
1/26   production of the asset, and may also include a reasonable proportion of indirect costs as well as any interest paid on money borrowed to finance the asset in question. The inclusion of distribution costs is specifically prohibited.

## ALTERNATIVE VALUATION METHODS

1/31   Alternative methods of valuation are permitted. Fixed assets and stocks may be included at current cost. Revaluations are

1/34

allowed for tangible fixed assets. Investments can be stated a
market value. In any of these cases, however, disclosure must b
made of:

1   The items affected, and the basis of valuation adopted
    and

2   The comparable historic cost amount for each of th
    affected items (except stocks), or the difference betwee
    the historic cost amount and the amount shown.

**REVALUATION RESERVE**   1/34

Any profit or loss which arises from stating an asset on an
basis other than historic cost must be taken to a revaluatior
reserve. This rule applies equally in respect of any revaluation
(or other departure from historic cost) that have taken plac
before the Act comes into force. Detailed rules govern th
circumstances in which transfers can be made from this reserv
to the profit and loss account.

**FIXED ASSETS**   1/18

1/32

All fixed assets with a limited useful life must be depreciated
Where the assets are stated on an alternative basis (other thar
historic cost) depreciation must be charged on that same basis

1/19

Long-term investments *may* be written down to reflect curren
market value. Any fixed asset *must* be written down where th
diminution in value is thought to be permanent. Suck
provisions should be shown separately, and must be writter
back where there is evidence that they are no longer required

**DEVELOPMENT COSTS**   1/20

Development costs can only be capitalised in 'specia
circumstances' (which are not described). Where they ar
included in the balance sheet, disclosure must include th
reason for capitalising them and the period over which they ar
to be written off.

**GOODWILL**   1/66

1/21

Where goodwill acquired by the company is shown as an asset
it must be written off – over a period chosen by the directors bu
which must not exceed its useful economic life. The perioc
chosen, and the reason for choosing it, must be disclosed. Thes
requirements expressly do not apply to goodwill arising or
consolidation. (It is notable that the provisions for depreciating
goodwill through the profit and loss account only apply 'wher
goodwill is treated as an asset'. Where goodwill is not shown as
an asset, i.e. where it is written off on acquisition, the write off
can presumably be made direct to reserves.)

| **OTHER INTANGIBLES** | 1/3 | Preliminary expenses, expenses in connection with a share or debenture issue, and costs of research (as opposed to development) must not be capitalised. |
|---|---|---|

**STOCKS** 1/27 The purchase price or production cost of stock may be determined by the FIFO, LIFO, weighted average cost, or any other similar method. The method chosen must be that which in the directors' opinion is most appropriate in the circumstances of the company. Any material difference between the amount at which stock is stated and its current replacement cost must be disclosed.

**RELATED COMPANIES** 1/91 A 'related' company is defined in terms similar to those which define an associated company in SSAP1 (see page 194), with a similar réference to the exercise of control or influence and with the same presumption that the relationship exists once the holding reaches 20 per cent.

1/65 Disclosure is required of the related company's share capital and reserves, and of its latest reported profit or loss. There is a proviso that these details need not be given where the related company is accounted for on the equity basis, i.e. where the investing group includes in its own profit and loss account its full share of the profit or loss of the related company. This treatment is only permitted in the case of group accounts and is not permitted in the individual accounts of the investing company.

**DIRECTORS' REPORT** S.13 The Act amplifies the previous and rather imprecise requirement for directors to include a comment in their report on the company's 'state of affairs'.

Directors' reports will now have to include a review of the development of the company's business during the year and of its position at the end of it. They are also required to include a comment on its likely development in the future, a description of any significant post-balance sheet events, and an indication of any activities in the field of research and development.

S.14 Detailed disclosure is required in the Directors' Report of any transactions whereby the company has acquired its own shares during the year or has provided financial assistance for a similar purpose. This requirement follows the major innovation in UK law (introduced elsewhere in the new Companies Act) whereby companies may now purchase their own shares.

S.16 Certain information which previously had to be given in the

Directors' Report is now required in equivalent form in the notes to the accounts:

analysis of turnover;

employee information;

details of share and debenture issues.

S.13(4)

The previous requirement to disclose exports is repealed. So is the option (S.163, 1948 Companies Act) by which certain information required to be disclosed in the accounts could alternatively be presented in the Directors' Report. Details of directors' interests in shares may now alternatively be disclosed in the notes.

S.15

Auditors now have a duty to consider whether the information contained in the Directors' Report is consistent with the accounts on which they are reporting. If, in their opinion, it is not, they must report accordingly.

**FORMATS: GENERAL RULES**

1/1

Balance sheets and profit and loss accounts must be presented in accordance with one of the legally prescribed formats. Two alternative formats are provided for the balance sheet (allowing for vertical or horizontal presentation) and four alternatives for the profit and loss account (horizontal and vertical, and each analysing costs on either an operating basis – cost of sales, distribution costs, etc. – or by type of expenditure – raw materials, wages and salaries, etc.).

**FORMATS: CONSISTENCY**

1/2

Once a format has been chosen it must be adopted in all subsequent years unless there are 'special reasons' for not doing so – in which case the change and the reasons for it must be disclosed.

**FORMATS: FLEXIBILITY**

1/1

For any given format, the order in which the items are listed and the headings and the sub-headings which describe them must be strictly followed. A degree of flexibility is permitted, however, by the following provisos:

1   Items may be shown in greater detail then required.
2   New headings may be inserted.
3   Certain information may alternatively be presented in notes to the accounts.
4   Arrangements and headings may be adapted where the special nature of the company's business requires it.
5   Items may be combined where, individually, they are immaterial.
6   Headings may be omitted where the amounts for the current and preceding year are both nil.

**ILLUSTRATION:
DOVETAILS' ACCOUNTS**

In order to illustrate the shape of accounts in the future, Dovetails' 1982 accounts are re-presented on the following pages in accordance with the requirements of the 1981 Companies Act. The illustration includes – in the form of summarised headings – an outline of the matters to be included in the Directors' Report.

The choice of format adopted in the example is one that represents least change from existing practice. This is the principle that a good number of companies can be expected to follow when assessing the various options and alternatives offered in the Act. Thus Dovetails' balance sheet and profit and loss account are both presented in vertical form, and detail is always relegated to the Notes where the law would alternatively permit it to be shown on the face of the two main statements.

The illustration provides a convenient summary of the impact of the new legislation on company accounting. To ease the comparison with Dovetails' existing accounts (see pages xv–xxii) the main areas of change in the new formats are shaded. It is emphasised that the shading is specifically in terms of new *statutory* requirement: it is not new to accounting practice that accounting policies, for example, should be disclosed, or that stock should be analysed into its major components, but it is new that these matters should be required to be disclosed by law.

The shading indicates that the main burden of additional disclosure falls in the area of the profit and loss account, most particularly in the detail which companies will now have to reveal regarding their cost of sales, gross profit and operating expenses. Turnover must be analysed by both geographical market and class of business (see Note 2), and the class of business analysis is also required in respect of operating profit (Note 4). Additional information and analysis is required in respect of staff costs (Note 6).

As far as the balance sheet is concerned, the only change in presentation is that the amounts for debenture loan and deferred taxation now have to be shown as deductions in the top half of the balance sheet. That apart, the main difference is one of terminology. Thus all balance sheets will in future have to include, for example, the caption 'total assets less current liabilities'. Otherwise, the main areas of additional disclosure in Dovetails' case are in respect of investments – which are classified in the statutory formats as fixed assets, and for which details of movements during the year will therefore be required – and bank overdrafts – where details must now be provided of any assets pledged as security.

It should be said, in the re-presentation of Dovetails' accounts, maximum advantage has been taken of the permission to aggregate and combine any amounts which can be deemed individually to be immaterial. In circumstances other than Dovetails, the additional balance sheet disclosure required under the new law could be substantial. The combined amount for debtors, for example, might have to be broken down into sub-headings for trade debtors, group companies, related companies, other debtors and prepayments if any of those sub-headings were individually material; and for each of the items shown under debtors in the balance sheet, separate disclosure is required for any amounts falling due after more than one year. Similar details and analyses are required in respect of creditors. For many companies, a further area of additional balance sheet disclosure will arise in respect of fixed assets – where details (including the amounts involved) are required of any deviation from the principle of historic cost.

---

**DOVETAILS LIMITED**

**Directors' Report for 1982**

Principal activities and any significant changes.

Review of the development of the business during the period and of its position at the end of it.

Recommended dividend.

Proposed transfers to reserves.

Particulars of any important events since the end of the year.

Indication of likely future developments in the business.

Indication of activities in field of research and development.

Details of own shares acquired.

Significant changes in fixed assets and differences between market and book value of property.

Directors' names.

Directors' interests in shares (may alternatively be presented in Notes).

Disabled persons employment policy.

Political and charitable donations.

**DOVETAILS LIMITED**

**Profit and loss account**
**For the year ended 31 December 1982**

| | Note | 1982 | 1981 |
|---|---|---|---|
| | | £ | £ |
| TURNOVER | 2 | 2,424,900 | 1,993,400 |
| Cost of sales | | 1,786,474 | 1,435,856 |
| GROSS PROFIT | | 638,426 | 557,544 |
| | | | |
| Distribution costs | | 98,637 | 72,005 |
| Administrative expenses | | 95,129 | 96,811 |
| Other operating charges (net) | | 314,827 | 254,510 |
| | | 508,593 | 423,326 |
| | | | |
| PROFIT ON ORDINARY ACTIVITIES BEFORE TAXATION | 4 | 129,833 | 134,218 |
| Tax on profit on ordinary activities | 7 | 49,736 | 71,408 |
| | | | |
| PROFIT ON ORDINARY ACTIVITIES AFTER TAXATION | | 80,097 | 62,810 |
| Extraordinary charge | 8 | 18,342 | – |
| | | | |
| PROFIT FOR THE FINANCIAL YEAR | | 61,755 | 62,810 |
| Dividend | 9 | 21,600 | 20,400 |
| | | | |
| Retained profit transferred to reserves | 17 | 40,155 | 42,410 |

**DOVETAILS LIMITED**

**Balance sheet
at 31 December 1982**

| | Note | 1982 | 1981 |
|---|---|---|---|
| | | £    £ | £ |
| **FIXED ASSETS** | | | |
| Tangible assets | 10 | 488,061 | 454,384 |
| Investments | 11 | 26,000 | 22,000 |
| | | 514,061 | 476,384 |
| **CURRENT ASSETS** | | | |
| Stocks | 12 | 435,289 | 404,095 |
| Debtors | | 584,537 | 416,756 |
| Cash | | 26,333 | 29,745 |
| | | 1,046,159 | 850,596 |
| **CREDITORS: AMOUNTS FALLING DUE WITHIN ONE YEAR** | | | |
| Bank overdraft | 13 | 111,966 | 85,599 |
| Trade creditors | | 461,958 | 329,877 |
| Taxation | | 46,061 | 16,831 |
| Dividend | | 21,600 | 20,400 |
| | | 641,585 | 452,707 |
| NET CURRENT ASSETS | | 404,574 | 397,889 |
| **TOTAL ASSETS LESS CURRENT LIABILITIES** | | 918,635 | 874,273 |
| **CREDITORS: AMOUNTS FALLING DUE AFTER MORE THAN ONE YEAR** | | | |
| Debenture loan | 14 | (140,000) | (140,000) |
| **PROVISION FOR LIABILITIES AND CHARGES** | | | |
| Deferred taxation | 15 | (99,107) | (94,900) |
| | | 679,528 | 639,373 |
| **CAPITAL AND RESERVES** | | | |
| Called-up share capital | 16 | 120,000 | 120,000 |
| Share premium account | | 243,336 | 243,336 |
| Profit and loss account | 17 | 316,192 | 276,037 |
| | | 679,528 | 639,373 |

**DOVETAILS LIMITED**

**Statement of source and application of funds
for the year ended 31 December 1982**

|  | | 1982 | 1981 |
|---|---|---|---|
|  | £ | £ | £ |
| **SOURCE OF FUNDS:** | | | |
| Profit before taxation | | 129,833 | 134,218 |
| Extraordinary charge | | (18,342) | – |
| **ADJUSTMENTS FOR ITEMS NOT INVOLVING THE MOVEMENT OF FUNDS:** | | | |
| Depreciation | 65,404 | | 59,926 |
| Profit on sale of fixed assets | (3,907) | | (1,320) |
| | | 61,497 | 58,606 |
| Funds generated from operations | | 172,988 | 192,824 |
| **OTHER SOURCES:** | | | |
| Sale of fixed assets | | 5,500 | 3,250 |
| | | 178,488 | 196,074 |
| **APPLICATION OF FUNDS:** | | | |
| Purchase of fixed assets | | 100,674 | 83,499 |
| Taxation paid | | 16,299 | 12,101 |
| Purchase of trade investment | | 4,000 | – |
| Dividend paid | | 20,400 | 18,000 |
| | | 141,373 | 113,600 |
| Increase in working capital | | 37,115 | 82,474 |
| **COMPRISING CHANGES IN:** | | | |
| Stock | | 31,194 | 28,967 |
| Debtors | | 167,781 | 52,390 |
| Creditors | | (132,081) | (33,523) |
| Net liquid funds | | (29,779) | 34,640 |
| | | 37,115 | 82,474 |

## DOVETAILS LIMITED

### Notes to the accounts
### year ended 31 December 1982

1    *Accounting policies*
The principal accounting policies adopted by the company in the preparation of its accounts are as follows:

(a)    *Depreciation*
Depreciation is not charged in respect of freehold land. On other assets it is charged in equal annual instalments over their anticipated useful lives. The rates of depreciation used are as follows:

| | | |
|---|---|---|
| Freehold buildings | – | 2 per cer.t per annum |
| Tools and equipment | – | 15 per cent per annum |
| Motor vehicles | – | 25 per cent per annum |

(b)    *Stocks and work-in-progress*
Stocks and work-in-progress are stated at the lower of cost and net realisable value. Cost comprises materials, direct labour and attributable production overheads, in respect of work-in-progress and finished goods.

(c)    *Deferred taxation*
Provision is made for taxation deferred because of timing differences between the treatment of certain items for accounting and taxation purposes, but only where there is a reasonable probability of payment.

(e)    *Foreign currencies*
Transactions denominated in foreign currencies are recorded at the rate of exchange ruling at the date of the transaction. Assets and liabilities denominated in foreign currencies are translated at the rate of exchange ruling at the balance sheet date.

2    *Turnover*
Turnover represents the invoiced value of goods supplied during the year, excluding value added tax. The analysis of turnover by class of business and by geographical market is as follows:

| | 1982 | 1981 |
|---|---|---|
| | £ | £ |
| United Kingdom | 2,308,567 | 1,872,867 |
| European Community | 116,333 | 120,533 |
| | 2,424,900 | 1,993,400 |
| Domestic furniture | 1,672,281 | 1,508,077 |
| Office furniture | 752,619 | 485,323 |
| | 2,424,900 | 1,993,400 |

*(Continued)*

|  |  | 1982 | 1981 |
|---|---|---:|---:|
|  |  | £ | £ |
| 3 | **Other net operating charges** | | |
|  | Other operating charges include: | | |
|  | Directors' emoluments (Note 5) | 43,500 | 42,000 |
|  | Depreciation | 65,404 | 59,926 |
|  | Hire of plant and machinery | 16,416 | 12,210 |
|  | Auditors' remuneration | 5,000 | 4,500 |
|  | Staff costs (Note 6) | 646,863 | 575,817 |
|  | *Interest payable* | | |
|  | Bank interest | 13,686 | 11,008 |
|  | Interest on long-term loan | 12,600 | 12,600 |
|  |  | 26,286 | 23,608 |
|  | and are arrived at after crediting: | | |
|  | Income from investments | | |
|  | Listed | 1,078 | 741 |
|  | Unlisted | 1,200 | 1,000 |
|  |  | 2,278 | 1,741 |

| 4 | **Profit on ordinary activities** | 1982 | 1981 |
|---|---|---:|---:|
|  | The analysis of profit before tax by class of business is as follows: | | |
|  |  | £ | £ |
|  | Domestic furniture | 88,426 | 103,396 |
|  | Office furniture | 41,407 | 30,822 |
|  |  | 129,833 | 134,218 |

|  |  | £ | £ |
|---|---|---:|---:|
| 5 | **Directors' emoluments** | | |
|  | Fees | 500 | 500 |
|  | Other remuneration including pension contributions | 39,000 | 32,500 |
|  | Compensation for loss of office | – | 5,000 |
|  | Pension paid to former director | 4,000 | 4,000 |
|  |  | 43,500 | 42,000 |
|  | Remuneration of Chairman | 9,500 | 8,500 |
|  | Remuneration of the highest-paid director | 13,000 | 10,000 |

|  | Number of directors | |
|---|---:|---:|
| Up to £5,000 | 1 | 1 |
| £5,001 to £10,000 | 3 | 4 |
| £10,001 to £15,000 | 1 | – |

*(Continued)*

| 6 | Staff costs | 1982 | 1981 |
|---|---|---|---|
| | | £ | £ |
| | Wages and salaries | 596,062 | 531,952 |
| | Social security costs | 50,801 | 43,865 |
| | Pension costs | – | – |
| | | 646,863 | 575,817 |

| | | Number of employees | |
|---|---|---|---|
| | The average weekly number of employees during the year, analysed by functions, was as follows: | | |
| | Works | 186 | 202 |
| | Sales and administration | 20 | 21 |
| | Total | 206 | 223 |

| 7 | Tax on profit on ordinary activities | | |
|---|---|---|---|
| | Based on the profit for the year | | |
| | Corporation tax at 52% (1981 – 52%) | 45,015 | 15,538 |
| | Transfer to deferred taxation | 4,721 | 55,870 |
| | | 49,736 | 71,408 |

| 8 | Extraordinary charge | | |
|---|---|---|---|
| | Redundancy and other costs relating to the closure of Scunthorpe factory | 37,354 | – |
| | Corporation tax relief thereon | (19,012) | – |
| | | 18,342 | – |

| 9 | Dividend | | |
|---|---|---|---|
| | Proposed Ordinary dividend of 18p (1981 – 17p) per share | 21,600 | 20,400 |

(Continued)

10    Tangible fixed assets

| | Freehold property | Tools & equipment | Motor vehicles | Total |
|---|---|---|---|---|
| | £ | £ | £ | £ |
| **Cost:** | | | | |
| At 1 Jan 1982 | 227,575 | 391,789 | 35,557 | 654,921 |
| Additions | 50,715 | 43,913 | 6,046 | 100,674 |
| Disposals | – | (18,866) | – | (18,866) |
| At 31 Dec 1982 | 278,290 | 416,836 | 41,603 | 736,729 |
| **Depreciation:** | | | | |
| At 1 Jan 1982 | 27,309 | 159,161 | 14,067 | 200,537 |
| Charge for the year | 5,058 | 50,483 | 9,863 | 65,404 |
| Disposals | – | (17,273) | – | (17,273) |
| At 31 Dec 1982 | 32,367 | 192,371 | 23,930 | 248,668 |
| **Net book values** | | | | |
| At 31 Dec 1982 | 245,923 | 224,465 | 17,673 | 488,061 |
| At 31 Dec 1981 | 200,266 | 232,628 | 21,490 | 454,384 |

| Capital commitments | 1982 | 1981 |
|---|---|---|
| | £ | £ |
| Contracted for but not provided in the accounts | 4,600 | 28,100 |
| Authorised but not yet contracted for | 8,900 | 1,900 |

11    *Investments*

| | £ |
|---|---|
| Cost: | |
| At 1 Jan 1982 | 22,000 |
| Additions | 4,000 |
| Disposals | – |
| At 31 Dec 1982 | 26,000 |

*(Continued)*

|  | 1982 | 1981 |
|---|---|---|
|  | £ | £ |
| Listed investments | 14,000 | 14,000 |
| Unlisted investments | 12,000 | 8,000 |
|  | 26,000 | 22,000 |
| Valuation | | |
| Listed investments at market value | 17,963 | 15,236 |

The unlisted investment comprises 12,000 Ordinary shares in Legato Limited, representing 15% of the issued share capital of that company.

12 *Stocks*

|  | 1982 | 1981 |
|---|---|---|
| Raw materials | 211,579 | 195,026 |
| Work-in-progress | 202,993 | 187,792 |
| Finished goods | 20,717 | 21,277 |
|  | 435,289 | 404,095 |

At 31 December 1982 there was no significant difference between the amount at which stock is stated and its current replacement cost. The replacement cost of stock at 31 December 1981 was approximately £55,000 greater than the amount at which stock is shown.

13 *Bank overdraft*
The bank overdraft is secured by a fixed charge on the freehold property of the company.

14 *Debenture loan*

|  | 1982 | 1981 |
|---|---|---|
| 9% Unsecured loan stock 1990/95 | 140,000 | 140,000 |

The 9% unsecured loan stock is repayable at the company's option between 1990 and 1995 with a final redemption date of 31 December 1995.

15 *Deferred taxation*

|  | 1982 | 1981 |
|---|---|---|
|  | £ | £ |
| Accelerated capital allowances | 108,364 | 103,643 |
| Advance corporation tax | (9,257) | (8,743) |
|  | 99,107 | 94,900 |

If full provision were made, the potential liability would be as follows:

| | 1982 | 1981 |
|---|---|---|
| Accelerated capital allowances | 147,500 | 138,000 |

(Continued)

| 16  Share capital | 1982 | 1981 |
|---|---|---|
| | £ | £ |
| Authorised: | | |
| 150,000 Ordinary shares of £1 each | 150,000 | 150,000 |
| Issued and fully paid: | | |
| 120,000 Ordinary shares of £1 each | 120,000 | 120,000 |
| 17  Profit and loss account | | |
| At 1 Jan 1982 | 276,037 | 233,627 |
| Retained profit for the year | 40,155 | 42,410 |
| At 31 Dec 1982 | 316,192 | 276,037 |

**DISCLOSURE CHECKLIST**

For those who wish to assess the overall impact, the full details of the new, prescribed formats for accounts are included at the end of Chapter 15 (pages 186-9). Chapter 15 itself may be useful to company directors who wish to ensure that their published accounts comply with statutory and other requirements. Its length is indicative of the disclosure burden which companies now have to bear. It does, however, provide a comprehensive working document for checking compliance with the disclosure requirements of the 1948-81 Companies Acts, Statements of Standard Accounting Practice and, for listed companies, the additional requirements of the Stock Exchange.

**EXEMPTIONS**

The formats and disclosure which have so far been described apply to the accounts which all companies prepare for their shareholders. A major innovation in the 1981 Act, however, is the distinction which is drawn between accounts prepared for shareholders and accounts which are filed with the Registrar of Companies. The exemptions described below apply only in respect of accounts which are prepared for filing purposes.

S.5(3)    The permitted exemptions are determined by the size of the company in question (see below). They are not, however, available to public companies, or to banking, shipping or insurance companies (as defined), or to companies belonging to a group which includes an ineligible company.

**SMALL COMPANIES**

S.6    Small companies may file a modified balance sheet (equivalent to the items marked with an X in the formats illustrated in the Appendix) and only limited information by way of notes. They need not file:

> a profit and loss account;
> a directors' report;
> notes to the accounts, except for those dealing with
> > accounting policies
> > share capital
> > creditors due after more than one and five years
> > details of security given
> > debtors due after more than one year
> > basis of foreign currency translation
> > details of subsidiaries and associates
> > transactions with directors (but not emoluments)

**MEDIUM-SIZED COMPANIES**

S.6    Medium-sized companies need not disclose the amount (or any analysis) of their turnover. They may also file a modified form of profit and loss account which combines the amounts for turnover, cost of sales, and other operating income (or equivalent headings under alternative formats) into one figure under the caption 'gross profit or loss'.

In all other respects the accounts filed by medium-sized companies must conform to the accounts they prepare for shareholders.

**QUALIFYING CONDITIONS**

S.8(1)   To qualify for the filing exemptions, a company must satisfy at least two of the following three conditions for both the year in question and the preceding year:

|                                      | *Small* | *Medium* |
|--------------------------------------|---------|----------|
| Turnover not more than               | £1.4 m  | £5.75 m  |
| Balance sheet total not more than    | £0.7 m  | £2.8 m   |
| Average number of employees not more than | 50 | 250 |

Balance sheet totals are taken as total assets – before deducting any creditors, current or otherwise. Average employees are to be calculated by dividing the aggregate of weekly numbers by 52. The turnover threshold is reduced proportionately for accounting periods of less than a year.

S.9(2)   A holding company can take advantage of the appropriate exemptions when filing its own accounts only if the qualifying conditions are met by the figures drawn from its group accounts.

S.10(2)   Where they are, the holding company may also file appropriately modified group accounts. Subsidiary companies qualify (or not) as of their own right – regardless of the qualifying status of the group.

Although the general rule is that the conditions have to be met for two successive years, there is a proviso wherby, once a company has qualified, it will not lose the exemptions in the

S.8(5)   first year in which it ceases to qualify. Thus a company which qualifies for two years, but which fails to do so in year three, can continue to file modified accounts for that third year. If it reverts to qualifying status in year four, it can also file modified accounts for that year – the one year failure to qualify is disregarded. Effectively, therefore, a company only loses the appropriate exemptions if it fails to meet the qualifying conditions for two consecutive years.

Conversely, for the first year – following two or more consecutive years of non-exemption – in which a company qualifies for exemption, it will still have to file full accounts; the exemptions only become available in the following year (assuming the conditions are met in that year).

S.8(8)   In respect of the first accounts to be prepared under the 1981

Act, there is a transitional provision whereby the exemptions will be available if the qualifying conditions are satisfied in either that or the preceding year. New companies will qualify for the appropriate exemptions in their first set of accounts if they meet the conditions in that year.

## DIRECTORS' STATEMENT

**S.7(2)** Where a company takes advantage of any filing exemptions, the modified accounts must include a statement by the directors, immediately above their signature, that they:

1. Have relied on the exemptions.
2. Have done so on the grounds that the company is entitled to the benefits of those exemptions as a small (or medium-sized) company.

## SPECIAL AUDIT REPORT

**S.7(5)** Where modified accounts are filed with the Registrar, they must include a special report by the auditors which:

1. Reproduces their report on the full accounts.
2. States that, in their opinion, the modified accounts have been properly prepared in the manner permitted for small (or medium-sized) companies, and that the company is entitled to the appropriate exemptions.

## PUBLICATION

The new Act also introduces new rules regarding the publication of accounts.

**S.21(3)** A company will be regarded as having 'published' a balance sheet or other account if it 'publishes, issues or circulates it or otherwise makes it available for public inspection in a manner calculated to invite members of the public generally, or any class of members of the public, to read it'. These provisions cover publication in newspapers, and may extend to accounts which are issued in simplified or abridged form, for example to employees.

**S.11** Whenever a company or group publishes 'full individual accounts' it must also publish the relevant auditor's report. For the purpose of these provisions full individual accounts include both the full accounts prepared for shareholders and any

**S.11(9)** modified accounts that might be delivered by small or medium-sized companies for filing purposes. The 'relevant auditors' report' will therefore be either the normal report on the accounts for shareholders or the special form of report required on modified accounts.

**S.11(8)** Where a company or group publishes 'abridged' accounts (which will occur whenever a balance sheet or profit and loss

S.11(6)
account is published otherwise than as part of full individual accounts), it must also publish a statement indicating:

1  That the accounts are not full accounts.
2  Whether full (or modified) accounts have been filed.
3  Whether the full accounts have been audited, and whether the audit report was unqualified.

S.11(9)   A full audit report must not be published with abridged accounts.

**SUMMARY: PLANNING POINTS**

Amongst the matters arising out of the new Act company directors may need to give early thought to the following:

- The decision as to the first year for which accounts are to be prepared on the new basis; companies with December year ends, for example, will be required to present accounts in the new format for the first time in respect of the year ended December 1983. However they may wish to plan for that event at an earlier date – particularly bearing in mind the need to present corresponding amounts on a comparable basis.

- The choice of format for the accounts (particularly for the profit and loss account) including any adaptations which the company may wish to make, headings which it may be able to merge, and the information which might alternatively be presented in the notes.

- A review of the company's accounting policies, to ensure conformity with legal requirements.

- A review of any assets shown at valuation, in order to identify original cost and, where necessary, to establish the required revaluation reserve.

- An assessment of the new disclosure requirements: in some cases the information required may involve amendments to the accounting system, e.g. the analyses of turnover and profit before tax, staff costs broken down by 'appropriate category' and the comparable historic cost information required when items are stated on some other basis.

- For small and medium-sized companies, the decision as to whether they are to avoid certain disclosures, but perhaps incur additional cost, by filing modified accounts.

# 15 Appendix: disclosure checklist for accounts

This appendix provides a checklist of compliance with the disclosure requirements of the 1948–81 Companies Acts (as varied by Statutory Instrument), Statements of Standard Accounting Practice and, for listed companies, the Stock Exchange listing agreement.

The requirements are organised into sections, as far as possible according to the usual arrangement of a company's accounts:

| Section | | Paragraphs |
|---|---|---|
| A | Directors' Report | 1–6 |
| B | Profit and loss account | 7–22 |
| C | Balance sheet | 23–41 |
| D | Funds statement | 42 |
| E | General matters | 43–51 |
| F | Group accounts | 52 |
| G | Current cost accounts | 53–58 |

*Appendix*

1. Listed companies (additional disclosure)
2. Profit and loss account (vertical format 1)
3. Profit and loss account (vertical format 2)
4. Balance sheet (vertical format)

In each section the information that is required to be disclosed is listed in abbreviated form: each entry is drafted in a style that assumes the unwritten preface: 'disclosure is required of . . .'. Explanatory notes are included where the need for disclosure is subject to particular conditions or definitions.

The checklist is believed to be comprehensive. For those who wish to use it as a working document it takes the form of an *aide-memoire* which provides a relatively quick means of ensuring that a company's published accounts include all the information that they should. To this end, boxes have been provided after each point for the user to complete with, for example, YES, NO or N/A (for not applicable). (For any one company, of course, a good deal of the information listed may not need to be given because the circumstances or transactions that are the subject of the particular disclosure requirement have not arisen during the year.)

Of necessity, the checklist is a summary. In cases of doubt reference should always be made to the specific wording of the provisions in the relevant Act or SSAP. For this purpose, references are included in the left-hand column of the checklist as follows:

| | |
|---|---|
| C8 | 1948 Companies Act |
| C7 | 1967 Companies Act |
| C0 | 1980 Companies Act |
| C1 | 1981 Companies Act |
| S | Section |
| C1/1/ | First Schedule, 1981 Companies Act |
| C1/3/ | Third Schedule, 1981 Companies Act |
| SI | Statutory Instrument |
| P | Statement of Standard Accounting Practice – |
| SE2 | Chapter 2 (listing agreement – companies) of the Stock Exchange 'Admission of securities to listing' |
| SE10 | Chapter 10, ditto. |
| ( ) | Paragraph No. |

*Note:* The checklist does not cover references in the Companies Acts to:

1 The authority given to the Department of Trade to grant certain exemptions where, in the opinion of the directors, disclosure would be harmful to the company;
2 The special provisions and exemptions relating to banking, shipping and insurance companies.

## Section A: Directors' Report

### ACTIVITIES

| | | |
|---|---|---|
| C7.S16(1) | 1.1 | The principal activities during the year and any significant changes. |
| C1.S13(1) | 1.2 | A review of the development of the business during the year and its position at the year-end. |
| C1.S13(3) | 1.3 | An indication of likely future developments in the business. |
| C1.S13(3) | 1.4 | An indication of R&D activities. |
| C1.S13(3) | 1.5 | Particulars of important events since the end of the year. (*See also* Section C.48) |
| C8.S157(1) | 1.6 | The amount of recommended dividend. |
| C.8.S157(1) | 1.7 | The amount proposed to be set aside to or withdrawn from reserves. |

### INTERESTS IN OWN SHARES

| | | |
|---|---|---|
| C1.S14 | 2.1 | Where company purchases any of its own shares during the year:<br>(a) number and nominal value of shares purchased;<br>(b) aggregate consideration paid;<br>(c) reasons for the purchase;<br>(d) percentage of the called-up share capital which the shares represent. |
| C1.S14 | 2.2 | Where a company has an interest in its own shares and such shares:<br>– are acquired by forfeiture or by surrender in lieu of forfeiture; or<br>– have been acquired otherwise than for valuable consideration or in a reduction of capital; or<br>– are acquired from a third party by a nominee without financial assistance from the company but in which the company has a beneficial interest; or<br>– are acquired by any person with financial assistance from the company; or<br>– where its own shares are made subject to a lien or charge taken by the company itself:<br>(a) the number and nominal value of the shares so acquired or charged during the year;<br>(b) the maximum number and nominal value of such shares held at any time during the year;<br>(c) the number and nominal value of such shares disposed of or cancelled during the year and, where applicable, the amount or value of the consideration in each case; |

(d) in relation to *(a)* to *(c)* above the percentage of the called-up share capital which such shares represent;

(e) where any of the shares have been charged, the amount of the charge in each case.

## FIXED ASSETS

C7.S16(1)(a)   3.1   Any significant changes in fixed assets of the company or of any of its subsidiaries during the year.

C7.S16(1)(a)   3.2   Any significant difference between the market value and book value of land and buildings.

## DIRECTORS

C7.S16(1)   4.1   The names of those who were directors at any time during the year.

C7.S16(1)(e)   4.2   For those who were directors at the end of the year, particulars of their interests, as recorded in the register, in shares or debentures of the company or any group company at the beginning (or date of appointment if later) and end of the year.

SI(1968)865
C7.S27(13)
SI(1968)1533
SI(1967)1594

*Note:* Excluding *(a)* nominee holdings in 100 per cent subsidiaries *(b)* directors of 100 per cent GB incorporated subsidiaries who are also holding company directors *(c)* holdings in parent company or other overseas group companies if 100% subsidiary or a parent company incorporated outside GB.

C7.S16(1)(e)   4.3   If any director has no interest in the shares or debentures of the company, a statement of that fact.

C1.S13(4)   *Note:* Information in 4.2 and 4.3 may alternatively be disclosed in the notes to the accounts.

## EMPLOYEES

SI(1980)1160   5.1   A statement describing the policy adopted during the year in respect of the employment of disabled persons covering, *inter alia,* employment, training, career development and promotion.

*Note:* Required if the average number of employees over the financial year exceeds 250, excluding employees working wholly or mainly outside the UK.

## POLITICAL AND CHARITABLE DONATIONS

C7.S19(1)
SI(1980)1055

6.1   The separate totals of *(a)* political and *(b)* charitable contributions made during the year (if together they exceed £200).

C7.S19(1)  6.2  For individual political contributions exceeding £200, the amount
SI(1980)1055  and the name of the recipient.

C7.S19(2)  *Note:* 6.1 and 6.2 not required if the company is a wholly owned
subsidiary of a company incorporated in GB. For companies with
subsidiaries, disclosure required on a group basis.

## Section B: Profit and Loss Account

*Note 1* The profit and loss account must be presented in the order
and under the headings required by either of the formats detailed
in Appendices 2 or 3. (The information may alternatively be
presented in horizontal form.)

*Note 2* Profit (or loss) on ordinary activities before taxation,
dividends and the amount set aside to reserves must be disclosed in
the profit and loss account. Other information may alternatively
be presented in the notes to the accounts and may be combined
where individually they are not material.

*Note 3* If a consolidated profit and loss account is prepared, a
separate profit and loss account for the holding company is not
required.

### TURNOVER

7.1  Amount and method of computation.

C1/1/94  *Note:* (1) Representing amount derived from ordinary activities;
C1/1/94  (2) to be stated exclusive of trade discounts, VAT and other sales
P5(8)  taxes.

C1/1/55(1)  7.2  Where substantially different classes of business have been carried
out, an analysis showing:
(a)  the amount of turnover attributable to each class;
(b)  the amount of profit or loss before taxation attributable to
each class.

C1/1/55(2)  7.3  Where substantially different markets have been supplied, a
geographical analysis of turnover attributable to each market.

*Note:* Disclosure of 7.2 and 7.3 above is not required if in the
directors' opinion it would prejudice the company's interests, but
the fact that information has not been disclosed must be stated.

## INCOME FROM RELATED/ASSOCIATED COMPANIES

C1/1/F
P1(18)

8.1   In the investing company's profit and loss account the income from shares in related/associated companies: dividends received and receivable (where necessary separately disclosing income from listed investments, see 9.2 below).

P1(24)

8.2   Where consolidated accounts are not prepared by the investing company (except where it is itself a wholly owned subsidiary) the information required by 8.3 and 8.4 below should be disclosed either in supplementary form or by preparation of a separate profit and loss account.

8.3   In the investing group's consolidated profit and loss account:

P1(19)   (a)   the share of the associate's pre-tax profits (less losses);
P1(20)   (b)   the tax attributable to that share;

*Note:* To be disclosed separately within the tax charge.

P1(21)   (c)   the share, if material, of extraordinary items dealt with in the associated company accounts;
P1(22)   (d)   the share of net profits (less losses) retained by the associated company.

P1(23)

8.4   If the results of one or more associated companies are significant in relation to the true and fair view:
(a)   total turnover and depreciation;
(b)   total profits before tax.

P1(37)

8.5   If accounting periods of associated companies are not co-terminous, the facts and dates of year-ends.

P1(39)

8.6   In the investing group accounts, adjustments, where material should be made similar to those adopted for consolidation, e.g. the elimination of unrealised profits on assets transferred between the associate and the group and adjustments to achieve consistency with group accounting policies.

## OTHER INCOME

C1/1/F        9.1   Income from shares in group companies.

C1/1/53(4)    9.2   Income from listed investments.

C1/1/F        9.3   Income from other fixed asset investments.

P8(25)               *Note:* Dividends from UK companies to be included gross, i.e. cash received/receivable plus tax credit.

C1/1/F        9.4   Other interest receivable and similar income.

C1/1/F               *Note:* In respect of 9.3 and 9.4 above, separate disclosure of any amounts received from group companies.

| | | |
|---|---|---|
| C1/1/53(5) | 9.5 | Rent receivable, less outgoings (if material). |
| C1/1/F | 9.6 | Other operating income. |
| C1/1/F | 9.7 | Where Format 2 is adopted (see Appendix 3):<br>*(a)* increase in stocks of finished goods and work-in-progress;<br>*(b)* credit for any expenses capitalised on own work. |

## DEPRECIATION

| | | |
|---|---|---|
| C1/1/19 | 10.1 | Total charge for depreciation, or diminution in value of fixed assets (and amount of any provision for diminution written back). |
| | 10.2 | For each major class of depreciable asset: |
| P12(22) | | *(a)* the depreciation methods used; |
| P12(22) | | *(b)* the useful lives or the depreciation rates used. |
| P12(20) | 10.3 | Effect on depreciation charge of any changes in the methods of depreciation, if material. |
| P12(6) | 10.4 | Surplus or deficiency compared with book value on disposal of fixed assets, if material. |

| | | |
|---|---|---|
| C1/1/(18) | | *Notes:* |
| P12(12)(16) | | 1 Depreciation should be provided on all fixed assets – including buildings (but excluding investment properties) – which have a limited useful economic life. |
| P19(10) | | 2 With regard to investment properties, depreciation should only be provided on those which are leasehold and the term of the lease is less than 20 years. |
| P19(7)(8) | | 3 An investment property must be held for its investment potential, any rental income being negotiated at arms length, construction must be fully complete but excludes property occupied by any group company. |
| P19(17) | | 4 Where, in order to comply with SSAP19, no depreciation is provided on investment properties, this will represent a departure from Companies Act requirements and the information in 49.2 will have to be disclosed. |
| C1/1/(32)<br>P12(21) | | 5 To the extent that assets are revalued in the accounts, depreciation should be based on the revalued amount. The effect of the revaluation, if material, should be disclosed in the year of change. |

## DIRECTORS' EMOLUMENTS

| | | |
|---|---|---|
| C8.S196 | 11.1 | *(a)* Aggregate emoluments (including those receivable from subsidiaries), fees, benefits in kind, pension contributions paid on directors' behalf. |

C8.S196   (b) Aggregate directors' and past directors' pensions (excluding pensions from schemes maintained by contributions).

C8.S191   (c) Aggregate compensation for loss of office (and other terminal
C8.S196       payments) paid to directors or past directors, divided between the company, subsidiaries and others.

(d) Distinguishing *(a)–(c)* above, between:
1 Amounts receivable in respect of services as directors.
2 Amounts in respect of other offices.

11.2   With regard to emoluments as in *(a)* above, but excluding pension contributions:

C7.S6        *(i)* The number of directors whose emoluments fall in each
SI(1979)1618       bracket of a scale in £5,000 multiples.

*(ii)* The emoluments for each chairman during year.

*(iii)* The emoluments of highest-paid director, if above chairman.

C7.S7        *(iv)* The number of directors who have waived rights to emoluments, and the aggregate amount waived in the year.

*Note: (i)–(iii)* do not apply to directors whose duties were wholly or mainly outside the UK.

SI(1979)1618   *(i)–(iv)* do not apply to a company which is neither a holding company nor a subsidiary and of which the aggregate directors' emoluments do not exceed £40,000.

## EMPLOYEES

C1/1/56(1)   12.1   The average weekly number of employees.

C1/1/56(1)   12.2   An analysis between appropriate categories of the average weekly number of employees.

C1/1/56(4)   12.3   Aggregate remuneration during the year, detailing:
*(a)* wages and salaries;
*(b)* Social Security costs;
*(c)* pension costs.

C7.S8        12.4   In respect of employees earning in excess of £20,000 (excluding
SI(1979)1618       pension contributions), the number of employees whose emoluments fall within each bracket of a scale in £5,000 multiples above £20,000.

*Note:* For 12.4 above, excluding *(a)* directors and *(b)* employees working wholly or mainly outside the UK.

## OTHER EXPENSES

13.1   Interest payable and similar charges:
C1/1/F       *(a)* in respect of group companies;

C1/1/53(2)            *(b)* on bank loans and overdrafts and other loans repayable wholly or in part within five years;

C1/1/1/53(2)         *(c)* on other loans, not so repayable.

C1/1/53(6)    13.2    Charges for hire of plant and machinery.

C1/1/53(7)    13.3    Auditors' remuneration, including expenses.

C1/1/F       13.4    Amounts written off investments.

C1/1/F       13.5    Where Format 1 (Appendix 2) has been adopted, the following expenses (including related depreciation):
                          *(a)* cost of sales;
                          *(b)* distribution costs;
                          *(c)* administration expenses.

C1/1/32(3)           *Note:* Where assets have been revalued, historic cost depreciation may be included in the above items, provided the additional charge is separately disclosed.

C1/1/F       13.6    Where Format 2 (Appendix 3) has been adopted:
                          *(a)* *(i)* raw materials and consumables;
                                 *(ii)* other external charges;
                          *(b)* exceptional amounts written off current assets;
                          *(c)* other operating charges.

## EXCEPTIONAL ITEMS

C1/1/57(3)
P6(14)      14.1    The size and nature of the items involved.

P6(11)
C1/1/57(3)           *Notes:*
                          1 Limited to items which derive from the ordinary activities of business but which require separate disclosure on account of their abnormal size or incidence.

P6(14)                 2 To be included in arriving at profit for the year from ordinary activities before taxation.

## TAXATION

C1/1/54(1)(3a)    15.1    Charge for and basis of computing UK corporation tax for the year.

C1/1/54(3b)
P8(22a)       15.2    Relief for overseas taxation

C1/1/54(3c)     15.3    UK income tax and basis of computation.

C1/1/54(3d)     15.4    Total overseas taxation on profits, income and, so far as charged to revenue, capital gains.

P8(22a)        15.5    Tax attributable to franked investment income.

| P8(22a) | 15.6 | Irrecoverable ACT. | |

P8(22a)    15.7   *(a)*  Transfers to/from deferred taxation.
P15(34)

P15(36)           *(b)*  Adjustments to balance on deferred taxation resulting from a change in the rate of taxation.

P15(35)           *(c)*  An indication of the extent to which the tax charged has been reduced by accelerated capital allowances, other timing differences and stock relief.

C1/1/54    15.8   Tax on profit on ordinary activities.

P1(15)     15.9   Tax attributable to share of related/associated companies' results.

C1/1/54    15.10  Tax on extraordinary profit or loss.

P8(23)     15.11  Rate of corporation tax used.

C1/1/54    15.12  Other taxes.

C1/1/54(2) 15.13  Any special circumstances affecting the tax liability:
                  *(a)*  for the year;
                  *(b)*  for succeeding financial years.

C1/1/34(5) 15.14  The taxation treatment of amounts transferred to or from revaluation reserves.

## EXTRAORDINARY ITEMS

C1/1/57(2) 16.1   The size and nature of the items in question (including the share of any such items dealt with in the accounts of related/associated companies) distinguishing separately between income and charges.

C1/1/F     16.2   The aggregate extraordinary profit or loss.

P6(11)            *Notes:*
                  1  Limited to items which derive from transactions outside the ordinary activities of the business and which are material and not expected to recur.

P6(15)            2  Aggregated amount (less attributable taxation) distinguishing separately between income and charges, to be shown in the P&L account after results derived from ordinary activities.

P15(36)           3  Adjustments to deferred tax consequent upon a fundamental change in the basis of taxation should be treated as extraordinary.

## PRIOR YEAR ADJUSTMENTS

C1/1/57(1) 17.1   The size and nature of the items involved.
C1/1/4(2)

| | | |
|---|---|---|
| P6(16) | 17.2 | The consequent adjustment to the opening balance of retained profits. |
| P6(16) | 17.3 | Where practicable, the effect on the prior year comparatives. |
| P6(12) | | *Notes:* |
| | | 1 Limited to adjustments arising from either |
| | | (a) changes in accounting policies, or |
| | | (b) correction of fundamental errors. |
| P6(16) | | 2 To be accounted for by restating prior years. |
| P6(17) | | 3 A statement of retained profits/reserves showing any prior year adjustments should immediately follow the profit and loss account. |

## APPROPRIATIONS

| | | |
|---|---|---|
| P8(24)<br>C1/1/3(7b) | 18.1 | The aggregate amount of dividends paid and proposed (excluding related ACT). |
| C1/1/53(3) | 18.2 | The amount provided for the redemption of share capital and/or loans. |
| C1/1/3(7a) | 18.3 | The amount set aside or proposed to be set aside to or withdrawn from reserves. |

## PROVISIONS

| | | |
|---|---|---|
| C1/1/19 | 19.1 | The amount of any provision in respect of a diminution in value of intangible assets or investments (and the amount of any such provision written back). |
| C1/1/71(2) | | *Note:* In the case of an investment company any such provision should be reflected in the revaluation reserve. |

## GENERAL

| | | |
|---|---|---|
| C1/1/3(6) | 20.1 | Profit on ordinary activities before taxation. |
| C1/1/F | 20.2 | Profit on ordinary activities after taxation. |
| C1/1/F | 20.3 | Profit for the financial year. |
| C1/1/F | 20.4 | In the case of Format 1 (Appendix 2), gross profit. |

## FORMAT

| | | |
|---|---|---|
| C1/1/2(2) | 21.1 | Details of any change in format compared with the previous year, together with the reasons for the change. |
| C1/1/1(1) | | *Note:* The format of the profit and loss account must accord with either of the formats detailed in Appendices 2 or 3. (Subject to alternative horizontal presentation.) Once a |

format has been adopted it should only be changed in subsequent years for 'special' reasons.

## CONSOLIDATED PROFIT AND LOSS ACCOUNT ONLY

C1.S1(5)  22.1  The extent to which the consolidated profit or loss for the year is dealt with in the holding company accounts.

C1.S1(6)  22.2  The fact that no company profit and loss account has been prepared should be stated.

# Section C: Balance Sheet

*Note 1* The balance sheet must be presented in the order and under the headings required by the Format detailed in Appendix 4. (The information may alternatively be presented in horizontal form.)

*Note 2* Items that must be disclosed on the face of the balance sheet are indicated by an asterisk. Other information may alternatively be presented in the notes to the accounts and may be combined where individually they are not material.

## FIXED ASSETS

C1/1/16  *Note 1* The primary method of valuation should be the historic cost of purchase or production. Alternative methods of valuation are permitted for certain classes of asset: intangible assets other than goodwill may be included at current cost; tangible fixed assets may be included at valuation or at current cost; investments may be included at market value or at directors' valuation.

C1/1/25  *Note 2* Tangible assets may be carried at a fixed amount if they are constantly being replaced and the amount is not material or subject to material variation.

C1/1/33  23.1  Where fixed assets are not included at historic cost:
(a) the items affected and the basis of valuation;
(b) the comparable historic cost of each item or the difference between the historic cost amount and the amount shown.

C1/1/26(3)  23.2  The amount of any interest capitalised and included in production cost.

C1/1/F  23.3*  The aggregate amount of all classes of fixed assets.

## INTANGIBLE FIXED ASSETS

C1/1/F 24.1 *(a)* The aggregate amount of development costs.
C1/1/20(2) *(b)* The reason for capitalising development costs and the period over which they are being written off.
P13(27) *(c)* Movements on deferred development expenditure and
P13(28) the amount carried forward at the beginning and end of the year.
P13(29) *(d)* An explanation of the accounting policy.

P13(21) *Note:* Development (but not research) expenditure should be deferred only to the extent that its recovery can, in the following circumstances, reasonably be regarded as assured:
1 There is a clearly defined project of which the commercial viability and technical feasibility have been reasonably assessed.
2 The related expenditure is separately identifiable and all costs, present and future, are expected to be recovered in full from future revenues.
3 Adequate resources exist, or are expected to be available, to complete the project.

C1/1/F 24.2 The aggregate amount of concessions, patents, licenses, trademarks and similar rights and assets.

C1/1/F *Note:* Capitalise only if they were acquired for valuable consideration; or they were created by the company.

C1/1/F 24.3 *(a)* The aggregate amount of goodwill.
C1/1/21(4) *(b)* The period over which it is being amortised, and the reasons for choosing that period.

C1/1/F *Notes*
C1/1/21 1 Goodwill should only be capitalised to the extent that it was acquired for valuable consideration. Where capitalised, it must be amortised over a period not exceeding its useful economic life.
2 The above requirement does not apply to goodwill arising on consolidation.

24.4 The aggregate amount of payments on account.

C1/1/42 24.5 Details of the movements in tangible assets during the year as in 25.1 below.

C1/1/43 24.6 For tangible assets included at valuation, the information in 25.2 below.

C1/1/F 24.7* The aggregate amount of all classes of intangible assets.

C1/1/3(2) *Note:* The following items must not be capitalised:
*(a)* preliminary expenses;

*(b)* expenses or commission in connection with a share or debenture issue;

*(c)* research costs.

## TANGIBLE FIXED ASSETS

C1/1/F    25.1    In respect of each major class of asset (including land and buildings; plant and machinery; fixtures, fittings, tools and equipment; and payments on account and assets in the course of construction):

C1/1/42
P12(22)

*(a)* aggregate cost or valuation at year beginning and end;

*(b)* aggregate additions and disposals during the year;

*(c)* aggregate revaluations during the year;

*(d)* aggregate internal assets capitalised or disposed of during the year;

*(e)* aggregate accumulated depreciation at year beginning and end;

*(f)* total depreciation charge for the year;

*(g)* the amount released on disposal during the year;

*(h)* other adjustments to the provision during the year;

C1/1/43    25.2    Where fixed assets are included at a valuation:

*(a)* the years in which assets were valued;

*(b)* the amount of each valuation;

*(c)* for assets valued during the period:

     *(i)* the names or qualifications of the valuers;

     *(ii)* the bases of valuation used.

C1/1/44    25.3    For land and buildings, the separate amounts for freehold, long leasehold (over 50 years unexpired at balance sheet date) and short leasehold.

P19(11)

*Notes*

1   Include investment properties at open market value.

P19(12)

2   If investment properties are valued by an employee or officer of the company a note is required to that effect.

C1/1/F    25.4*    The aggregate amount of all classes of tangible assets.

## INVESTMENTS IN GROUP COMPANIES (AND RELATED INDEBTEDNESS)

C1/1/F    26.1    Aggregate amount of shares in group companies.

C1/1/F    26.2    Aggregate amount of indebtedness *(a)* from and *(b)* to group companies analysed as appropriate between loans, current and deferred.

C1/1/59    26.3    Aggregate amounts of *(i)* investments in and *(ii)* indebtness with group companies analysed between the totals for:

*(a)* amounts attributable to any holding company and/or fellow subsidiary;

*(b)* amounts attributable to any other subsidiaries.

C7.S3(1-5)     26.4     In respect of each subsidiary owned at the end of the financial year:
*(a)* its name;
*(b)* its country of incorporation (if outside GB) or, if different from holding company, its country of registration;
*(c)* the identity and proportion of each class of shares held *(i)* directly by the company or its nominees and *(ii)* indirectly by subsidiaries or their nominees.

*Note:* Required only in respect of principal subsidiaries where particulars would otherwise be of excessive length.

C1/1/60     26.5     In the case of a holding company, the number, amount and description of any shares or debentures of the company held by its subsidiaries or their nominees.

*Note:* Disclosure is not required where the interest is that of a personal representative or non-beneficial trust.

C7S.5(1&2)     26.6     The name of the ultimate holding company and its country of incorporation.

C1/1/42     26.7     The movement in cost of fixed asset investments during the year as detailed in 25.1 above.

C1/1/43     26.8     For fixed asset investments other than listed investments included at valuation, the information in 25.2 above.

C1/1/45     26.9     In respect of listed investments the information in 28.1 below.

## RELATED/ASSOCIATED COMPANIES (AND INDEBTEDNESS)

C1/1/91
P1(13)

*Note 1* A company is associated/related where the interest is substantial, long term and the investing company participates in the commercial/financial decisions. An associate also applies where the interest forms part of a consortium or joint venture.

*Note 2* SSAP1 permits the inclusion of the group's interest in determining the proportion held of the associated company's equity, whereas indirect holdings do not fall within Companies Acts definition of a related company.

P1(55)

*Note 3* If all investments falling within the scope of related companies are dealt with as associated companies, the term related does not have to be used in the balance sheet or profit and loss account. The notes should state there are no other related companies other than those treated as associates.

P1(25)  27.1  In the investing company's balance sheet, the amount of the interest in associated companies should be stated at the cost of investments, less any amounts written-off (unless shown at valuation).

P1(35)  27.2  Where consolidated accounts are not prepared by the investing company (and except where it is itself a wholly owned subsidairy) the information required by 27.3 and 27.7 should be disclosed either in supplementary form or by preparation of a separate balance sheet.

P1(26)  27.3  In the investing group's balance sheet:
(a) the share of net assets, other than goodwill
(b) the share of goodwill
(c) the premium paid (or discount) on acquisition of the interest, to the extent that it has not been written off or amortised

Note: (a) above should be disclosed separately but (b) and (c) may be aggregated.

C1/1/F
P1(27)(28)  27.4  Loans to/from related/associated companies.

C1/1/F
P1(29)  27.5  Amounts owed to/by related/associated companies analysed as appropriate between current and deferred.

P1(30)  27.6  Information in respect of the associated company's tangible and intangible assets and liabilities if materially relevant for the members' appreciation of the investment.

P1(31)  27.7  The share of post acquisition accumulated reserves and any movement thereon.

P1(49)  27.8  For each principal associated company:
(a) its name
(b) the proportion of each class of shares held
(c) an indication of its nature of business.

P1(40)  27.9  Extent of any restrictions on the ability of the associated company to distribute its profits (other than those designated non-distributable).

P1(38)  27.10  If the investing company or group holds in excess of 20 per cent of the equity voting rights of a company other than a subsidiary but does not account for the investment as an associated company, the treatment adopted and the reasons for doing so should be disclosed.

Notes
1  The directors may, after consultation with their auditors, omit this reason, if it would be harmful to the business.
2  The information in 52.8 below is also required where the investment is not treated as an associate.

P1(38)     27.11     If the investing company or group hold less than 20 per cent of the equity voting rights but accounts for its investment as an associate, the basis on which significant influence is exercised should be stated.

C1/1/42     27.12     The movement in cost of fixed asset investments during the year as detailed in 25.1 above.

C1/1/43     27.13     For fixed asset investments other than listed investments included at valuation, the information in 25.2 above.

C/1/45     27.14     In respect of listed investments the information in 28.1 below.

C1/1/31     27.15     For investments included at directors' valuation the information in 28.2 below.

## INVESTMENTS (OTHER THAN GROUP OR RELATED/ASSOCIATED COMPANIES)

    28.1     In respect of listed investments:
C1/1/45(1)         *(a)* the aggregate amount;
C1/1/45(2)         *(b)* the aggregate market value (and, individually, the Stock Exchange value, if less);
C1/1/45(1)         *(c)* separate aggregate amounts for those listed on a recognised Stock Exchange and other listed investments.

C1/1/31     28.2     Where investments are included at directors' valuation:
        *(a)* the method used;
        *(b)* the reason for adopting it.

C1.S3     28.3     If at the balance sheet date *(i)* the company holds more than 10 per cent of any class of the allotted shares of another company or *(ii)* holds more than 10 per cent of the nominal value of the allotted share capital of another company or *(iii)* the shareholdings in any one company exceed 10 per cent of the total assets of the investing company:
        *(a)* the name of the other company;
        *(b)* the country of incorporation (if outside GB) and of registration (if incorporated in GB but different from the investing company);
        *(c)* the description and proportion of the classes of shares held.

C7.S4(4)(5)     *Note:* Required only in respect of principal investment where particulars would otherwise be of excessive length.

C1/1/42     28.4     The movement in cost of fixed asset investments during the year as defined in 25.1 above.

C1/1/43     28.5     For fixed asset investments other than listed investments included at valuation, the information in 25.2 above.

## STOCKS AND WORK-IN-PROGRESS

C1/1/F      29.1\*     The aggregate amount of all classes of stock.

C1/1/F
P9(29)      29.2     The amount of each category of stock and work-in-progress sub-classified as appropriate to the business, but to include:
- (a) raw materials and consumables;
- (b) work-in-progress;
- (c) finished goods and goods for resale;
- (d) payments on account.

     29.3     For long-term contracts:

P9(27)      (a) the amount of work-in-progress (stated at cost plus attributable profit, less foreseeable losses);

P9(30)      (b) cash received and receivable at the accounting date as progress payments.

P9(27)      *Note:* Where losses on individual contracts exceed costs to date less progress payments, such excesses to be shown separately as provisions.

C7/2/11(8b)      29.4     An explanation of the accounting policies used in calculating:
- (a) cost;
- (b) net realisable value;
- (c) attributable profit and foreseeable losses.

*Notes*

P9(26)      1    Stocks and work-in-progress (other than long-term contracts) to be stated at the lower of cost or net realisable value of the separate items or of groups of similar items.

C1/1/26      2    The purchase price or production cost at which stock is stated may include attributable overheads and interest to finance production.

C1/1/26(4)      3    Distribution costs must not be included in production cost.

C1/1/27
C1/1/31(5)      4    Cost should be determined by the method most appropriate to the business, but may be based on the FIFO;LIFO; weighted average price; or any other similar method. Stock may alternatively be stated at current cost.

C1/1/26(3)      29.5     The amount of any interest included in the stated value of stock.

C1/1/27(3-5)      29.6     Where the stated value of stock differs materially from its replacement cost at the balance sheet date (or, if more appropriate from its latest actual purchase price/production cost before that date) the amount of that difference should be stated.

## OTHER ASSETS

C1/1/23(1)      30.1     Current assets should be included at net realisable value if this is less than purchase price or production cost.

C1/1/24(1)  30.2  Where an amount repayable on a liability of the company exceeds the value of consideration received at the time the liability arose, the aggregate amount of the difference.

C1/1/24(2)  *Note:* The amount should be subject to annual amortisation and be completely written-off prior to repayment.

C1/1/51(2)  30.3  The aggregate amount of loans to employees to acquire shares in the company or its holding company.

*Note:* For transactions involving directors see 45 and 46 below.

C1/1/F  30.4  The aggregate amount in respect of:
(a) loans (other than to group or related companies or employees);
(b) the company's own shares acquired together with their nominal value;
(c)* all classes of fixed asset investments;
(d)* called-up share capital not paid;
(e)* current assets;
(f)* all classes of current asset debtors;
(g) trade debtors;
(h) other debtors;
(i) prepayments and accrued income;
(j)* all classes of current asset investments;
(k)* cash at bank and in hand;
(l)* prepayments and accrued income not treated as current assets;
(m)*net current assets;
(n)* total assets less current liabilities.

C1/1/F  30.5  For each class of asset included under current asset debtors the amounts falling due after more than one year should be shown separately.

## DEBENTURES, LOANS AND BANK OVERDRAFTS

C1/1/48(1)  31.1  The aggregate amount of liabilities repayable wholly or in part more than five years after the balance sheet date, distinguishing between:
(a) those repayable by instalments;
(b) others not so repayable.

*Note:* The aggregate amount of instalments falling due for repayment after the five year period should be separately disclosed.

C1/1/48(2)  31.2  In respect of each liability included in 31.1 above:
(a) the terms of repayment;
(b) rate of interest;

*Note:* A general indication of repayment terms and interest rates is sufficient where the above details would be of excessive length.

C1/1/F | 31.3 | The aggregate amount of bank loans and overdrafts analysed as appropriate between those falling due within and those falling due after twelve months.

C1/1/41(2) | 31.4 | Particulars of any redeemed (but re-issuable) debentures.

C1/1/F | 31.5 | The aggregate amount of debentures in issue, disclosing convertible loans separately.

C1/1/41(1) | 31.6 | For any debentures issued during the year, the amount, class, consideration received and reason for the issue.

C1/1/41(3) | 31.7 | For any of the company's debentures held by nominees of, or trustees for, the company, the nominal amount and the book value of the holding.

C1/1/48(4) | 31.8 | The aggregate amount of secured liabilities and an indication of the security given,

## PROVISIONS FOR LIABILITIES AND CHARGES

C1/1/F | 32.1 | The aggregate amount of provisions (other than for depreciation) analysed between:
(a) pensions and similar obligations;
(b) other provisions (separately disclosed if material).

C1/1/46(2) | 32.2 | For each sub-heading:
(a) the balance at the beginning and end of the year together with the amount transferred to or from the provision during the year;
(b) the source and application of any such movement.

## GOVERNMENT GRANTS

P4(9) | 33.1 | Where grants relating to fixed assets are treated as deferred credits, the amount of the deferred credit (if material).

## PROPOSED DIVIDENDS

C1/1/51(3)
P8(26) | 34.1 | The aggregate amount payable to shareholders (to be shown as a current liability).

## TAXATION

C1/1/47 | 35.1 | The amount of any taxation provisions.

*Notes*

P8(14) | 1 If corporation tax liability is not disclosed as current liability, the due date for payment should be shown.

P8(26&27) | 2 ACT on proposed dividends to be included as a current tax liability and, if recoverable, deducted from deferred tax account (or, in the absence of such an account, shown as a deferred asset).

|  | 35.2 | Deferred taxation: |
| P15(37)  C1/1/F |  | (a) the amount of the deferred taxation account balance (to be shown in the specified place in the balance sheet). |
| P15(37) |  | (b) an indication (by way of note) of (i) the nature and (ii) the amount of the major elements of which the balance in (a) is composed; |
| P15(30) |  | (c) a description of the method of calculation adopted, including – where the full potential amount is not provided – an explanation of the assumptions on which the partial amount not provided is based; |
| P15(33) |  | (d) the potential amount (by way of note) of deferred tax for all timing differences, distinguishing the principal categories and showing, for each category, the amount provided in the accounts. |

## OTHER CREDITORS

C1/1/F       36.1    Aggregate amounts in respect of:
(a) payments received on account, in so far as not deducted from stock;
(b) trade creditors;
(c) bills of exchange payable;
(d) social security;
(e) other creditors;
(f)* all classes of creditors falling due within one year;
(g)* all classes of creditors falling due after one year;
(h)* accruals and deferred income [not included in (f) and (g) above];
(i)* all classes of provisions for liabilities and charges.

## CAPITAL

C1/1/38(1)    37.1    (a)* The aggregate amount of the called-up share capital.
(b) The authorised share capital.

C1/1/38(1)    37.2    Where more than one class of shares have been allotted, the number and aggregate nominal value of each class.

C1/1/39       37.3    For any shares allotted during the year, the number, aggregate nominal value, class, consideration received and reason for the allotment.

C1/1/38(2)    37.4    For redeemable shares, the earliest and latest dates of redemption; whether mandatory or at company's option, and premium payable.

C1/1/40 | 37.5 | For options on unallotted shares, the number, amount and description of shares under option, the price, and the year during which exercisable.

C1/1/49 | 37.6 | For arrears of fixed cumulative dividends, the amount and period of arrears for each class of share.

P8(28) | *Note:* For preference shares issued before 6 April 1973, at a fixed rate of dividend, the new rate should be shown in the balance sheet description.

## REVALUATION RESERVE

C1/1/F | 38.1* | The aggregate amount of the revaluation reserve.

C1/1/34 | 38.2 | If any asset is stated other than at historic cost the surplus or deficit must be transferred to a separate reserve.

*Notes*

P19(13) | 1 | In the case of investment properties, if a deficit is not covered by the balance on the revaluation reserve the excess should be reflected in the profit and loss account.

C1/1/34 | 2 | 38.2 above applies equally to revaluations incorporated in a company's accounts prior to the 1981 Companies Act becoming effective.

C1/1/71 | 3 | Not required in the case of an investment company.

## OTHER RESERVES

C1/1/F | 39.1 | The aggregate amounts in respect of:
(a)* share premium account;
(b)* all classes of other reserves;
(c) capital redemption reserve;
(d) reserves for own shares;
(e) any reserves provided for by the company's Articles;
(f)* profit and loss account;
(g) other reserves.

C1/1/46(2) | 39.2 | For each class of reserve:
(a) the amount transferred to or from the reserve during the year;
(b) the source or application of any such movement.

## INVESTMENT COMPANIES

C0/3/39(2) | 40.1 | Where an investment trust company [as defined in C1/1/73 and C041(3)] makes a distribution which reduces the value of its net assets below the total of its called-up share capital and undistributable reserves, a note to that effect.

**FORMAT**

C1/1/2(2)   41.1   Details of any change in format compared with the previous year, together with the reasons for the change.

C1/1/1(1)   *Note:* The format of the balance sheet must accord with the format detailed in Appendix 4 (subject to alternative horizontal presentation). Once a format has been adopted it should only be changed in subsequent years for 'special' reasons.

## Section D: Funds Statement

P10(10)   42.1   A statement of source and application of funds for both the current and corresponding previous year, showing:

P10(11)   *(a)*   the profit or loss for the year together with adjustment for items which did not use/provide funds,
and if material:
*(b)*   dividends paid;
*(c)*   acquisitions and disposals of fixed and other non-current assets;
*(d)*   funds raised by (or used in) increases (or decreases) in medium or long-term loans or share capital;
*(e)*   increase or decrease in working capital (sub-divided into components);
*(f)*   movements in net liquid funds.

*Notes*

P10(9)   1   Statement not required if turnover or gross income is less than £25,000 per annum

P10(12)   2   For group accounts, the statement should reflect the
P10(5)   operations of the group. The effect of acquisition or disposals of subsidiaries should be reflected either (1) as separate items or (2) by showing their effect on the individual assets and liabilities.

P10(4)   3   Amounts should be stated with a minimum of 'netting off'.

## Section E: General Matters

**ACCOUNTING POLICIES**

C1/1/10-15   43.1   If accounts are prepared on the basis of assumptions which differ
P2(17)   materially from any of the generally accepted fundamental concepts ('going concern', 'accruals', 'consistency' and 'prudence'), a clear explanation of the facts.

C1/1/36   43.2   Explanations of all accounting policies followed for dealing with
P2(18)   items which are judged material or critical in determining the result for the year and in stating the financial position.

## FOREIGN CURRENCIES

C1/1/58          44.1    The basis on which foreign currencies have been translated into
                        sterling.

## TRANSACTIONS INVOLVING DIRECTORS AND CONNECTED PERSONS

C0.S54(1)(2)     45.1    In respect of any:

                        1  Transaction or arrangement (as defined – see Note 1 below)
                           entered into by the company (or its subsidiary) for a person
                           who, at any time during the year, was a director of the
                           company or of its holding company, or was connected with
                           such a director; or

C0.S54(1)(2)             2  Any agreement to enter into any such transaction or
                           arrangement; or

C0.S54(1)(2)             3  Any other transaction or arrangement with the company or its
                           subsidiary in which a person who, at any time during the year,
                           was a director of the company or its holding company and had,
                           directly or indirectly, a 'material interest' (see Note 2 below):

C0.S55                  (a)  the principal terms of the transaction, arrangement or
                             agreement;

                        (b)  a statement that the transaction, arrangement or
                             agreement was either made or subsisted during the year;

                        (c)  the name of the person for whom it was made;

                        (d)  where that person is or was connected with a director of
                             the company or its holding company, the name of
                             the director;

                        (e)  where 45.1.3 applies:

                             (i) the name of the director with the material interest;

                             (ii) the nature of that interest;

                        (f)  in the case of a loan, an agreement for a loan, the
                             assignment or assumption of a loan or a loan under a
                             mutual arrangement:

                             (i) the amount of the liability of the person to whom the loan
                             was (or was agreed to be) made, showing the amount of
                             principal and interest at the beginning and end of the year;

                             (ii) the maximum amount of the liability during the year;

                             (iii) the amount of any interest due but unpaid;

                             (iv) the amount of provision made in respect of any
                             known or anticipated repayment failure by the
                             borrower.

                        (g)  in the case of a guarantee or security, or assignment or
                             assumption of a guarantee or security;

                             (i) the amount for which the company (or its subsidiary)
                             was liable under the guarantee or in respect of the
                             security at the beginning and end of the year;

*(ii)* the maximum amount for which the company (or its subsidiary) may become so liable;

*(iii)* any amount paid and any liability incurred by the company (or its subsidiary) for the purpose of fulfilling the guarantee, or discharging the security including any loss incurred by reason of the enforcement of the guarantee or security;

*(h)* in the case of any other transaction, arrangement or agreement, the value involved.

*Notes*

C0.S56(1)    1  The transactions or arrangements referred to include: loans; quasi-loans; credit transactions and guarantees or security in connection therewith, the assignment of any rights, obligations or liabilities under such transactions; and any arrangement by the company for another person to enter into such a transaction.

C0.S54(4b)    2  An interest in such a transaction is not material, if, in the opinion of the majority of the directors (other than the director concerned) it is not material.

C0.S54(6)    3  The disclosure requirements do not apply in relation to the following transactions, arrangements and agreements:

C0.S54(6a)    *(a)* one between one company and another in which a director of the first company, or its subsidiary or holding company, is interested only by virtue of his being a director of the other;

C0.S54(6b)  C1/3/51(c)    *(b)* contracts of service;

C0.S58(1)(2)    *(c)* credit transactions, if the aggregate of the amounts involved for any one person did not, at any time during the year, exceed £5,000;

C1/3/(53)    *(d)* transactions under 45.1.3 if the aggregate values of each transaction or arrangement *(i)* did not at any time during the year exceed £1,000 or, if more; *(ii)* at the end of the year did not exceed the lesser of £5,000 or one per cent of the value of the net assets of the company.

## TRANSACTIONS INVOLVING OFFICERS OF THE COMPANY

C0.S56(2)    46.1  In respect of any transactions, arrangement or agreement (as defined, see Note 1 below) made by the company or its subsidiary for a person who, at any time during the year, was an officer of the company (but not a director):

C0.S56(2)(8)    *(a)* the total at the year-end of the amounts outstanding (being the amount of the outstanding liability of the person for whom the transactions, etc., in question were made or, in the case of a guarantee or security, the amount guaranteed or secured).

*(b)* the number of officers for whom the transaction, etc. falling within each heading in Note 1 below was made.

*Notes*

1  The transactions, arrangements or agreements referred to include:

*(a)* loans;

*(b)* quasi loans;

*(c)* credit transactions.

Each of these transactions should include related guarantees and securities, arrangements for assignment or assumption or mutual arrangements, and agreements to enter into any of the transactions and arrangements outlined.

C1/3/52  2  Disclosure not required where the amount outstanding at the year-end in respect of each officer, does not exceed £2,500.

## CONTINGENCIES AND COMMITMENTS

C1/1/50(1)  47.1  Particulars (and amount if practicable) of any charge on the assets of the company to secure the liabilities of any other person.

C1/1/50(3)  47.2  The estimated amount, where practicable, of future capital expenditure:

*(a)* contracted for but not provided,

*(b)* authorised by the directors but not contracted for.

C1/1/50(4)  47.3  Particulars of pension commitments:

*(a)* provided for in the accounts,

*(b)* not provided for in the accounts,

*(c)* which relates to pensions payable to past directors.

C1/1/50(5)  47.4  Particulars of any other financial commitments which are not provided for in the accounts, but which are relevant to assessing the company's state of affairs.

C1/1/50(6)  *Note:* Commitments in 47.2 to 47.4 above should be separately disclosed if undertaken on behalf of or for the benefit of *(a)* a holding company or fellow subsidiary, or *(b)* any subsidiary [and analysed between *(a)* and *(b)* above].

C1/1/50(2)  47.5  In relation to any material contingent losses not provided for
P18(16)(20)  (and any material contingent gains where it is probable that the gain will be realised):

*(a)* the legal nature of the contingency;

*(b)* the uncertainties that are expected to affect the ultimate outcome;

*(c)* the amount or a prudent estimate of the financial effect before tax (or, in the case of a gain, a statement that it is not practicable to make such an estimate);

(d) an explanation of the taxation implications, where necessary for a proper understanding of the financial position;

(e) whether any valuation security has been given in respect of the liability, and if so the details of the security.

P18(15)(17)

*Note:* Material contingent losses should be provided for where it is probable that a future event will confirm a loss which can be estimated with reasonable accuracy at the date on which the accounts are approved by the board. Contingent gains should not be accrued.

## POST-BALANCE SHEET EVENTS (See also Section A.1.5)

P17(23a)(24) (25)

48.1 In respect of 'non-adjusting' events, i.e. those which concern conditions which did not exist at the balance sheet date:

(a) the nature of the event;

(b) an estimate of the financial effect, before taxation, or a statement that it is not practicable to make such an estimate;

(c) an explanation of the taxation implications, where necessary for a proper understanding of the financial position.

P17(21)(22) C1/1/12(b)

*Note:* 'Adjusting' events, i.e. those which provide additional evidence of conditions existing at the balance sheet date, as well as going concern considerations, require changes in the amounts included in the accounts.

P17(23b)

48.2 Details, as in 48.1 above, of any transactions entered into before the year-end, the substance of which was primarily to alter the appearance of the company's balance sheet.

P17(26)

48.3 The date on which the accounts are approved by the board of directors.

## ADDITIONAL INFORMATION

C1.S.1(3)

49.1 Any other information which is necessary in order that the accounts show a true and fair view.

C1.S.1(4)

49.2 Where any departure from Companies Act requirements is made in order that the accounts show a true and fair view, particulars of the departure, the reasons for it and the effect on the accounts must be disclosed.

## PRIOR YEAR COMPARATIVES

C1/1/4

50.1 The corresponding amounts for the preceding financial year for all items shown in the balance sheet and profit and loss account and notes thereon.

C1/1/58(3)  *Note:* Not required in respect of proportion of share capital held in subsidiaries and related companies or transactions in 45 and 46 above.

### DIRECTOR'S SIGNATURE

C8.S155&156  51.1  The signature, on the balance sheet, of two directors (or sole director).

## Section F: Group Accounts

C.8.S150
P14(19)  *Note 1*  Group accounts are required where a company *(a)* has a subsidiary at the end of its financial year and *(b)* is not itself a wholly owned subsidiary of another company incorporated in GB.

C8.S150
C8.S152
C1.S2  *Note 2*  Group accounts should normally deal with the state of affairs and profit or loss of the holding company and all its subsidiaries. For subsidiaries excluded from group accounts, see 52.1.

C.8.S151(1)
P14(15)
C1/1/68  *Note 3*  Group accounts should normally be presented in the form of a single set of consolidated accounts. For subsidiaries excluded from consolidation, see 52.2–52.4.

52.1  Where a subsidiary is excluded totally from group accounts:

C1/1/69(2a)
P14(20)  *(a)*  the reasons for the exclusion;

C1/1/69(3)  *(b)*  the net aggregate amount of profits less losses of omitted subsidiaries *(i)* dealt with and *(ii)* not dealt with in the consolidated accounts for the current year and for the previous years since acquisition.

C1/1/69(4)  *Note:* Not required if the company is a wholly owned subsidiary and the directors state that in their opinion the value of the investment is not less than the amount at which it is stated in the holding company balance sheet.

C1/1/69(2b)  *(c)*  any material qualifications in the auditors' report.

*Notes*

C8.S150(2)  1  A subsidiary may be excluded totally from group accounts only on grounds of *(a)* impracticability, *(b)* insignificance, *(c)* disproportionate expense, *(d)* dissimilar activities, or if its inclusion would be *(e)* misleading or *(f)* harmful [but as to *(d)* see also 52.3].

2  If any of the information required in 52.1 *(a)* and *(b)* above is not obtainable a statement to that effect.

52.2  Where a subsidiary is excluded from consolidation:
*(a)*  the reasons for the exclusion;
*(b)*  the names of the principal subsidiaries excluded.

P14(23)          52.3     Where a subsidiary is excluded from consolidation because of
                          dissimilar activities:
                          (a) the separate accounts for that subsidiary, which should in
                              in turn include:
                          (b) a note of the holding company's interest;
                          (c) particulars of intra-group balances;
                          (d) the nature of transactions with the rest of the group;
                          (e) a reconciliation with the amount included in the consolidated
                              accounts for the group's investment in the subsidiary.

                          *Note:* The group's investment in the subsidiary should be stated in
                          the consolidated accounts under the equity method of accounting.

P14(26)          52.4     Where a subsidiary is excluded from consolidation because of
                          severe restrictions on control:
                          (a) the net assets of the subsidiary;
                          (b) its profits or losses for the year;
                          (c) any amounts included in the consolidated profit and loss
                              account in respect of *(i)* dividends received and *(ii)* writing
                              down the investment.

P14(25)                   *Note:* The group's investment in the subsidiary should be stated at
                          the amount at which it would have been included under the equity
                          method at the date the restrictions came into force, with no further
                          accruals for subsequent profits or losses except in respect of any
                          permanent impairment of value, where each investment should be
                          considered separately.

P14(16)          52.5     Where uniform accounting policies are not adopted by group
                          companies:
                          (a) the different accounting policies used,
                          (b) an indication of the amounts of assets and liabilities involved,
                          (c) where practicable, an indication of the effect on results and
                              net assets that arises from using different policies from those
                              of the group,
                          (d) the reasons for the different treatment.

P14(18)          52.6     Where the financial periods of any subsidiaries are not co-
C8.S152(4)                terminous with that of the holding company:
C1.S2
                          (a) the names of the principal subsidiaries with different
                              accounting dates,
C1/1/70(a)                (b) the reasons for their not being co-terminous,
C1/1/70(b)                (c) the accounting dates on which the relevant subsidiaries'
                              financial years ended.

P14(30)          52.7     For subsidiaries acquired or sold during the year, sufficient
                          information concerning their results to enable shareholders to
                          appreciate the effect on the consolidated results.

C1.S4     52.8     Where a company holds in excess of 20 per cent of the allotted share capital of another company which is not consolidated or included under the equity method of valuation, if material *(a)* the aggregate amount of capital and reserves at the end of the year or latest available year-end before that date, *(b)* the profit or loss for the year in *(a)* above.

P14(33)     52.9     The names of principal subsidiaries and, for each:
          *(a)*   the proportion of the nominal value of issued shares of each class held by the group;
          *(b)*   an indication of the nature of the subsidiary's business;
P14(18)          *(c)*   the length of the accounting period, if different from that of the holding company.

        52.10     Minority interests:
P14(34)          *(a)*   in the consolidated balance sheet: separately but not as part of shareholder's funds;
P14(35)          *(b)*   in the consolidated P&L account: separately after group profit or loss on ordinary activities after tax but before extraordinary items.

P14(36)     52.11     Extent of restrictions on the holding company's ability to distribute group profits (other than those designated non-distributable).

C1/1/63     52.12     Disclosure is required only on a company (rather than a consolidated) basis in respect of:
          *(a)*   directors' and employees' emoluments (11 and 12.4 above);
          *(b)*   transactions involving directors, officers and connected persons (45 and 46 above);
          *(c)*   interests in other companies (28.3 and 52.8 above).

## Section G: Current Cost Accounts

### PROFIT AND LOSS ACCOUNT

P16(55)     53.1     *(a)*   the current cost operating profit or loss;
P1(46)          *(b)*   the share of the associated companies' current cost profit or loss before taxation but after interest;
          *(c)*   interest/income relating to net borrowing on which the gearing adjustment has been based;
          *(d)*   the gearing adjustment; (stating separately the amount relating to associated companies)
          *(e)*   taxation;
          *(f)*   extraordinary items; and
          *(g)*   current cost profit or loss (after tax) attributable to shareholders.

P1(47)         *Note:* Where associated companies do not prepare current cost accounts and the information is included based on directors' best estimate, this fact should be disclosed.

P16(56)    53.2   A reconciliation between the current cost operating profit and the profit or loss before charging interest and taxation, calculated on the historical cost basis, giving the respective amounts of the following:
(a) depreciation adjustment;
(b) cost of sales adjustment;
(c) monetary working capital adjustment;
(d) where appropriate, interest relating to monetary working capital.

*Note:* Adjustments *(b)* and *(c)* may be combined.

(e) other material adjustments made to profits calculated on the historical cost basis when determining current cost operating profit.

P16(59)    53.3   For listed companies, the current cost earnings per share based on the current cost profit attributable to equity shareholders before extraordinary items.

## BALANCE SHEET

P16(57)    54.1   The totals of net operating assets and net borrowing and their main elements.

*Note:* The balance sheet may be in summarised form.

P1(45)     54.2   The investment in associated companies should be shown:
(a) as the share of current cost net assets, other than goodwill;
(b) provided fair values were attributed to the net assets on acquisition, goodwill and any premium paid should be shown at their historical cost.

## NOTES TO THE ACCOUNTS

P16(58)    55.1   The bases and methods adopted in preparing the accounts, particularly in relation to:
(a) fixed assets valuation and depreciation;
(b) stock valuation and the cost of sales adjustment;
(c) the monetary working capital adjustment;
(d) the gearing adjustment;
(e) the translation of foreign currencies and treatment of differences arising;
(f) other material adjustments to the historical cost information; and
(g) the corresponding amounts.

P16(52)    55.2   Where it is not practicable to treat them in a manner consistent with the definition of profit set out in the SSAP16, the treatment within the current cost profit and loss account of the items set out below:

(a)  gains and losses on asset disposals;
(b)  extraordinary and exceptional items;
(c)  prior year items;
(d)  income from related/associated companies;
(e)  group consolidation adjustments;
(f)  minority interest; and
(g)  translation of foreign currencies.

P16(53c)    55.3    Where the directors' valuation of a listed investment is materially different from mid-market value, the basis of valuation and the reasons for the difference.

P16(57)    55.4    A summary of fixed asset accounts.

P16(57)    55.5    Movements on reserves.

## GROUP ACCOUNTS

P16(60)    56.1    In the case of a holding company, the current cost accounts should be prepared only on a group basis.

## CORRESPONDING AMOUNTS

P16(61)    57.1    Corresponding amounts for the preceding year.

*Note:* Only required in the first year if they are readily available, unless the current cost accounts are the main accounts.

## MAIN ACCOUNTS

P16(48c)    58.1    If current cost accounts are the main accounts:
(a)  at least sufficient information to enable the user to ascertain the historical cost profit of the period under existing conventions;
(b)  in the case of a group, the separate accounts of the holding company;
C1/1/33    (c)  particulars required in 23.1 above.

*Note:* If current cost accounts are the main accounts, they should be reviewed for compliance with the other sections of this checklist.

## Appendix 1: Listed Companies (Additional Disclosure)

### AFFAIRS

| | | |
|---|---|---|
| SE2/10(b) | 1.1 | An explanation why trading results differ materially from any published forecast. |
| SE2/10(a) | 1.2 | The reasons for any significant departues from standard accounting practices. |

### ACTIVITIES

| | | |
|---|---|---|
| SE2(10)(d) | 2.1 | The principal country of operation of each significant subsidiary. |
| SE2(10)(e) | 2.2 | Principal country of operation of each company (not a subsidiary) in which the group interest is 20 per cent or more. |
| SE2(10)(c) | 2.3 | A geographical analysis of overseas turnover and trading results (see Section B.7.2). |

*Notes*

SE2/Note 40

1  Analysis should be by continent unless 50 per cent or more of the overseas operations relate to one continent, in which case further analysis by country is required.
2  No further analysis of trading results is required unless the contribution from a specific area is abnormal.

### DIRECTORS' INTERESTS

| | | |
|---|---|---|
| | 3.1 | In addition to the particulars regarding directors' interests in shares or debentures of the company required under C7.S16 (see Section A.4.2). |
| SE2(10)(h) | | *(a)* a distinction between beneficial and non-beneficial interests, indicating any duplication; |
| SE2(10)(h) | | *(b)* details, by way of note, of any changes in those interests occurring between the year-end and a date not more than one month prior to the date of the notice of meeting. |
| SE2(10)(1) SE2/Note 47 | 3.2 | If, regarding the requirement to disclose details of significant contracts in which directors have an interest there have been no such contracts subsisting during the year, a statement to that effect. |

*Note:* For Stock Exchange purposes, a 'significant' contract is one which represents not less than 1 per cent of the relevant account's amount.

| | | |
|---|---|---|
| SE2(11)(d) | 3.3 | In the Directors' Report, the period unexpired for any service contract of any director proposed for re-election at the forthcoming AGM. |

## WAIVERS

SE2(10)(m)    4.1    Particulars of any arrangement under which a director has agreed to waive any emoluments.

SE2(10)(n)    4.2    Particulars of any arrangement under which a shareholder has agreed to waive any dividends.

SE2/Note 49    *Note:* Waivers of a minor amount may be disregarded provided that some payment has been made on each share during the year.

## SUBSTANTIAL SHAREHOLDINGS

SE2(10)(i)    5.1    Particulars at a date not more than one month prior to the date of
SE2/Note 45    notice of meeting, of any shareholding (other than by a director) of 5 per cent or more in any class of voting share capital of the company, or, if there is no such holding, a statement of that fact.

## STATUS

SE2(10)(j)    6.1    A statement as to whether the 'close' company provisions of the ICTA 1970 apply (and whether there has been any change in that respect since the year-end).

6.2    For investment trust companies:
SE2(10)(k)    *(a)* The company's taxation status and any change since the year end.
SE9(2)(g)    *(b)* A statement confirming their approval under the provisions of Section 359 of the ICTA 1970;
*(c)* stating the last accounting period in respect of which approval was given;
*(d)* confirmation that the company has subseqently directed its affairs in order to continue approved status.

## LOANS AND INTEREST

SE2(10)(f)    7.1    The aggregate amounts repayable at the end of each financial year in respect of both *(i)* bank loans and overdrafts and *(ii)* other borrowings:
*(a)* in one year or less or on demand;
*(b)* between one and two years;
*(c)* between two and five years;
*(d)* in five years or more.

SE2(10)(g)    7.2    The amount of interest capitalised during the year together with the amount and treatment of any related tax relief.

## EARNINGS PER SHARE

P3(14)    8.1    The amount of earnings per share (with comparatives), calculated on the 'net basis'.

*Note:* To be shown on the face of the profit and loss account. If the tax charge includes either *(a)* irrecoverable ACT or *(b)* unrelieved overseas tax due to dividend payments, the amount of earnings per share, calculated on the nil distribution basis should also be shown, if materially different.

P3(15)    8.2    The basis of the calculation detailing the amount of earnings and the number of equity shares used.

P3(16)    8.3    Where the company has, at the balance sheet date, contracted to to issue further shares after the end of the year, or where it has already issued shares which will rank for dividend later (or where it has issued convertible loan stock or debentures, or granted options to subscribe for equity shares), and if the dilution is material (not less than 5%).

*(a)*   the amount of fully diluted earnings per share;

*Notes*
1   Wherever both are disclosed, equal prominence should be given to basic and fully diluted earnings per share:
2   Comparative fully diluted earnings per share should not be shown unless assumptions on which it was based still apply.

*(b)*   the basis of calculation.

## INVESTMENT COMPANIES

SE9(4)(b)    9.1    The aggregate amount of realised and unrealised surpluses, analysing separately profits and losses on listed and unlisted investments.

SE9(6)    9.2    A list of investments whose value exceeds 5 per cent of the fund, and at least the ten largest investments.

SE9(6)    9.3    The following should be disclosed, together with the comparatives in respect of investments listed in 9.2 above:
*(a)*   a brief description of the business;
*(b)*   proportion of share capital owned;
*(c)*   cost;
*(d)*   directors' valuation;
*(e)*   dividends received in the year (indicating any abnormal dividends);
*(f)*   dividend cover or underlying earnings;
*(g)*   extraordinary items;
*(h)*   net assets attributable to the investments.

SE9(6)    9.4    An analysis of any provision for diminution in value of investment giving details of the name, cost, provision made and book value of each investment against which a provision has been made.

## INVESTMENT TRUSTS

SE9(2)    10.1    A geographical analysis (based on country of incorporation) of the investment portfolio.

10.2    An analysis of the portfolio by industrial or commercial sectors.

10.3    A list of the largest investments by market value, stating their value.

10.4    An analysis of the portfolio between:
(a)    equity share capital;
(b)    capital with an equity element;
(c)    fixed income securities.

10.5    An analysis of income between:
(a)    dividends and interest;
(b)    other income distinguishing, where material, underwriting income and the results of dealing by subsidiaries.

10.6    Where more than 15 per cent of the group's assets are invested in or lent in respect of (a) securities not listed on a recognised stock exchange or (b) holdings representing in excess of 20 per cent of the equity capital, excluding interests in approved investment trusts:
(a)    an analysis, where material, of realised and unrealised profits or losses between listed and unlisted investments.

10.7    The name of the managing group or company and an indication of their terms of appointment.

## Appendix 2: Profit and Loss Account (Vertical Format 1)

Note: All formats included in the appendices may alternatively be presented in horizontal form. In such cases items marked with an asterisk need not be disclosed.

X  Represents minimum headings which must be included on the face of the balance sheet or profit and loss account (as appropriate).

O  Represents items which may alternatively be presented in the notes to the accounts, and may be combined where individually they are not material.

|  | £ | £ |
|---|---|---|
| TURNOVER | | 0 |
| Cost of sales | | (0) |
| GROSS PROFIT (OR LOSS)* | | 0 |
| Distribution cost | | (0) |
| Administrative expenses | | (0) |
| Other operating income | | 0 |
| Income from shares in group companies | | 0 |
| Income from shares in related companies | | 0 |
| Income from other fixed asset investments | | 0 |
| Other interest receivable and similar income | | 0 |
| Amounts written off investments | | (0) |
| Interest payable and similar charges | | (0) |
| PROFIT (OR LOSS) ON ORDINARY ACTIVITIES BEFORE TAXATION | | X |
| Tax on profit (or loss) on ordinary activities | | (0) |
| Profit (or loss) on ordinary activities after taxation | | 0 |
| Extraordinary income | 0 | |
| Extraordinary charges | (0) | |
| Extraordinary profit (or loss) * | | 0 |
| Tax on extraordinary profit (or loss) | | (0) |
| Other taxes not shown under the above items | | (0) |
| PROFIT (OR LOSS) FOR THE FINANCIAL YEAR | | 0 |
| Dividends paid and proposed | | (X) |
| AMOUNT SET ASIDE TO RESERVES | | X |

# Appendix 3: Profit and Loss Account (Vertical Format 2)

| | £ |
|---|---|
| TURNOVER | 0 |
| Change in stock of finished goods and work-in-progress | 0 |
| Own work capitalised | 0 |
| Other operating income | 0 |
| Raw materials and consumables | (0) |
| Other external charges | (0) |
| Staff costs: | |
|   Wages and salaries | (0) |
|   Social Security costs | (0) |
|   Other pension costs | (0) |
| Depreciation and other amounts written-off tangible and intangible assets | (0) |
| Exceptional amounts written-off assets | (0) |
| Other operating charges | (0) |
| Income from shares in group companies | 0 |
| Income from shares in related companies | 0 |
| Income from other fixed asset investments | 0 |
| Other interest receivable and similar income | 0 |
| Amounts written-off investments | (0) |
| Interest payable and similar charges | (0) |
| PROFIT OR LOSS ON ORDINARY ACTIVITIES BEFORE TAXATION | X |
| Tax on profit (or loss) on ordinary activities | (0) |
| Profit (or loss) on ordinary activities after taxation | 0 |
| Extraordinary income | 0 |
| Extraordinary charges | (0) |
| Extraordinary profit (or loss)* | 0 |
| Tax on extraordinary profit (or loss) | (0) |
| Other taxes not shown under the above items | (0) |
| PROFIT (OR LOSS) FOR THE FINANCIAL YEAR | 0 |
| Dividends paid and proposed | (X) |
| AMOUNT SET ASIDE TO RESERVES | X |

**Appendix 4: Balance Sheet (Vertical Format)**

|  | £ | £ | £ |
|---|---|---|---|
| CALLED-UP SHARE CAPITAL NOT PAID |  |  | X |
| FIXED ASSETS |  |  | X |
| Intangible assets |  | X |  |
| Development costs | 0 |  |  |
| Patents, licences, trademarks, etc. | 0 |  |  |
| Goodwill | 0 |  |  |
| Payments on account | 0 |  |  |
| Tangible assets |  | X |  |
| Land and buildings | 0 |  |  |
| Plant and machinery | 0 |  |  |
| Fittings, tools and equipment | 0 |  |  |
| Payments on account and assets in course of construction | 0 |  |  |
| Investments |  | X |  |
| Shares in group companies | 0 |  |  |
| Loans to group companies | 0 |  |  |
| Shares in related companies | 0 |  |  |
| Loans to related companies | 0 |  |  |
| Other investments other than loans | 0 |  |  |
| Other loans | 0 |  |  |
| Own shares | 0 |  |  |
| CURRENT ASSETS |  |  | X |
| Stocks |  | X |  |
| Raw materials and consumables | 0 |  |  |
| Work-in-progress | 0 |  |  |
| Finished goods and goods for resale | 0 |  |  |
| Payments on account | 0 |  |  |
| Debtors |  | X |  |
| Trade debtors | 0 |  |  |
| Amounts owed by group companies | 0 |  |  |
| Amounts owed by related companies | 0 |  |  |
| Other debtors | 0 |  |  |
| Called-up share capital not paid | 0 |  |  |
| Prepayments and accrued income | 0 |  |  |
| Investments |  | X |  |
| Shares in group companies | 0 |  |  |
| Own shares | 0 |  |  |
| Other investments | 0 |  |  |
| Cash at bank and in hand |  | X |  |
| PREPAYMENTS AND ACCRUED INCOME |  |  | X |

*(Continued)*

|  | £ | £ | £ |
|---|---|---|---|

CREITORS: AMOUNTS FALLING DUE WITHIN ONE YEAR (X)

| | | |
|---|---|
| Debenture loans | 0 |
| Bank loans and overdrafts | 0 |
| Payments received on account | 0 |
| Trade creditors | 0 |
| Bills of Exchange payable | 0 |
| Amounts owed to group companies | 0 |
| Amounts owed to related companies | 0 |
| Other creditors, taxation, and Social Security | 0 |
| Accruals and deferred income | 0 |

*NET CURRENT ASSETS (LIABILITIES)        X

*TOTAL ASSETS LESS CURRENT LIABILITIES        X

CREDITORS: AMOUNTS FALLING DUE AFTER MORE THAN ONE YEAR (X)

| | | |
|---|---|
| Debenture loans | 0 |
| Bank loans and overdrafts | 0 |
| Payments received on account | 0 |
| Trade creditors | 0 |
| Bills of Exchange payable | 0 |
| Amounts owed to group companies | 0 |
| Amounts owed to related companies | 0 |
| Other creditors, taxation, and Social Security | 0 |
| Accruals and deferred income | 0 |

PROVISIONS FOR LIABILITIES AND CHARGES (X)

| | | |
|---|---|
| Pensions and similar obligations | 0 |
| Taxation, including deferred taxation | 0 |
| Other provisions | 0 |

ACCRUALS AND DEFERRED INCOME (X)

          X

CAPITAL AND RESERVES        X

| | | |
|---|---|
| Called-up share capital | X |
| Share premium account | X |
| Revaluation reserve | X |
| Other reserves | X |

| | | |
|---|---|
| Capital redemption reserve | 0 |
| Reserve for own shares | 0 |
| Reserves provided for by the Articles of Association | 0 |
| Other reserves | 0 |

Profit and loss account        X

          X

# Part Six

# ACCOUNTING POLICIES AND BUSINESS 'PERFORMANCE'

# 16 Policies and 'performance'

**INTRODUCTION**

One of the purposes of this book has been to underline the extent to which the preparation of a set of accounts – and the reading they give of a business's performance – is subject to a considerable degree of estimation and opinion. This chapter reverts to the general question of accounting principles and the alternative methods by which certain of the items appearing in a set of accounts might be arrived at. Its particular relevance will be for those who wish to use accounts in order to assess the strength and profitability of other companies – whether that be small, remote shareholders assessing the company in which they have invested their savings or a businessman who is looking at another company with a view to acquisition. The fairness of the story told in the accounts will depend very largely on the fairness of the accounting policies which have been adopted in preparing them. The ability to assess the fairness of the adopted policies requires both an awareness of 'standard practice' – in the areas where that has been established – and an awareness of the possible alternatives in those areas for which no one generally accepted method of accounting has yet been developed. This chapter points to some of the items in accounts to which anyone reading them should pay particular attention.

**STATEMENTS OF STANDARD ACCOUNTING PRACTICE (SSAPs)**

One of the consequences of a series of financial collapses during the 1960s was that the question of accounting principles – and particularly the multiplicity of alternative accounting treatments that appeared to be available – came under sharp criticism. As a result, in 1970, the accountancy bodies set up an Accounting Standards Committee with the purpose of developing and issuing approved methods of accounting so as to narrow the areas of difference between the methods adopted by different companies to account for similar items.

Nineteen SSAPs have been issued to date and references to the more important of them are included in the paragraphs that follow. There is no doubt that the issue of these statements has enhanced the level of comparability between different companies' accounts: not only are companies now required to disclose the accounting policies that they have adopted, but they are also required to disclose and explain any deviation from standard practice. In addition, the requirement for consistency ensures that the accounts of any one company will be readily comparable – in terms of the bases on which the figures are drawn up – from one year to the next. Nevertheless it would be spurious to suggest that a particular, uniform method of accounting can always be developed to meet the variety of different circumstances in which different types of businesses operate. The level of standardisation achieved by the issue of SSAPs is constrained by the need to accommodate different business circumstances: for this reason a number of SSAPs have been drafted in order to allow a degree of flexibility and choice; and there remain a number of difficult accounting areas for which it has not yet proved possible to issue a Statement of Standard Accounting Practice.

## ASSOCIATED COMPANIES

An associated company is one in which the holding is less than 50 per cent (more than which would make it a subsidiary), but, which is sufficient to give the investing company 'significant influence' over the associate. Significant influence is measured by the extent to which the investing company participates in the policy decisions of the associate. The standard benchmark was that significant influence would automatically exist where the holding was 20 per cent or more (SSAP1) although a more recent revision proposes that the 20 per cent rule becomes less rigid, allowing for the possibility of significant influence arising from holdings of less than 20 per cent.

The assessment of whether or not the company is an associate is therefore a matter of some judgement. The accounting consequences are considerable. Whereas income from investments would normally be accounted for on the basis of dividends received, the standard treatment for associated companies has been for the investing group to include in its own profit and loss account its full share of the profits of the associate – regardless of whether or not those profits have been distributed. An amount equal to that share of profits is added to the value at which the investment is shown in the balance sheet.

The reader should therefore be aware of the extent to which the company's own performance has been enhanced by its participation in the profits of associated companies. Associated company profits only increase funds available to a company if they are paid up by way of dividend and, although the investing company may influence the distribution policy of the associate, it will not be able to control it. Those profits are therefore of a different order to the profits that the company has generated for itself and their degree of significance in the profit and loss account should be read in that context.

Equally important, the reader should attempt to assess by what basis the company has or has not decided that another company should be treated as an associate. Despite the existence of an SSAP, the Institute's 1981/82 *Survey of Published Accounts* revealed that of 238 companies which disclosed holdings of between 20 and 50 per cent in other companies, 72 did not treat them as associated. The reasons for not so treating were given as:

| | |
|---|---|
| Not material | 28 |
| Not sufficient influence | 14 |
| Prudence | 2 |
| No reason | 27 |
| | —— |
| | 72 |

Note that the majority of these reasons (materiality, sufficiency of influence, etc.) are matters of subjective opinion. There is a possibility that the figures might be regarded as material, and the influence significant, where the investing company wants to reflect a share of a profitable associate, but that it might wish to disclaim any influence (and therefore avoid taking any share of the loss) over an unprofitable associate.

**EXTRAORDINARY AND EXCEPTIONAL ITEMS**

The distinction between extraordinary and exceptional items – and the impact their alternative treatment can have in the profit and loss account – has been described in Part Two. This topic is the subject of SSAP6. The essential point as far as the reader of accounts is concerned is that exceptional items should be taken into account before arriving at operating profit from normal trading operations, whereas extraordinary items are excluded from that figure and disclosed 'below the line'. Once again, the point to be aware of is that what is exceptional and what is extraordinary in the particular circumstances of a given business will often resolve to a question of subjective opinion.

The following figures are extracted from the 1981/82 Survey. They illustrate the extent to which different companies will form different views as to how similar items should be accounted for. The third column indicates a treatment which avoids the profit and loss account altogether – the items in question being accounted for directly to reserves:

| | Exceptional | Extraordinary | Reserve movements |
|---|---|---|---|
| | % | % | % |
| Foreign exchange differences | 9 | 25 | 66 |
| Goodwill, etc, written off | 3 | 32 | 65 |
| Profits and losses on closures | 5 | 93 | 2 |
| Reorganisation expenses | 12 | 87 | 1 |
| Profit and loss on sale of fixed assets | 45 | 55 | – |
| Redundancy costs | 75 | 25 | – |
| Surplus on redemption of debentures | 29 | 54 | 17 |

## LEASING

Largely because of favourable tax treatment, the incidence of leasing amongst companies as a means of financing their operations has grown tremendously in recent years. Because the lessee company had not had legal ownership of the assets in question, usual accounting practice has been to omit any mention of the assets in the balance sheet and to account only for the annual rentals in the profit and loss account.

This choice – between leasing and outright purchase – and their alternative accounting treatments has led to severe difficulties of comparison between companies. Two identical companies will appear to be quite differently profitable if the capital employed by one includes assets that it has purchased while the capital employed by the other excludes any amount for the cost of similar assets which it happens to have leased. Nevertheless the lessee company will by the terms of the lease often have committed itself to leasing commitments of significant amounts for a number of years.

No standard accounting practice presently exists in this area but a recent exposure draft by the ASC proposes that, where the terms of a lease substantially transfer all the risks and rewards of ownership of an asset to the lessee, the leased asset should be capitalised in the balance sheet and the corresponding liability included to reflect the future commitments. In the meantime, in the absence of any further and voluntary disclosure, the reader of any company's accounts might attempt to assess the incidence of any leasing by looking for the amount of the rentals paid during the year – which, where significant, are required to be disclosed by law.

## PENSION COSTS

Pension costs are another area where at present there is no standard or generally accepted accounting treatment. They can nevertheless amount to a very significant element of a company's costs, and they are costs the measurement of which involve a very high degree of assumption, estimation and opinion. The central difficulty is in assessing what level of present costs will be sufficient to fund the benefits due to employees in later years. That assessment involves critical assumptions regarding future levels of inflation, future levels of salary, the expected rate of return on pension fund investments and the life expectancy of employees. Although much of this will be a matter for actuarial assessment, the question of whether a company's present contributions are at a level which is sufficient to meet its future liabilities can have a critical bearing on the profit and loss account. Unfortunately – and perhaps not surprisingly in view of the enormous difficulties of measurement which are involved – the matter of present contributions and future commitments is one to which companies tend to give very little disclosure.

## RESEARCH AND DEVELOPMENT

Until the issue of an accounting standard (SSAP17) in 1977, the variety of methods by which companies treated their research and development expenditure were numerous. For the most part, R&D costs are intangible and the question as to whether any future benefit will derive from them is particularly intractible. The relevant accounting principle is one of matching: if a cost is not to be written off as an expense to the profit and loss account, then it must be carried forward as an asset in the balance sheet. The consequence for accounts is that any reluctance to write of R&D costs increasingly leads to the accumulation of an asset from which the future benefit to be derived is at best uncertain and at worst spurious.

Standard Accounting Practice now distinguishes between expenditure on pure research (the advance of knowledge), expenditure on applied research (directing pure research towards commercial possibilities) and expenditure on specific development projects (work directed at the introduction or improvement of a specific product or process). No tangible benefit can immediately be related to research costs and therefore they should be written off as incurred. With regard to development costs, however, where there is a clearly defined project and where its ultimate commercial viability can be assessed with reasonable certainty, it is permissable to carry them forward as an asset to be matched against the revenues they will help to generate in the future.

## STOCK

The valuation of a company's stock at the balance sheet date is a matter that affords a great deal of room for subjective judgement. Part Two describes how Dovetails' stock was valued by reference to the actual cost of producing it – without reference to its replacement cost or subsequent resale value – and how the choice of 'costs' from the range of different purchase prices during the year significantly affected not only the value of stock but also the calculation of profit. Reference was also made to the level of estimation and opinion involved in those instances where stock is written down to less than its cost, e.g. in order to provide for obsolesence.

SSAP9 established some of the ground rules that should be adopted in valuing stock. Nevertheless, it is a good example of the way in which an accounting 'standard' can do no more than establish some basic rules, without attempting to be prescriptive in the more detailed aspects of valuation in order to permit the flexibility which different businesses will need in order fairly to value totally different types of stock and work-in-progress.

The basic principle is that the costs to be included in stock should be limited to those expenses which have been incurred in bringing the stock to its present condition and location at the balance sheet date, subject only to the general rule that stock should be stated at the lower of cost and net realisable value. The methods that should be adopted in arriving at that cost are not prescribed, other than that they should be those which are most appropriate to the circumstances of the business in order to arrive at an approximation of actual cost. Companies vary greatly in the level of information they disclose and, amongst the difficulties confronting any reader of accounts, two particular problems will be assessing the method that has been used to arrive at cost and the extent to which overheads have or have not been included in the valuation.

Of those companies that did provide some further information, the 1981/82 *Survey of Published Accounts* revealed the following variety of methods adopted by companies in their assessment of cost of stock:

| | |
|---|---:|
| FIFO method | 45 |
| Average cost | 16 |
| Standard or unit cost | 6 |
| Retail prices less average sales margin | 20 |
| Base stock | 5 |
| LIFO method | 3 |
| | 95 |

All of these are methods adopted in order to arrive at an approximation of actual cost. The FIFO method (first in first out) attributes later material costs to stock valuation (and earlier costs to the cost of goods sold). The LIFO method (last in first out) attributes earliest costs to the valuation of stock in hand. The method by which estimated profit margins are deducted from retail selling prices is one that is used primarily by retail stores.

The following figures – also extracted from the 1981/82 Survey – summarise the extent to which companies included in the Survey provided more specific information as to their policy for including overheads in stock valuation, and the sort of description which they gave:

| | |
|---|---:|
| Production, works or manufacturing overheads included | 146 |
| 'Appropriate' overheads included | 69 |
| Administrative overheads included in addition to manufacturing overheads | 7 |
| All overheads specifically excluded | 9 |
| No information given | 69 |
| | 300 |

Even less information is usually given regarding any amounts by which stock may have been written down in order to state it at net realisable value.

With regard to long-term contracts, SSAP9 permits work-in-progress to be valued, in given circumstances, at more than cost, i.e. to recognise a proportion of profit before the contract is completed. For companies engaged in this sort of work the estimates of what the eventual profit might be and how much of it can reasonably be recognised in the current year will be subject to a good degree of uncertainty; but those estimates will be critical to the reported results.

**DEPRECIATION**

The level of judgement inherent in assessing the annual charge for depreciation expense – and its consequence for accounts – has been covered in Part Two. The relevant SSAP (No. 12) is a further example of an accounting standard which can do no more than establish the basic rule: all assets which have a finite useful life should be depreciated over the accounting periods expected to benefit from their use; the method of calculating depreciation – and in particular the expected life of a particular asset – will be a matter on which different companies will have different views. This again is an area in which the reader – in his attempt to assimilate information from accounts – is largely at the mercy of the willingness or otherwise of the particular company to provide further detail: some companies offer precise and detailed statements of their depreciation policies; others provide information in only the very broadest of terms. In general, the reader should beware that the older the assets then, in times of inflation, the more understated will be the cost of using them, i.e. the depreciation expense, compared with what those costs would be if the assets needed to be replaced at current prices.

**GROUPS:
CONSOLIDATION**

The 1948 Companies Act introduced the requirement that, in addition to separate accounts for each individual company, the existence of a group of companies under common control should be recognised by producing consolidated accounts that combine the separate accounts of each member of the group. [A holding company controls another (subsidiary) company if it owns more than 50 per cent of its equity share capital.]

The process of consolidation is one whereby the assets and liabilities of each member of the group, and their profits or losses for the period, are aggregated into one figure in the accounts for the group as a whole. For the most part, the accounts of a group are constructed on exactly the same bases as the accounts for an individual company, although there are one or two adjustments which are made on consolidation in order that the group accounts portray a fair picture of the financial position and performance of the group *vis-à-vis* the outside world. Thus any amount due to or from companies within the same group are eliminated on consolidation (because as far as the outside world is concerned no such assets or liabilities exist) and any trading between group companies is excluded from the combined figures for turnover and profit on the basis that a profit only accrues to the group as a whole when a sale is made to external third parties. That apart, there are two further areas of accounting which have particular relevance in the context of groups – goodwill and foreign currencies.

**GOODWILL**

Goodwill is a term used to describe the amount paid in order to acquire any rights or facilities (such as the right to sell or produce a product, or the acquisition of business connections or 'know-how'), or an amount paid in excess of the value of any tangible assets acquired. In a group context, goodwill will usually arise in the consolidation process in so far as it represents the surplus paid on the acquisition of a subsidiary over and above the value ascribed to the subsidiary's net assets at the time of acquisition.

One point which should be made quite clear is that, where it appears in a balance sheet, the amount shown against goodwill is not an estimate of the total 'goodwill' attaching to the business concerned. A balance sheet is very largely an accumulation of costs incurred by a company: a company may possess a good number of other 'assets' (its workforce, its market reputation, its management skill) which never appear in a balance sheet because accounts do not attempt to put any value on them. It should be underlined, therefore, that the appearance of goodwill does not mean that the balance sheet purports to reflect the value of the business – in the sense of what could be obtained for it if it were sold as a going concern. Goodwill in accounting terms is no more than the amount paid in the past in order to acquire some intangible benefit.

The alternative accounting treatments for goodwill are various. Some companies take the view that, once it has been acquired, goodwill is maintainable and should continue to be shown in the accounts at its original cost, unless there is evidence that its value has been permanently impaired. The alternative view – and one which is supported by prudence – is that balance sheets should not be confused by including assets of dubious or intangible value. The compromise position is that goodwill is an asset which has a finite life, which eventually expires, and which should therefore be written-off over a number of years – although that number is something which is totally at the discretion of the company concerned.

All that can be said is that the reader should be put on warning where goodwill appears in a balance sheet and should be concerned to read the accounting policy which has been adopted in respect of it and the extent to which that policy has an affect on the profit and loss account. The 1981/82 Survey shows the following breakdown:

| | |
|---|---:|
| Goodwill shown at cost | 29 |
| Goodwill written down or amortised | 30 |
| Goodwill written off in year of acquisition | 195 |
| | 254 |

Of the companies writing off goodwill in the year in which it was acquired, 145 indicated that this was done through reserves (thus avoiding the profit and loss account totally), 43 treated it as an extraordinary item (thus avoiding any impact on operating profit) and 7 gave no indication as to how the writing off would be treated. The majority of the companies who stated that their policy was to amortise goodwill over a period of years gave no indication of how long that period was.

**FOREIGN CURRENCY TRANSLATION**

Where a group has overseas subsidiaries, the problem arises as to how the operations of the foreign company are to be translated from the local currency into sterling for inclusion in the UK consolidated accounts.

Different methods of translation are possible, and it is an area of accounting for which it has proved difficult to establish any one generally accepted treatment. The latest proposal is that it should be standard practice to translate overseas profit and loss accounts at the average rate of exchange ruling during the year and to translate overseas balances at the closing rate of exchange ruling on the balance sheet date. (An alternative treatment would be to translate foreign currency assets and liabilities at the rates ruling at the time each transaction was entered into.) Because of wide fluctuations in foreign currency exchange rates, the differing methods of translation can have a marked impact on the results disclosed by a group with significant overseas operations.

More importantly, there is considerable dispute as to how any differences that arise from the translation process should be treated in the accounts – in particular, whether they should be included in the profit and loss account or accounted for direct to reserves. The emerging consensus is that exchange rate differences that have no cash flow implications for the company concerned should not be allowed to distort its reported results for the year. Thus the 'differences' that arise merely from the accounting process of expressing figures recorded in one currency into the domestic currency have nothing to do with the operating performance of the group (unless and until overseas profits are repatriated, i.e. funds are transferred from one currency to another) and should not therefore be reflected in the profit and loss account.

Whether the process of translation will result in a 'profit' or 'loss' in any one year will depend on how sterling has moved against the particular foreign currency during the year in question. Here again, all that can be said is that the reader should scrutinise the method by which the company has dealt with these differences: despite the requirement for consistency, it has not been unknown in recent years for companies to switch their accounting policy in this respect according to whether or not the movement in sterling has given rise to a 'profit' on translation (in which case it becomes attractive to account for that profit in the profit and loss account) or a 'loss' (in which case the reasons for accounting direct to reserves become more persuasive).

By way of illustration of the alternative policies which companies adopt, the 1981/82 Survey shows the following analysis:

|  | Profit and loss account | Reserves |
|---|---|---|
| Unrealised differences on translation of: | | |
| Fixed assets and long-term borrowing | 27 | 112 |
| Current assets | 18 | – |
| Other (unspecified) assets and liabilities | 81 | 83 |
|  | 126 | 195 |

# Appendix 1   Glossary of terms

**Accounting bases**    The (sometimes alternative) methods that have been developed for applying basic accounting concepts to business transactions and for measuring certain items in the accounts, e.g. various methods for depreciation of fixed assets.

**Accounting concepts**    The basic assumptions underlying the preparation of accounts, including 'going concern', 'accruals', 'consistency' and 'prudence'.

**Accounting policies**    The specific accounting bases judged by the business to be most appropriate to its circumstances and therefore adopted in the preparation of its accounts, e.g. of the various methods of accounting for depreciation, the policy adopted may be to depreciate plant plant over a five-year period.

**Accounting records**    The 'books' in which a business records the transactions it has entered into. For companies, minimum standards of accounting records are required by law.

**Accrual**    An expense or a proportion thereof not invoiced prior to the balance sheet date but included in the accounts – sometimes on an estimated basis.

**Accruals concept**    Income and expenses are recognised in the period in which they are earned or incurred, rather than the period in which they happen to be received or paid.

**Advance corporation tax**    The tax a company is required to pay (at the basic income tax rate) when it makes a distribution. The amount paid can be subsequently set off against the company's corporation tax liability for that year.

**Asset**    Any property or rights owned by the company that have a monetary value.

**Associated company**    *See* Related company.

**Balance sheet**    A statement describing the financial position of a business at a particular date.

**Capital allowance**    An allowance against profits given for tax purposes in respect of expenditure on fixed assets during the period.

**Capital employed**    The aggregate amount of long-term funds invested in or lent to the business and used by it in carrying out its operations.

| | |
|---|---|
| **Capitalisation** | The treatment of costs as assets to be included in the balance sheet rather than as expenses to be written off in the profit and loss account. |
| **Cash flow** | A statement – often a projection – of future, anticipated cash balances based on estimated cash inflows and outflows over a given period. |
| **Consistency concept** | The requirement that once an accounting policy for a particular item in the accounts has been adopted the same policy should be used from one period to the next. Any change in policy must be fully disclosed. |
| **Consolidation** | Method of combining the accounts of a group of companies into one balance sheet and profit and loss account for the group as a whole. |
| **Contingent liability** | A liability dependent upon the outcome of a future event. |
| **Costs of goods sold** | Those costs (usually raw materials, labour and production overheads) directly attributable to goods that have been sold. The difference between sales and cost of goods sold gives a measure of gross profit. |
| **Creditors** | Amounts due to those who have supplied goods or services to the business. |
| **Current asset** | An asset which, if not already in cash form, is expected to be converted into cash within twelve months of the balance sheet date. |
| **Current cost convention** | A basis of accounting under which revenue is compared with the current (rather than the historic) cost of resources used up in earning it and assets are stated in the balance sheet at their current value to the business (usually equivalent to net current replacement cost). |
| **Current liability** | An amount owed which will have to be paid within twelve months of the balance sheet date. |
| **Current ratio** | The comparison between current assets and current liabilities in a balance sheet, providing a measure of business liquidity. |
| **Debentures** | Long-term loans, usually secured on the company's assets. |
| **Debtors** | Amounts due from customers to whom goods or services have been sold but for which they have not yet paid. |
| **Deferred asset/liability** | An amount receivable or payable more than twelve months after the balance sheet date. |
| **Deferred taxation** | An estimate of a tax liability payable at some estimated future date, resulting from timing differences in the taxation and accounting treatment of certain items of income and expenditure. |
| **Depreciation** | An estimate of the proportion of the cost of a fixed asset which has been |

consumed (whether through use, obsolesence or the passage of time) during the accounting period.

**Distribution**

The amount distributed to shareholders out of the profits of the company, usually in the form of a cash dividend.

**Dividend cover**

The relationship between the amount of profit reported for the year and the amount distributed.

**Dividend yield**

The relationship between the amount of dividend per share and the market share price of listed companies.

**Double entry**

A system of bookkeeping whereby the amount of each transaction the business enters into is recorded in two places – according to the manner in which the transaction increases or decreases any one or more of the business's assets, liabilities, capital, revenue, or expenses.

**Earnings per share**

The amount of profit (after tax, but before any extraordinary items) attributable to shareholders divided by the number of Ordinary shares in issue.

**Exceptional item**

Income or expenditure that, although arising from the ordinary course of business, is of such unusual size or incidence that it needs to be disclosed separately.

**Expense**

A cost incurred, or a proportion of a cost, the benefit of which is wholly used up in the earning of the revenue for a particular accounting period.

**Exposure draft**

A document issued by the Accounting Standards Committee for comment prior to the formalisation of a Statement of Standard Accounting Practice.

**Extraordinary item**

Any significant amount of income or expenditure arising from events outside the ordinary activities of the business and which, because of its unusual nature, needs to be separately disclosed.

**Fixed asset**

Assets held for use by the business rather than for sale.

**Fixed cost**

A cost that does not necessarily vary with changes in the scale of operations, e.g. rent.

**Gearing**

The ratio of debt to equity, usually expressed as the proportion which long-term borrowings bear to shareholders' funds.

**Going concern concept**

The assumption that the business will continue in operation for the foreseeable future, i.e. that there is no intention to curtail or significantly reduce the scale of operations.

**Goodwill**

Any surplus consideration paid over and above the value of net tangible assets acquired.

**Gross profit**            The difference between sales and the cost of goods sold.

**Group**                   A number of companies operating under the same controlling ownership.

**Historic cost convention**    The convention by which assets are valued on the basis of the original cost of acquiring or producing them.

**Holding company**        A company that controls another company as a result of owning more than 50 per cent of its equity share capital.

**Interest cover**         The relationship between the amount of interest payable during a period and the amount of profit (before interest and before tax).

**Liability**              An amount owed.

**Liquidity**              A term used to describe the cash resources of a business and its ability to meet its short-term obligations.

**Listed investments**     Investments the market price for which is quoted on a recognised Stock Exchange.

**Long lease**             A lease with an unexpired term in excess of 50 years.

**Long-term liability**    An amount payable more than twelve months after the balance sheet date.

**Materiality**            A subjective judgement of the extent to which any amount is significant in the context of the financial position of a business as described in the balance sheet or its reported profit or loss.

**Minority interest**      That part of a group's net assets owned by shareholders other than the holding company.

**Net assets**             The net amount of total assets less total liabilities.

**Net book value**         The cost (or valuation) of fixed assets less accumulated depreciation to date.

**Net realisable value**   Amount at which an asset could be sold in its existing condition at the balance sheet date, after deducting any costs to be incurred in disposing of it.

**Nominal value**          The face value of a share or other security.

**Overhead**               An expense that cannot be attributed to any specific part of the company's operations.

**Post balance sheet event**    Any event occurring after the balance sheet date, but before the accounts are issued, which is sufficiently significant to be either reflected or noted in the accounts.

**Prepayment**

The part of a cost which is carried forward as an asset in the balance sheet to be recognised as an expense in the ensuing period(s) in which the benefit will be derived from it.

**Price/earnings ratio**

The relationship between the latest reported earnings per share and the market price per share.

**Prior year adjustment**

A retrospective adjustment to the previous years' accounts which is reflected by revising comparative figures in the current year's accounts.

**Profit**

The difference between the revenues earned in the period and the costs incurred in earning them. A number of alternative definitions are possible according to whether the figure is struck before or after tax, extraordinary items, distributions, etc.

**Profit and loss account**

A statement summarising the revenues earned and the costs incurred in earning them during an accounting period.

**Provision**

The amount written off in the current year's profit and loss account in respect of any known or estimated loss or liability.

**Prudence concept**

The philosophy which says that when measuring profit provision should be made for all known or expected losses and liabilities, but that revenue should only be recognised if it is realised in the form of cash or near-cash.

**Quick ratio**

The relationship between those current assets readily convertible into cash (usually current assets less stock) and current liabilities.

**Related company**

A company in which the investing company holds a substantial (generally not less than 20 per cent) and long-term interest and over which it exercises significant influence.

**Reserves**

The accumulated amount of profit less losses, and any other surpluses, generated by the company since its incorporation and retained in it.

**Revenue**

Money received from selling the product of the business.

**Share capital**

Stated in the balance sheet at its nominal value and (if fully paid, and subject to any share premium) representing the amount of money introduced into the company by its shareholders at the time the shares were issued.

**Shareholders' funds**

A measure of the shareholders' total interest in the company, represented by the total of share capital plus reserves.

**Share premium**

The surplus over and above nominal value received in consideration for the issue of shares.

**Statement of Standard Accounting Practice**  Statements issued by the accountancy bodies which describe approved methods of accounting. (*Abbrev.* SSAP.)

**Stock appreciation relief**  A taxation relief given in order to allow for any increase in the cost of financing stock which results from increased prices. It is calculated by applying, to the carrying value of stock at the beginning of the period, the movement in a Government-produced price index during the period.

**Subsidiary company**  Any company in which the investing company has an interest of more than 50 per cent in the voting share capital, or otherwise is a member of it and controls the composition of its board of directors.

**Tax credit**  The amount of tax deducted at source (at the basic rate of income tax) by a company from any dividend payment.

**Timing difference**  An adjustment to accounting profit in order to arrive at taxable profit which arises from the difference between the accounting and taxation treatment of certain items of income and expenditure.

**Translation (of foreign currencies)**  The conversion of foreign currency amounts into sterling for the purposes of preparing UK accounts.

**Turnover**  Revenue from sales.

**Variable cost**  A cost that increases or decreases in line with changes in the level of activity.

**Working capital**  Current assets less current liabilities, representing the amount a business needs to invest – and which is continually circulating – in order to finance its stock, debtors and work-in-progress.

**Work-in-progress**  Goods (or services) in the course of production (or provision) at the balance sheet date.

# Appendix 2 Sources of comparative business statistics

Part Three laid some emphasis on the benefit a businessman can derive from comparing the performance of his own business with that of similar businesses or the industry as a whole. This appendix provides further information on the possible sources of comparable business statistics.

**TRADE ASSOCIATIONS**  Some 2,000 trade and related associations serve the business interests of British industry. A good number of them collect, analyse and distribute business statistics drawn from their particular industrial sector. The resulting publications in most cases can be purchased, or occasionally obtained free, by any interested party.

The chart at the end of this appendix gives a first, and very broad, indication of the sort of information which is made available by a cross section of associations. It has been prepared from responses to direct enquiries of the trade associations concerned. All of the associations contacted proved most helpful in their willingness to provide details of the statistical services they offered. Addresses and telephone numbers are included for those who wish to enquire for greater detail than can be included in this summary.

The chart covers a cross section of British business, but excludes nationalised industries and those dominated by very large companies. It is necessarily selective. Usually, only one association appears under each trade. This is not to suggest that the association given is the only one within the sector that provides statistics, but rather that it is a good example of one which does. In some cases – where a body has been set up within a sector for the sole purpose of collecting and disseminating statistics and information – it is the natural choice for the purpose of this summary.

The sort of information made available varies widely. All of it is useful to the businessman, but for present purposes it has been classified into three broad types – according to its immediate usefulness in terms of assessing comparable business performance.

The first class of information is of the sort which provides specific indicators of profitability within the sector, and which is often published in the form of ratios and percentages which are immediately comparable with the forms of analyses described in Part Three of this book. Associations publishing this information will usually compile their statistics from a variety of sources, including individual business results and responses to statistical questionnaires. The resultant publications provide members with an immediate basis for comparing their own business performance with those of a similar size, while at the same time keeping in touch with the more general developments within the trade.

The second level of statistics are those which provide an analysis by product or sub-sector within the industry. In these cases the statistics will often cover trends in sales, production, average selling prices, and order book levels. Here again information is compiled from a variety of sources (for example Business Monitors – see below) and is collated and made available to members – often with a commentary – in a single publication. This sort of information will enable the businessman to assess his share of the sector, to compare his sales trends and price experience with those of his competitors, and generally to keep in touch with the state of the market for his product.

The third category of statistics are those which summarise such things as sales, production and price trends for an industry as a whole, or which otherwise provide no more than broad economic indicators of the levels of demand and output within the whole sector. Usually, this information will be collated from other – often Government – publications and will be presented as a background to annual reports.

For each association, the publications considered relevant are listed and their contents summarised. Many publications span more than one category. Available booklists are indicated by the symbol *.

## BUSINESS MONITORS

*Business Monitors* is the series through which the Government publishes the statistics it gathers on industrial activity and performance. They are published by HMSO on behalf of the Business Statistics Office, and separate series are available for production and for service and distribution sectors.

Trade associations often include statistics extracted from the relevant *Business Monitor* for the purposes of their own publications. Potentially most useful are the *Quarterly Production Monitors* (PQ series). They provide up-to-date sales figures for any one of nearly 4,000 individual products manufactured by firms in some 160 industries. Where available, import and export figures, employment statistics and movements in wholesale and retail prices are also included in the quarterly issue for the particular product.

This information can help the businessman to assess sales and price trends for his own products, to measure the efficiency of different parts of his business, and to compare his own performance with that of the industry as a whole. *Business Monitors* can also provide him with a basis for keeping up-to-date with trends in the industries that supply him.

Further details, and the complete listing of the product headings under which *Business Monitors* are issued, are available from the Business Statistics Office, Cardiff Road, Newport, Gwent NPT 1XG (Tel. 0633 56111).

**OTHER SOURCES**

A number of independent organisations issue publications summarising comparative business performance. The annual *Times 1000* offers financial extracts and selective profitability ratios for the largest 1,000 UK-listed companies, ranked by size of turnover. Jordans publish similar information for the private sector in their *Britain's Top 2,000 Companies.* In this case the companies included are listed in alphabetical order. In both of these publications a description of trading activity is given for each company, but the information is not presented or classified by industrial category.

Dunn & Bradstreet compile an annual series of *Management Ratios* which offer a detailed analysis of the comparative performance within some 22 separate industrial sectors. The analysis within each sector is broken down to give separate statistics for large, medium and small businesses. Inter Company Comparisons publish an annual *Industrial Performance Analysis* which includes 14 business ratios for 150 separate sectors.

All of these publications draw their source data from the annual published accounts of the companies concerned. The time-lag between the period to which the figures relate and the publication of comparative statistics can be up to two years.

## TRADE ASSOCIATIONS: BUSINESS AND INDUSTRY STATISTICS

| Trade and Trade Association | Specific Indicators of Business Performance | Statistics by sub-sector and/or by product | Statistics for the sector as a whole |
|---|---|---|---|
| AGRICULTURAL CHEMICALS<br>British Agrochemicals Association, 93 Embankment, London SE1 7TU<br><br>01-735 8471 | | *Annual Report and Handbook*<br>Sales by broad product type | Sales – total, UK. export; UK pesticide usage |
| BAKING (Inc. CHOCOLATE AND CONFECTIONERY)<br>The Cocoa, Chocolate and Confectionery Alliance,<br>11 Green Street, London W1Y 3RF<br><br>01-629 8971 | | *Annual Report*<br>Despatches (UK) by product type (tonnes), ingedients purchased (tonnes)<br><br>*Statistical Summaries (monthly)*<br>Despatches as above on a monthly basis (with previous year's equivalent) | Sales – total UK; consumer and trade values; imports and exports<br><br>Summary of despatches, stocks and values, total and average invoice values and consumer values; stocks; wholesale price indices |
| BOOKSELLING*<br>Booksellers Association of Great Britain & Ireland, 154 Buckingham Palace Road, London SW1W 9TZ<br><br>01-730 8214/5/6 | *BA Charter Group Economic Survey (Annual)*<br>Comparative analysis of business results<br><br>Net profit as a percentage of total sales, net profit by size of book sales; performance by specialisation | Analysis of sales by size of business | Overall trading results within the sector |
| BREWING<br>Brewers Society, 42 Portman Road, London W1H OBB<br><br>01-486 4831 | | *Statistical Handbook (Annual)*<br>Production and consumption statistics<br><br>Inter-drink comparisons; prices and expenditure; Customs and Excise Duty; licensing statistics | Production and consumption statistics |

BUILDING
The Building Services
Research and Information
Association,*
Old Bracknell Lane,
Bracknell,
Berks RG12 4AH

0344 25071

*Statistics Bulletin (Quarterly)*
Production, imports and
exports; price indices; new
orders by sector; trade
expectations within sectors

Output of products and equipment; trade expectations

Housebuilding starts and
completions; expectations

National Federation of
Building Trades
Employers,*
82 New Cavendish Street,
London W1M 8AD

01-580 5588

*State of Trade Enquiry (Quarterly)*
Anticipated volume of work;
current capacity levels

Availability of labour within
trades

National Council of
Building Material
Producers,
33 Alfred Place,
London WC1E 7EG

01-580 3344

*BMP Statistical Bulletin (Monthly)*
Value of new orders and
output

Building materials;
production and sales; price
indices; imports and exports

Housebuilding approvals
starts, completions,
renovations

Building Societies – share
deposits and mortgages;
private architects – estimated
workload and value of new
commissions

CARPETS
British Carpet
Manufacturers
Association,
26 St James's Square,
London SW1Y 4JH

01-839 2145

*Annual Report*
Sales by product type; fibres
used

Exports, imports

*(Continued)*

| Trade and Trade Association | Specific Indicators of Business Performance | Statistics by sub-sector and/or by product | Statistics for the sector as a whole |
|---|---|---|---|
| CHEMICALS<br>Chemical Industries Association,<br>Alembic House,<br>93 Albert Embankment,<br>London SE1 7TU<br><br>01-735 3001/8 | | *UK Statistics Handbook (annual)*<br>Production, sales, employees, exports, imports, consumption of materials, fuel and energy, price indices | As opposite, for sector as a whole |
| ELECTRICAL<br>British Electrical & Allied Manufacturers Association,<br>8 Leicester Street,<br>London WC2N 7BN<br><br>01-437 0678 | No regular publications but confidential information; service available to members only; statistical collections with product areas | | |
| FOOD<br>Food Manufacturer's Federation,<br>6 Catherine Street,<br>London WC2B 5JJ<br><br>01-836 2460 | | *Annual Statistics, Food Industry*<br>Processed food production; employment statistics | Imports and exports |
| FOOTWEAR<br>British Footwear Manufacturers Federation,*<br>Royalty House,<br>72 Dean Street,<br>London W1V 5HB | Sales and net output per enterprise and per head. Cost of sales in the footwear industry – analysis. Production and profitability | *Footwear Industry Statistical Review (Annual)*<br>Consumption of materials; footwear deliveries; average selling prices; import penetration and sales<br><br>*Quarterly Statistical Supplement*<br>Sales, domestic supplies and import penetration by sector | Sales, exports, imports, import penetration, employment, earnings<br><br>Wholesale and retail prices<br><br>Exports/imports |

**FURNITURE**

Furniture Industry
Research Association (FIRA),*
Maxwell Road,
Stevenage
Herts ST1 2EW

0438 3433

*Statistical Digest of the Furniture Industry*
Number of companies, turnover, employees, materials consumed, overseas trade, price indices

*Quarterly Bulletin*
Updates of *Statistical Digest* (above)

*Monthly statistics*
Costs and prices

Deliveries, orders, supplies
Employment
Retail sales

**GLASS**

British Glass Industry
Research Association,
Northumberland Road,
Sheffield S10 2UA

0742 686201

Confidential information available to members

**GROCERY & PROVISION TRADE**

Institute of Grocery
Distribution,*
Grange Lane,
Letchmore Heath,
Watford WD2 8DQ

Radlett 7141

NOTE: This association provides a wide range of financial and economic information apart from the publications listed

*The Retail Grocery Business (Annual)*
Analysis of financial performance

*Companies in the Food Industry 1979/80*
Summary of financial performances of member companies (sales, pre-tax profits, capital employed, financial ratios)

*The Grocery Business 1970–80*
Economic environment, consumer habits and profiles, the food manufacturing sector, the food distribution sector

Size and structure of the retail grocery business; trade changes

Employees and remuneration

*Food Industry Statistics Digest (Annual, updated monthly)*
National consumption, turnover, number and size of shops

Retail prices, costs and profits, stocks and capital

Long-term forecasts

(Continued)

| Trade and Trade Association | Specific Indicators of Business Performance | Statistics by sub-sector and/or by product | Statistics for the sector as a whole |
| --- | --- | --- | --- |
| KNITTING<br>HATRA (was Hosiery & Allied Trades Research Association).*<br>7 Gregory Boulevarde, Nottingham NG7 6LO<br><br>0602 623311 | | KNITSTATS (half-yearly)<br>Home consumption; imports as a percentage of home consumption; exports as a percentage of sales<br><br>Materials used in production | Exports, imports, employment, pay and prices<br><br>Price indices |
| LEATHER<br>British Leather Federation, 9 St Thomas Street, London SE1 9SA<br><br>01-407 1582 | Confidential information available to members only; emphasis on market research | | |
| MOTOR TRADE<br>Motor Agents Association, 201 Gt Portland Street, London W1N 6AB<br><br>01-580 9122 | | Monthly Statistical Digest<br>New car registration by make; best-selling models; vehicle production | Manufacturer's market shares; average weekly production; turnover; average earnings of employees<br><br>Consumption and deliveries of petroleum products; price and rates of duty on petrol |
| OFFICE PRODUCTS<br>British Stationery & Office Products Federation, 6 Wimpole Street, London W1M 8AS | Statistical function being developed: no statistics produced at present | | |

| Organization | Publication | Contents |
|---|---|---|
| **PAPER AND PACKAGING** PIRA (The Research Association for the Paper, Board Printing & Packaging Industries),* Randall Road, Leatherhead, Surrey KT22 7RU | *Statistical and Economic Review of the Packaging Industries 1976-80.* | UK industrial and manufacturing production by volume; retail sales by volume |
| | *Outlook 1981/82 United Kingdom* Consumption, price movements, end uses of materials, competition, sales – UK and export | |
| | Outlook-demand, price-movements and competition | |
| | *Cost and Availability of Packaging 1980-85* Demand, production and capacity, price movements; production costs, availability of raw materials Estimated movement in individual production costs. | Estimated movement in total direct production costs General economic factors and assumptions. RPI forecast, forecast of UK industrial production, forecast of exchange movements |
| **PHARMACEUTICALS** Association of the British Pharmaceutical Industry,* 12 Whitehall, London SW1A 2DY 01-839 3961 | *The Pharmaceutical Industry and the Nation's Health* UK output by therapeutic group Profit as a percentage of home sales; net output per employee | Output, growth; home sales; exports and imports; trade surpluses of industry |
| | Exports and imports; wholesale price increases | R&D expenditures; wholesale price increases; promotion expenditure; sales to NHS |
| **PLASTICS AND RUBBER** Rubber & Plastics Research Association, Shawbury Shrewsbury, Salop SY4 4NR 0939 250383 | *West European Trade in Rubber Products* – available also as 'Trade by Product' and 'Trade by Country' Production and consumption; analysis of import shares | Imports and exports |
| | *The Market for Plastics Processing Machinery in the UK* UK production, imports, exports and consumption; future prospects and trends | |
| | *The future of the Plastics Industry* Supply of raw materials; market trends; replacement of traditional products | Basic data and forecasts on the plastics processing market |

(Continued)

| Trade and Trade Association | Specific Indicators of Business Performance | Statistics by sub-sector and/or by product | Statistics for the sector as a whole |
|---|---|---|---|
| PUBLISHING<br>Publishers Association,*<br>19 Bedford Square,<br>London WC1B 3JH<br><br>01-580 6321 | *Quarterly Statistics Bulletin*<br>Profit as percentage of assets, sales, capital employed and per employee | *Quarterly Surveys +*<br>Value of turnover, total units, average prices<br><br>*Yearly Surveys +*<br>As above, plus financial structure of companies<br><br>Price indices; sales (home and export) by product category; market analyses | |
| TEXTILES<br>British Textile Employers Association,*<br>5th Floor,<br>Royal Exchange,<br>Manchester M2 7ED<br><br>061-834 7871 | | *Quarterly Statistical Review*<br>Detailed statistics of activity in each sector; imports and exports<br><br>(Also various statistical publications giving production, employment, machine activity, consumption of materials, exports and imports, within each sector.) | Main indicators of activity and foreign trade in textiles and clothing |
| TIMBER<br>Timber Trade Federation,<br>47 Whitcomb Street,<br>London WC2H 7DI<br><br>01-839 1891 | | *UK Year Book of Timber Statistics (and monthly supplements)*<br>Imports, exports, sales, consumption, stocks, price information | |

# Index